THE APPENDIX TO
DWELLY'S DICTIONARY

GAIRM: Leabhar 89

APPENDIX
TO
DWELLY'S
GAELIC-ENGLISH DICTIONARY

Compiled by
EDWARD DWELLY

Edited
from manuscripts in Dwelly's hand
in the National Library of Scotland
by
DOUGLAS CLYNE

Editing completed, and seen through the press
by
Derick Thomson

GAIRM PUBLICATIONS
GLASGOW

Published by
GAIRM PUBLICATIONS
29 Waterloo Street, Glasgow G2 6BZ, Scotland

Printed by Martin's of Berwick Ltd.

ISBN 1 871901 08 1

© 1991

Thug Comann Gaidhealach Ghlaschu cuideachadh don
Fhoillsichear le cosgaisean an leabhair seo, mar chuimhneachan air
an Lighiche Aonghas MacGhilleNaoimh (Angus MacNiven)

Dwelly's *Illustrated Gaelic-English Dictionary*
is available from Gairm Publications in the latest printing of 1988.

EDITOR'S PREFACE

In the Preface to Edward Dwelly's Illustrated Gaelic-English Dictionary, the author wrote: "An Appendix has since been compiled of additional words and meanings, received in proofs that arrived too late for their insertion in alphabetical order in the text, and also those found in books not accessible to me before the earlier parts were issued. That Appendix would in itself fill a considerable volume but the issue of it, however important, requires a considerable sum of money which up to the present is not forthcoming."

I have often wondered what had happened to the Appendix and a chance conversation on the telephone with the Reverend Dr Roderick MacLeod, MA, BD, PhD, Minister of Cumlodden & Lochfyne-side Parish and the present contributor of the Gaelic supplement 'Na Duilleagan Gàidhlig' to the Church of Scotland's monthly, 'Life and Work' provided me with the answer. After referring to the records, he informed me that it had been deposited with the manuscript section of the National Library of Scotland in Edinburgh, as MS 14957.

With the willing assistance of Mr I. F. Maciver, Curator of Manuscripts, I received three specimen photocopied pages from the Appendix and decided to purchase photocopies of the complete Appendix at a cost of some £115!

The whole Appendix, running to some 500 meticulously handwritten sheets in Dwelly's fair hand, is largely in alphabetical order. Rather surprisingly, however, nearly four-fifths of the Appendix relate to the letters A to D. As stated by Dwelly in his Preface, it contains not only additional words but also additional meanings for words contained in his Dictionary, and numbered in sequence to the meanings already given.

Another feature of the Appendix consists of words – some additional and others in Dwelly's Dictionary – which are followed by passages in which the word is used and for which Dwelly queried the translations. These have been most kindly and expertly provided by the Rev. Dr Roderick MacLeod and by Mr Kenneth MacDonald of the Department of Celtic Studies in the University of Glasgow. These translations form an important part of the Appendix, which is now made available to the public for the first time.

Early in the Appendix I came across a note which queried whether 188 words, mainly from the Highland Society's Dictionary and carrying the obsolete mark (†) were obsolete in fact. The uncertainty had, apparently, arisen because the slips on which these words were written by a Mr MacIsaac had been cut too closely to the left margin. All of these words have now been checked, firstly by Mr Angus Nicol a fellow member of The Highland Society of London, and more recently by me. Only those words from the H.S.D. which were really obsolete when Dwelly received them, now carry the obsolete sign.

When the photocopies of the Appendix arrived, Mr Maciver indicated that he had also sent me photocopies of MS 14958 which had been deposited with MS 14957. This consisted of 30 pages, to which Dwelly referred in the main Appendix in the majority of cases.

MS 14958 contains some interesting items such as Uist games, names for the political parties, Shinty, parts of a spinning-wheel and of a still, flower names, ritual drinks and various words and expressions for death. I have incorporated them alphabetically, along with the main text of MS 14957, as this is clearly what Dwelly intended.

In order to make the best possible use of the Appendix a complete Index is essential and I make no excuse for the fact that it runs to twenty-four pages of quarto paper with four columns to the page, equal to one-quarter of the length of the Gaelic text.

Finally I would like to thank Mr I. F. Maciver, Curator of

Manuscripts in The National Library of Scotland, for his willing assistance in photocopying the Appendix; my daughter, Verity, for her invaluable help in the preparation of the Index; the Reverend Dr Roderick MacLeod and Mr Kenneth MacDonald for all the trouble they took in translating more than a hundred passages from the text and for their help and advice in many other ways; and Mr Angus Nicol for painstakingly checking the doubtfully obsolete words from The Highland Society's Dictionary.

Last of all I would like to thank Professor Derick Thomson and Gairm Publications for agreeing to publish this final example of Edward Dwelly's painstaking research more than fifty years after his death on 25th January 1939.

DOUGLAS CLYNE   *June 1989*

An Additional Note

Unfortunately, Dr Douglas Clyne did not survive to see his labours on Dwelly's text in print. His last letter to me was dated 16th July 1989, and in it he said he was leaving for a Continental holiday on 24th July, and would be returning to Cornwall on 24th August. He expected to have about four days of typing to do on this work after his return, and promised to forward the completed typescript then. He did return to the typescript after his holiday, and the end came (on 2nd October) shortly after he had finally finished going over it again. Mrs Elizabeth Clyne and her daughters were meticulous in looking out all his papers and drafts relating to this book, and passing them on to me, to help with the final preparation of the typescript for publication.

I have consulted these papers in detail, and compared the typescript with the photocopies of Dwelly's notes, producing in the process occasional fresh readings of Dwelly's hand. In the light of this, it may be useful to give a little detail of the work Dr Clyne has done on these originals. He imposed an alphabetical ordering at frequent points, as well as incorporating into the alphabetical sequence the many additional notes that Dwelly had assembled in National Library of Scotland MS 14958. Dr Clyne further developed the often bare references to the published Dwelly, re-supplying the range of meanings (or the relevant ones) given there, and sometimes expanding the syntax of Dwelly's explanations (though retaining his terminology, which is occasionally quaint), or attempting some degree of re-definition where Dwelly's formulations seemed not quite clear. A number of these re-definitions have been put in square brackets, to indicate that they are not verbatim MS quotations. Also, a number of the *translations* of lines of verse quoted, e.g. from Donnchadh Bàn, were taken from editions completed after Dwelly's death. In the process of seeing the book through the press, I have added some further corrections and modifications (e.g. 'hair-brained' to 'hare-brained' sub *amsgaoidh*, and various obvious corrections which are made silently). This applies also to supplying accents where the length of vowels is not in doubt. Essentially, however, it is Dwelly's collection that is presented here, not a fundamental revision or up-dating of it.

We can hardly stress sufficiently the valuable additional dimenson Dwelly brought to his work through his extensive network of contacts. By this means he provided a rich expansion of published lexical explanations, and this process is strikingly illustrated in his MS notes, showing how much detail, e.g. regarding Gaelic usages in Caithness, Wester Ross, Lewis, Perthshire, Islay etc, has in this way been brought to bear. It was a process that he had developed while working on the published Dictionary, but we see some intensification of it in the early part of the Appendix, which is much fuller for the early letters of the alphabet. This is presumably because more of these diverse sources had already been incorporated in the later parts of the original Dictionary, which appeared over a number of years. Some of these contributions can be seen to be direct responses to the items published by Dwelly.

The users and students of Gaelic must always be extremely grateful to Edward Dwelly, and they should feel a similar gratitude to Douglas Clyne for making still more of Dwelly's work available. Douglas Clyne was a big man in many different ways.

Derick S. Thomson

AUTHORITIES QUOTED IN THIS WORK

Most of the words not marked are taken from MacLeod & Dewar's Gaelic Dictionary, but the sources of all important additions have been marked as follows. (The places in brackets show the districts whose localisms the various authorities specially represent.)

* *MacAlpine's Pron. Gaelic Dict.* (Chiefly Islay & neighbourhood.)

† Obsolete words or meanings. *MacBain's Etymological Gaelic Dict.* (Badenoch &c.)

Cameron's Gaelic Names of Plants.

Gaelic Names of Birds, collected by Dr Alex Carmichael for C. Ferguson, and inserted by the latter in Gaelic Society of Inverness Trans. xi and xii.

Dr H. Cameron Gillies' Names of Diseases.

** *Armstrong's Gaelic Dictionary* (Mid Perthshire.)

MacEachen's Gaelic Dictionary (Arisaig & Badenoch.)

Highland Society's Gaelic Dictionary.

Car. Gad. – Carmina Gadelica.

Celt. Mag. – Celtic Magazine.

CM – Celtic Monthly.

C. Rev. – Celtic Review.

Donn. Bàn – Dun. Macintyre's poems 5th edition.

DU – David Urquhart, Kyle, Lochalsh.

G – An Gaidheal (magazine 1872-1878).

G.na B. – Guth na Bliadhna (magazine).

GSI. – Gaelic Society of Inverness Transactions.

JGC.S – J. G. Campbell's 'Superstition'.

JGC.W – J. G. Campbell's 'Witchcraft'.

Leabh.-nan-c. – Leabhar nan cnoc.

Leabh.na Fèinne

M – Menzies' Orain Ghàidhealach.

McI – Dun. Macintyre's poems, 5th ed.

McMh.A. – Alex MacDonald's poems, 1902.

MS – Large manuscript English-Gaelic Dict. in possession of Rev. D. Walker Macintyre, Kilmonivaig. It was revised in Nov. 1, 1823 and purchased at the sale of Sir Wm. MacLeod Bannatyne's Library in 1834 by Donald Gregory, Edinburgh, who gave it to Angus MacDonnell, Inch. No compiler's nor reviser's name is given.

NGP – Nicolson's Gaelic Proverbs.

R – William Ross's songs, 1877.

RGG – Reid's Gaelic Grammar.

WH – Campbell's West Highland Tales.

W & S, WS – Waifs & Strays of Celtic Tradition.

AC – Dr Alex Carmichael, author of 'Carmina Gadelica' (Western Isles).

AF – Gaelic Names of Beasts, *et cetera*, by Alex Forbes, Edinburgh.

AH – Alex Henderson, Ardnamurchan.

CR – Rev. C. M. Morrison, Jura (Perthshire and West coast of Ross.)

DC – Rev. Dr Campbell, Broadford (Argyll & Uist.)

DJM – D. J. Matheson, Kyleakin.

DM – Duncan MacIsaac, Oban.

DMC – Rev. D. M. Cameron, Ledaig.

DMcL – Duncan MacLachlan, Connel.

DMK – Donald MacKenzie, Killimister, Wick.

DMu – Rev. D. Munro, Ferintosh.

DMy – Donald Murray, Aberdeen (Lewis).

G-J.F. – J. F. Gates, London.

JGM – J. G. MacKay, London.

JM – Rev. J. MacRury, Snizort (Skye & Uist.)

JMcF – John MacFadyen.

MM – Malcolm MacFarlane, Elderslie.

MMcD – Malcolm MacDonald, Stornoway.

MMcL – Malcolm MacLeod, Uig, Lewis (Lewis).

MMcN – Michael MacNeill, Castlebay, Barra.

PJM – P. J. MacIver, Kyle.

TS – Rev. T. Sinton, Dores.

WC – William Cameron, Poolewe.

ABBREVIATIONS

a.	active voice
a.	adjective
adv.	adverb
aff.	affirmative
art.	article
col.	colloquial
comp.	comparative degree

conj.	conjunction	poss.	possessive
conj. interr.	interrogative conjunction	poss. pron.	possessive pronoun
cont.	contraction	pref.	prefix
dat.	dative case	prep.	preposition
def.	defective verb	prep. pron.	prepositional pronoun
dim.	diminutive	part.	participle
f.	feminine	pr. pt.	present participle
fut.	future tense	pt. pt.	past participle
gen.	genitive case	pron.	pronoun
i.e.	that is	p. prov.	provincial
impers.	impersonal	rel.	relative
impr.	improper	rel. pron.	relative pronoun
ind.	indeclinable	s.	substantive
indic.	indicative	s.f.	feminine substantive
infin.	infinitive	sing.	singular number
int.	interjection	s.m.	masculine substantive
inter.	interrogative	sup.	superlative degree
m.	masculine	v.	verb
n., nom.	nominative case	v.a.	active verb
neg.	negative	v.n.	verbal noun
pass.	passive	v. irr.	irregular verb
pl.	plural	v. tr.	Transitive verb

Notes by Dwelly on the Appendix

Grammatical and other notes occur in various places in the Dictionary, e.g.

1. The subjunctive in -*eas* on page 216 (i.e. p. 216 of Dwelly's Illustrated Dictionary).
2. The past participle in *te* or *ta* on page 53.
3. The distinction between dialects by the use of *eu* and *ia*, see under *EU*, page 394.
4. The differentiation between *thu* and *sibh*, see under *sibh* on page 838 and under *thu* on page 948.

The Appendix consists of words or additional meanings received in proofs that arrived too late for their insertion in alphabetical order in the Dictionary, or those found in books which were not accessible to the compiler before the earlier parts of the work had been issued to the public.

Every diligence has been exerted to gather all the Gaelic words omitted in the text for insertion in this Appendix and it is hardly likely that many have been overlooked now, owing to the diligent and continued assistance received from many correspondents all over the world. Should, however, any reader come across a Gaelic word at any time that has not been included, the compiler will be most glad to hear from him with regard to the same, with the context in which he heard or saw it, so that it may be included in future editions of "Faclair".

Additional Words and Meanings to those in the Dictionary

A

a, *Prov.* for e, he
a'ad, see agad
aar, (AF), *s.* Eagle
abachail, *a.* Maturative.
abachd, *s.f.* 'Bha mi ann an abachd', said of one taking sanctuary.
abaid, (DU), *s.f.* Dirt. 2 Confusion. Cha'n fhaca mi a leithid de dh'abaid riamh, *I have never seen such confusion*, said of a house that is dirty and topsy-turvy.
abairteach, (DU), *a.* Self-opinionated and supercilious.
abalach, see ablach, *s.m.* D,p.3
àban, -ain, *s.m.* Backwater. 2 Disused or silted-up channel. Occurs in place-names. *Celtic Review*, II 384
abanta, *a.* Witty. Duine abanta, *a witty man.*
abantachd, *s.f.* Wittiness.
abantas, -ais, *s.m.* Wittiness.
abartach, (DU), *a.* Easily offended. 2 Conceited, pompous.
abartas, -ais, *s.m. See abartachd.* 2 *(MS)* Averment.
àbh, *gen. sing,* àibh, *s.m.* Hand-net.
abhach, (AF), *s.m.* See abhag, *s.f.* 2 Deer.
abhachd, *s.f.* Capability, profit.
abhag, *s.f.* Terrier. Plural abhaig in *Gairloch.* (DU).
abhair, (AF), *s.* Cart or plough horse.
àbhairt, *s.f.* See àbhaist, *s.f.* Habit.
abhall, -ail, *s.f.* Apple-tree. 2 Orchard. Fiùran ùr de'n t-sean abhall, *a new branch or sapling from the old apple tree. Duanaire*, 76.
abhardach, (DMK), *a.* Curious, anomalous. *Caithness*
abharn, *Sutherland* for abhainn.
a bharr, *adv.* Moreover.
àbhas, *s.m.* Grant.

àbhdan, (DU), pl.-anan, *s.m.* Finger. 2 *pl.* fingers, implying a whole hand.
abhras, *s.m.* 7 Tuft of flax or wool on a distaff. 8 The batch (in weaving). 9 (CR) Lower edge of a herring net. *West of Ross-shire.* 10 (DU). The meshed part of a net. A' cur a mach an abhrais, in casting a net, one man pays out the rope (an druim) while a second man puts out the mesher. This prevents entanglement.
abhrun, (AF), *s.m.* Three year old castrated goat.
abhsadh, *s.m.* Jerk. 2 The whole canvas of a boat or ship. *Sàr-Obair.*
abhsag, (AF), *s.f.* Plug-hole in a boat.
abhuilteach, (MS), *a.* Facetious.
ablach, *a.* Cripple. Ablach cuibhle, *a damaged wheel.*
abrach, -aich, aichean, (MMcD), *s.f.* A small portable quern, smaller than a brà. *Lewis.* (Abbreviation of brà Abrach, or *Lochaber quern*).
abrag or abragh. *Perthshire* for abradh.
àbruid, (MS), *s.f.* Ankle (HSD).
†aca, *int.* See! Behold! (HSD).
†acaidh, -e, -ean, *s.f.* Abode, habitation.
acaineachd, *s.f.* Plaintiveness (HSD).
acainn, See acfhuinn, *s.f.* Apparatus.
acair, *s.f.* Anchor. For illustrations and names of parts, see under bàta. 6 Stone to hold the thatch of a house in place.
acair, (CR), *s.f.* Part of a *sgamhan* (mow). *West of Ross-shire.*
acair-èiginn, *s.f.* Sheet-anchor.
acairseideach. *a.* Anchorable. (HSD).
acaiseach, *a.* Malicious.
acarra, *a.* 3 (DU) Careful, as in landing a fish with a rod and line.
acarrachd, (DU), *s.f.* 'Playing' a fish.
acarraich, (DU), *v.a.* Handle carefully. 2 'Play' a fish.
†accomar, *adv.* In hand, at one's mercy. †2 for faiceamaid. (HSD).
acfhuinn, *s.f.* Horses' harness.

ADDITIONAL TERMS FOR HARNESS, see page 4.

25 Bann-bràghad, *s.m. Hames-strap band of harness.*

26 Beart-dheiridh, *s.f. Breeching.*

27 Beart-bhronn, *s.f. Girth.*

28 Beart-dheiridh-dialta, *s.f. Crupper.*

29 Beulannach, *s.m. 'Bit' of a bridle.*

30 Bronnach-dialta, *s.f. Saddle-girth.*

31 Brùban, *s.f. Girth, belly-band. West coast of Ross-shire.*

32 brù-bheairt, *s.f. girth.*

32(a) Cab, *s.m. 'Bit' of a bridle.*

33 Cabstair, *s.m. Bit* (HSD).

34 Cairb, *s.f. Bent ridge of a girth saddle.*

35 Ceannasg, *s.m. Headstall.*

36 Ceum, *s.m. 7 Stirrup.*

37 Claigionn-srathrath, *s.m. Timbers of girth saddle.*

38 Clàir-shùl, *s.m. Blinders.*

39 Crios, *s.m. Belly-band.*

40 Copan-srèine, *s.m. Boss of a bridle* (HSD).

41 Crann-bhràighd, *pl.* crainn-bhraigh-dean, *s.m. Plough-horse's collar.*

42 Cromagan na briogais, *s.f. Breeching hooks of a cart.*

43 Cruipean, *s.m. Crupper.*

44 Droman, *s.m. Back-band of a horse when in a cart.*

45 Eislichean, *s.f. pl. Stretchers from the ends of the tail beam to corresponding sides of saddle-crupper and stretchers together correspond to the breeching.* (CR) The eisleach is the strap connecting the crupper with the saddle.

46 Gabhail, *s.f. & m. The Stirrup strap.*

47 Glomair, *s.m. Bridle.*

48 Guailneanan, *s. pl Traces of a carriage.*

49 Iall-srèine, (CR), *s.f. Bridle-rein.*

50 Iall-sròine, (CR), *s.f. Musrole, the band over a horse's nose.*

51 Lùb-mhurain, *s.f. Rope of grass, plaited or woven in a horse-collar.*

52 Meilleag, s.f. *Bridle-bit* (HSD).

53 Mireannach or mirfhionnach, *s.m. Bit. Uist.*

54 Muinghiall, -a, -an, *s.f. Head-stall of a halter or bridle.*

55 Muran, *s.m. Rope of grass, plaited or woven in horse-collar.*

56 Siola, -chan, *s.m.* (*s.f.* in Badenoch) *pl. Wooden hames for plough horses.*

57 Sròineall, *s.m. Musrole, nose-thong of a horse's bridle.*

58 Sròin-iall, *s.m.* Alternative spelling of 57..

59 Sròin-srèine, *s.m. Musrole, nose-thong of horse's bridle.*

60 Sròn-taod, *s. Halter.*

61 Suanach, *s.f. Plough-rein.*

62 Sùgan, *s.m. Horse's collar. Mull & Islay.*

63 Suigean, *s.m. Crupper* (HSD).

64 Tarrach, *s.f. Girth of a pack-saddle.*

65 Truis-bhràghad, *s.f. Band.*

66 Uchdach, (CR), *s.f. Breast band to keep the saddle from slipping backwards.*

acfhuinn-spreadhaich, (DMK), *s.f.* Piece of bright lead having several large hooks attached to it. It is thrown among a shoal of fish which its brightness attracts, and it is hauled in smartly, often with a fish impaled on each hook. It is also called a 'fishing-devil' and a 'destroyer'. *West coast of Ross-shire.*

-ach, *terminal prefix* of adjectives formed from substantives, signifying "having".

achailleag, (CR), *s.f.* Black and white wagtail. *Lairg.*

-achd, *s.f. ind.* Termination of substantives formed from adjectives (HSD).

achdaidh, *a.* Self-satisfied. *Sàr-Obair.*

achlasag, *s.f.* See achlasan, armful.

achlasaich, *v.* See achlaisich, to put under the arm.

achlasan, -ain, *s.m.* 4 Infant. 5 Haunch in heraldry (HSD).

a choidhche, (MM). The best form of a chaoidh.

††acmhuingeach, *a.* Rich, plentiful (HSD).

†acor, *s.m.* See acobhar, avarice. covetousness (HSD).

adag. The old practice of hooding stooks is still followed in parts of Gaeldom. The upper part of a sheaf is divided down to the band in two equal parts and placed with the stubble end uppermost so as to hang down both sides of the stook. Two or three hood-sheaves – the Scots name – suffice for a stook. The Gaelic word, *adag*, probably is derived from this hat-like covering, (CR).

†adaimh, *v.n.* See aidich, to confess. (HSD).

†adair, *s.m.* Hatter.

†adamh, s.m. Atom (HSD).

†adbhal, see àdhbhal, a. Vast, huge, awful.

†adbhath, *past def. v.* Died (HSD).

†adbuir, *v.n.* I swear. (HSD).

†adfed, *a.* Chaste (HSD).

†adfhuar, a. Very cold (HSD).

adh-alluidh, (AF), s. Buffalo, wild cow.

àdha, (MS), *s.m.* Lungs.

àdha, (DU), *pl.* àdhanan. Quarter of a sheep, cow, or slaughtered animal. 'Do cheithir àdhanan', applied to a person, means *your whole body*. 'Is beag aig do cheithir àdhanan e', *it is little enough for your whole body*; cheannaich mi àdha dheth a' mhart, *I bought a quarter (from off) of the cow*.

adha, *s.m.* The Gairloch form for àdha (liver) and there is another plural form *adhaichean* as well as the usual *àinean*.

†adhaigh, s. Night.

adhaisich, (MS), *v.n.* Pace.

adhaltrach, *s.m.* See adhaltraiche, adulterer.

adhamh, (DMK), *s.m.* Quarter of a carcase of beef or mutton. *West coast of Ross-shire.*

adharc-ballan, (MMcD), *s.m.* Cupping-horn. *Lewis.*

adharc-snothain, (MMcD), *s.m.* Snuff horn or 'mill'. *Lewis.*

adhartach, *a.* Progressive *in grammar.*

adhartanach, *a.* Cushioned.

adhartas, (DU), *s.m.* Progress.

adhbhalmhòr, *a.* See àdhbhal, vast, huge, awful. (HSD).

adhlacaidh, *a.* Funereal.

adhrus, *s.m.* See aoradh, worship (HSd).

african, -ain, *s.m.* Marigold, see bile-bhuidhe.

ag. In Arran, *he will go to do it*, is 'theid e 'a dhèanamh'; *he is going to do it*, tha e dol 'a dhèanamh; *he is doing it*, tha e 'g a dhèanamh. Bha e 'g a dhèanamh dh'innis e is mi 'bhacadh dha innis, means *he told after I had forbidden him to.*

ag, (AF), *s.* Cow 2 Deer.

agaid, (AF), -e, -ean, *s.m.* Magpie.

agairteach, -eich, -ean, *s.m.* Party, litigant.

agairteach, *a.* Sarcastic.

agall, (AC), *s.m.* Eloquence.

agallaidh, (MS), *v.n.* Antagonize.

agamas. *Sutherland* and parts of *Perthshire* for agam-sa.

agamhail, *a.* See agail, doubtful (HSD)

agartas, *s.m.* Remorse. *Leabhar nan cnoc.*

agh, (AF), *s.f.* Two year old cow.

àgha, *s.m.* See àdha, the liver.

aghaich, (MS), *v.a.* Foreshame.

aghaidheachd, (MS), *s.f.* Resistance.

aghair, *s.m.* See aoghair. Shepherd.

agh-alluidh, (AF), *s.f.* Buffalo, wild cow. 2 Stag.

aghan, (AF), *s.f.* Heifer, see agh.

aghan-goirridh, (AF), *s.m.* Fox-coloured heifer.

aghann-ghrìosaich, *s.f.* Frying-pan.

aghanntaiche, (MS), *s.m.* Adversary.

aghastar, (CR), *s.m.* 2 Bridle.

agh-fèidh, (AF), *s.f.* Fawn, hind. 2 Female of red-deer under one year old.

ag-na-dara, (AF), *s.f.* Heifer in calf.

aghnaiche, *s.m.* Pleader.

aghnaidhe, *s.m.* See adhna, advocate (HSD).

agrail, (MS), *a.* Argumental.

†ahaile, *prep.* Immediately after.

†aibghidheadh, *s.m.* See abachadh, ripening.

-aibh, extension of nominative ending in: Raimh mu'n dunadh na basaibh. Iain Lom T, p.48; Far 'n do shuidheachadh bordaibh. Iain Lom T, p.53.

aibhealaich, (MS), *v.a.* Bemonster.

aibheilt, -eile, *a.* Huge See †aidhbheil Wonder, boasting.

aibheilteachd, *s.f.* Hugeness, monstrosity.

aibheis, *s.f.* 9 Horizon. *Sàr-Obair.*

†aibhind, *a.* See aoibhinn, pleasant, comely.

aibhirsear, *s.m.* See aibhistear, The Devil, destroyer.

àibhisteach, *a.* Affrightful.

aibhseachd, *s.m.* See aibheiseachadh, exaggeration.

†aibhset for chaidh iad.

aic, (DU), for faic. 2 (DU) Pig-sty. 3

(DU) Badly-kept house.

†aicdhe, *s.f.* Veil (HSD).

†aicdhe, *prep.* According to HSD.

†aiceachd, *s.f.* Leading (HSD).

†aicead, for faic iad.

†aiceapta, *s.f.* Religious worship (HSD).

†aicesion for aige-san.

aicheamhaileach, *a.* See aichbheileach, revengeful, vindictive.

aichean, (AF), *s.m.* Cockle.

àicheannach, -aiche, *a.* Negative (HSD).

aichsheun, -ein, -an, *s.m.* See àicheadh, denial, refusal.

aichsheun, (MS), *v.a.* Gainsay.

aicideach, *a.* See acaideach, uneasy, painful, sickly, groaning.

aicidh, *s.f.* Indisposition, malady.

aicidhid, *s.f.* See acaid, pain, hurt.

aicle, *s.f.* Veil.

†aid, *s.* Cold.

aid, *a.* Equal, the same.

aid, *prov.* for iad.

aideal, *s.m.* Sandbank off the coast which is accessible only at low tides.

aidh, (CK), *Sutherland* for taidhe, attention. 'Thug e an aidh dha', *he noticed it*; toir an aidh dha, *take heed to it, attend to it.*

†aidhbhle, *pl.* of aidhbheil. 2 *pl.* of aibheall.

†aidheadh, *s.m.* Death.

†aidheir, *gen.* of adhar.

†aidheitighe, *a.* Very ugly.

aidhis, (AG), *s.* Curse. *Reay country.*

aidhis, (AG), *v.a.* Wish ill to. *Reay country.*

†aidhmhean, *v.* I confess.

†aidhneasair, *s.m.* Opponent.

†aidhniche, *s.m.* Pleader.

†aidhnios, *s.f.* Pleading.

†aidhniorachd, *s.f.* Business of an advocate.

†aidhnis, *v.a.* Debate, plead.

aidhre, (AF), *s.* Flocks. 'Greigh is aidhre Mhannain', *the herds and flocks of the Isle of Man.*

aidhre, *s.f.* See eithre, the tail of a fish.

aidhrine, *s.f.* See aithrine, calf.

†aidhte, *s.pl.* Instruments.

aidmheileach, *s.m.* 2 Professor.

aidreach, (AF), *s.* Milch cow.

aifrionn, *s.m.* MacEachen gives -ean as the plural.

aig. In the *Reay country* aig is used for *gu*, as in the phrase aig ìre= gu ìre. Gheuraich an nàmhaid aig ìre an càil-*Gaelic Elegy* by G. MacKay of Roster. 2 Also means *mac* in *Reay Country*, as Iain aig Iain (Eun aig Eun).

àigeach, *s.m. Gairloch* for òigeach, a stallion.

aigeal, *s.m.* Bottom. ''San t-slochd gun aigeal', *in the bottomless pit. Dain I. Ghobha.*

aigeannach, *a.* 5 High mettled, spirited, as a horse. 6 (MS) Alive.

†aigeidighe, *a.* Acid.

aigh, *s.m.* meaning deer, always has the plural *aighean* in prose.

aighbhirsear, *s.m.* The Devil.

†aighmheil, *s.m.* Fear.

aighear, (MS), *s.m.* Lawyer.

†aighthe, *gen.* of aghaidh, face, visage.

†aigid, *s.f.* Sourness.

aigilean, *s.m.* 4 Aglet (metal tag of a lace; tag or spangle, as a dress ornament). Now written *aiguillette* (Oxford Illustrated Dictionary, p.l.).

†aigill, *v.a.* Address.

aigionnach, (MS), *a.* Pleasant.

aigiontachd, *s.f.* See aigeannachd, stubbornness.

aigneach, *a.* 6 Gladsome.

aigne, (MS), *s.m.* Cue.

aignidheachd, *s.f.* Sprightliness.

ail, *s.f.* Prickle. 2 Stag.

ailbean, (DC), *s.m.* Part of the ebb where marine grass or *zostera marina* grows. *Uist.*

ailbh, *s.f.* See seilbh, possession, property. 2 (AF) Sheep.

ailbh, *s.f.* See †aoilbhinn, small flock.

ailbheag, (AH), *s.f.* Ring-bolt in a boat. No. 32 on D,p.76 (AF).

ailbhinn, *s.f.* 2 Sheep. 5 Sea. 6 Air space.

ail-cuach, (AF), *s.m.* Lizard.

àileadair, -ean, *s.m.* Airer. 2 Perfumer.

aileag, *s.f.* Hiccup. Always *accompanied*, but not always *preceded* by the article an 'Tha aileag a' bhàis air', *he has the death hiccup.*

aileag, (AF), *s.f.* Swallow, see gobhlan gaoithe. 2 Storm-petrel. 3 Meteorite. *Sutherland & Caithness* (DMK).

ailean, Na h-, *s.f.* Part 6 of *toirsgian*, a peat-spade; the socket in *blade-iron, in which the handle and step are inserted.* D,p.960.

ailean, *s.m.* Orts, stubble. 2 (AC) Island. (Reay Country) 3 Shiskine, Arran.

ailean, *s.m.* for airean, a ploughman, as in *Ailean an t-suic,* the space into which the "meargeal" and "uirthilleach" are inserted. See crann-nan-gad, an old-fashioned kind of plough. See D,p.26.

àilean-bhall, -an-bhall, *s.m.* Bowling green.

aileabeartach, s.m. Halberdier.

ailein, s. Delight.

àileis, (DU), *s.f.* Playing. Ag àileis *playing.* Not applied to horseplay, but only to *cluich chàirdeil,* or diversion.

aileiseach, (MS), *a.* Lazy.

ailghean, *a.* Soft, smooth, tender.

ailgheas, *s.* Resumptuousness, sauciness.

àilgheasach, (DMK), *s.* 4 Luxurious Chaidh a thogail glè *à., he was brought up very luxuriously.* 5 Lascivious. 6 Arbitrary (MS).

àilich, (MS), *v.a.* Air.

ailis, *prov.* for atharrais, *s.f.* Mimicry, foolish repetition. 'Sann mar mheagairt a' ghobhair tha ailis a' mhinnein, *according to the goat's bleating is the mimicry of the kid.*

ailitir, *s.f.* Pilgrimage.

†aill, *s.f.* 7 Turn.

aill, *a.* Another. 2 Noble.

àilleachd, *s.f.* 4 Decoration.

ailleagan, *s.m.* Ailleagan mo chluaise, *the hole in my ear.*

ailleanachd, s.f. ind. Bashfulness.

ailliubhar, (AF), *s.m.* Salmon.

ailliubhus, (AF), *s.m.* Salmon.

ailm, *s.f.* 6 Palm tree. †7 see ailmh, flint stone, boundary stone. 8 (AG) says never a boundary stone.

ailmeid, *s.f.* Green dye made by boiling heather tops and alum together (JGC. S., 103).

ailmhin, (AF), *s.* Brood.

ailn, (AC) = àilean, *s.m.* Green, plain, meadow (AG).

ailneachd, (MS), *s.f.* Amiability.

àilneagan, (MS), *s.m.* Trifle. 2 Beauty. 3 See àilleagan.

ailp, (AF), *s.* Elephant.

ailpe, (AF), *s.* Elephant.

ailrich, (MS), *v.a.* Accomplish.

ailsing, *s.f. Kintyre* for aisling, *s.f.* Dream.

†ailt, *s.pl.* Joints.

†ailtnighe, *a.* Sharp.

†ailtreachas, *s.m.* See altrumas *s.m.* Nursing.

ailt-sgèine, *s.f.* Sharp knife.

aimeasguidh (aimsgith), (JM), *a.* Inclined to shy or run away. Each *a.,* a horse inclined to bolt.

aimhealtas, (AG), *s.f.* Home-sickness, longing.

aimhidh, *a.* Sour, sulky, sullen, surly *Sàr-Obair.*

aimhleach, *a.* Dire.

aimhleasaich, *v.a.* Curry, damage.

aimhleig, (AF), *s.f.* Swallow, see gobhlan-gaoithe. 2 Stormy-petrel.

aimhleineachd, *s.f.* Scantiness.

aimhneas, *s.m.* See aoibhneas, gladness.

aimhreidheam, *v.* See aimhreitich, confound, entangle.

aimhreig, see aimreidh, *gen. sing.* of aimhreadh, disturbance, disagreement.

aimileid, (MS), *s.f.* Amulet.

aimlisg, (MS), *s.f.* Cumber. 2 Mischief. Ball aimlisg, *a mischievous person or thing.*

aimlisgeach, *a.* 6 Inconvenient. 7 Barful.

aimlisgeachadh, (MS), *s.m.* Annoyance.

aimlisgear, (MS), *s.m.* Aggressor.

aimlisgich, *v.a.* Ensnare. 2 Annoy. 3 Cumber.

aimsir-eòlas, -ais, *s.m.* Chronology.

ain, *s.m.* 2 see ainn.

ain, *s.f.* Year. 2 see aithne.

ainbheasach, *a.* Humoursome.

ainbheirt, *s.f.* See aimbeairt (for aimbeirt), *gen. sing.* of aimbeart, poverty, want, indigence.

ainbhfeitheach, *a.* Rude, ignorant.

ainbhfheirg, *s.f.* Rage.

ainbhfhial, *a.* Ungenerous.

†ainbhfhior, *a.* Untrue.

ainbhte, (CR), *s.m.* Stot, young bullock, *West of Ross-shire.* 2 see ainmhidh, *s.m.* Brute, animal, beast. 3 *s.f.* (CR) Heifer.

ainbhtean, *s.m.* See ainmhidh, *s.m.* Brute, animal, beast.

†ainble, *s.f.* Badness, malice.

aincheardachd, *s.f.* Buffoonery.

†ainchiallachd, see ainchiall, *s.f.* Peevishness.

†aindeagdha, *a.* Very hostile.

aindealbhaich, *v.n.* Antic.

aindeisealachd, *s.f.* Disadvantage.

ain-dioineachd, (MS), *s.f.* Mercy.

ain-dligheadh, (MS), *s.m.* Illegality, see ain-dlighe, s.m. Injustice.

ain-dlighich, *v.a.* Overtask.

aindreanna, *a.* Immoderately furious.

àine, (CR), *a.* For fàine, *a.* Lower. *Sutherland.*

†aineach, *s.m.* Horsemanship.

†aineachd, *s.m.* Misapplied prowess. 2 Casualty.

aineadas, (CR), *s.m.* Slight provocation. *West of Ross-shire.*

ainealadh, *pr. pt.* A variation of anaileadh. Breathing. 'Gaoth tuath cho cruaidh ri slait 'G ainealadh os cionn ar stuic', *a north wind as hard as a rod breathing above our gunwale.* D. Macpherson, *An Duanaire,* Edinburgh, 1868, p.97.

àineanach, (MS), *a.* Lunged.

†aineas, *s.m.* Acquaintance.

aineigneachd, *s.f.* Dishumour.

aineignidh, (MS), *a.* Surly.

aineis, (MS), *s.* Anise.

aineòlach, *a.* 2 Unknown. 'Is fheàrr an t-olc eòlach na'n t-olc aineòlach', *the known evil is better than the unknown.*

ain-eud, (MS), *s.m.* Bigotry.

ainfheoileach, -eiche, *a.* Proud, fungous, exuberant.

ainfhiach, (JM), *s.m.* Heavy (especially long-standing) debts.

ainfhioghair, see aindealbh, *s.m.* Unseemly figure. 2 Distorted picture. D,p.15.

†ainfine, s. pl. Foreigners.

aing, (CR), *s.* Hatred, spite, ill-will. *Sutherland.* 2 Anger, displeasure. *Lewis.*

aingeach, (CR), *a.* Malicious, spiteful.

aingealta, (MS), *a.* 3 Peevish. 4 Rude.

aingealtas, (MS), *s.m.* Huff.

†aingin, *s.f.* Disaster.

àingleach, (MS), *a.* Igneous 2 Angelic.

àingleachadh, (MS), *s.m.* Ignition.

aingleachd, (MS), see ainglidheachd, *s.f.* Angelicalness.

àinich, *v.n.* Pant, breathe with a noise.

†ainicthe, *s.f.* Purification. 2 Release.

†ainiceam, *v.* I shun, avoid, defend.

ainigidh, (AG), *a. Reay country* for aingidh, *a.* Wicked. D,p.16.

†ainleanach, *a.* Persecuting, oppressive.

ainleog, -oig, -an, *s.f.* Swallow.

ainlinn, *S.* Swallow.

ainignidh, *a. Uist* for aingidh, *a.* Wicked. D,p.16.

ainm, *s.m.* An ainm an àigh, *in the name of goodness! Goodness gracious!*

ainmach, see anmoch, *a.* Late. D,p.35.

ainmaideach, (AG), C' ainmaideach?, What do you call him? *Reay Country.*

ainmeachadh, *s.m.* Denomination.

ainmean, (AG), C' ainmean e?, *what-do-you-call-it? Reay Country.*

ainmeanach, *a.* Denominative.

ainmheadh, (AF), *s.* Cattle.

ainmhide, (CR), *s.m.* Beast. This is the primary meaning, those on D,p.16 being metaphorical. 3 Heifer. *Creich, Sutherland* and *West Ross-Shire.*

ainmhidean, (CK), *s.m.* One year old heifer, heifer-stirk. *Creich, Sutherland.*

ainmhidean, *s.pl.* of ainmhide. 2 In *Farr, plural* of ainmhidh.

ainmhidh, (CR), *s.* 2 Heifer. *Sutherland* pronounced in *Creich* and in *Farr* ana'i and ena'i (*n* long), while in ainmhidh (beast), the *v* sound of *mh* is retained in *Arran,* the word commonly meaning a horse. In *Farr,* ainmhidean, the *plural* of ainmhide is also used as the *plural* of ainmhidh.

ainmhidheil, see ainmhidheach, *a.* Brutal.

†ain-mhìn, *a.* Rough, fierce.

†ainmhinte, pl. of ainmhidh.

†ainmhire, s.f. Fury.

†ainmhireach, *a.* Furious, see anabhiorach *s.m.* Centipede. 2 Whitlow. D,p.30.

ainmiceachd, (MS), *s.f.* Rareness.

ainmiceas, -eis, *s.m.* Infrequency, see ainmigead, *s.m.* Rareness. D,p.17.

ainmig, see 'b'ainmig a leithid.' D,p.17, is more generally and usually expressed, 'B'ainneamh a leithid.'

ainmigeachd, *s.f.* Seldomness.

àinne, see ainn (fàinne), *s.f.* Ring. D, p.406.

ainneanta, *a.* 2 Stiff, obstinate.

†ainnear, -ir, see ainnir, *s.f.* Virgin. D,p.16.

ainneartaich, (MS), *v.a.* Ransack.

ainneartaich, (HSD), *v.a.* Gripe, oppress

ainneartair, (MS), *s.m.* Griper.

ainneist, see àirneis, *s.f.* Household furniture. D,p.21.

ainnich, -e, -ean, *s.f.* Sob.

†ainnimh, (HSD), s.f. Wilderness.

†ainnine, (HSD), a. Prodigal.

ainnis, (MS), s.f. 5 Emptiness, barrenness.

†ainniuid, (HSD), *a.* Prodigal.

†ainnsein, (HSD), for ann an sin.

ainriochdaich, (MS), *v.a.* Unmask, inmask.

ainsgeach, see ainsgeineach, a. D,p.17.

ainsgeanta, (HSD), -einte, *a.* Furious, ill-tempered.

ain-sheasgair, (HSD), *a.* 2 Rude.

ainstil, (HSD), *s.f.* Fury, disorder.

aintheas, see aintheasachd, *s.f.* Feverishness.

air, "Mar is lugha 'sann is fheàrr", is the usual expression for 'air a lughad 's fheàirrd', the smaller the better. D,p.18

air, over. In Arran, 'Dol air bèinn' means *going over the hill*, but in the *south* of Arran it also means *going to Lamlash.* 2 Or in *Sutherland*, 'Bheag air mhòr', means *little or much.*

air ais, *adv.* Back.

air banidh, (MS), *adv.* Bestraught.

†airbhe, *s.f.* Fence. Obsolete except in place-names.

†airbheart-bhith, s.m. Life.

†airce, *a.* Sudden.

†airceadol, *s.m.* Rhythmic history.

àircein, see àrcan, s.m. Cork. D,p.44.

†airceisin, *adv.* Therefore, on that account.

aircheadal, *s.m.* Doctrine, prophecy.

†airchealtrach, (AF), *s.* Hind of three years. 2 Cow. 3 Hind.

†aircheana, *adv.* From thence forward.

†aircheann, *s.m.* Border. 2 End.

airchios, *s.m.* Pity.

airchis, *s.f.* 4 see aircis below.

air chor, *adv.* So that.

†air cill, s.f. Lying in wait.

†aircinneach, *s.m.* Chief of a clan.

aircis, *s.f.* Pity, clemency, compassion. 2 Meeting. 3 Hide. 4 Rigour.

àird, *s.f.* 9 Activity. D,p.19.

àirdeachd, *s.f.* 'Cumaidh iad à. riut', *they will make a course for thee*, but in West Highland Tales it is mistranslated, *they will keep company with thee.*

airdeal, (DU), *a.* Orderly, well-kept. taigh airdeal, *a well-kept house.*

air deo, (air neo), *adv.* If not, except. *Arran.*

†airdhe, *a.* Bad.

†airdreanna, s.f. Constellation.

aire, *s.f.* In *Arran*, 'Tha e an aire dha', *he intends.*

àireach, -eich, *s.m.* See àrach. D, p. 43.

àireach, (MS), *s.m.* 5 Bowman. *Hebrides*

àireachas, (MS), *s.m.* 6 Dairy.

†aireachd, *s.f.* Band, company.

aireach-fada, (AF), *s.* Pack-horse.

†airead, *s.f.* Band, company.

†aireagal, -ail, *s.m.* House, habitation.

àireamh, *v.a.* Number, count, compute. see D,p.20. 2 Reckon, think. In *Arran*, "tha mi 'g airea' gu'n e th'ann", *I think that it is he.* 'Tha mi 'g airea' gu'n dèan sin feum'. *I think that will do.* It is airea', not àirea', except when the word stands last, as 'Is e seo e tha mi'g àirea' ', *I am at thinking*, and at Shiskine and the Northend it is "tha mi'g àireamh, the *mh* being pronounced as *v*, so that the prime meaning is *I reckon.*

àireamhach, *s.m.* 4 Arithmetician.

àireamhach, *a.* 2 Arithmetical.

àireamhail, *a.* Numerical.

àirean, (RGG), *s.m.* Green patches among hills. Hill dwellings.

aire-san, *adv.* Thereupon.

†airfear, for àirmhear, *fut.* Passive of *v.* àireamh. D,p.21.

†airg, v. Spoil, plunder.

airge, (AF), *s.* Cattle, herd.

airgeadh, *s.m. & pr. pt.* Rifling, consuming.

†airgeirne, s.f. Cow-calf.

airghe, (AF), *s.* Cattle, herd.

airgheannach-srèine, see arannachsrèine, *s.m.* Bridle-rein. D,p.43.

†airgin, v. See airg, *s.m.* Prince.

airgiodaich, *v.a.* Plate, cover with silver.

†airgneach, *a.* Boisterous, enraged.

†airgtheach, *s.m.* Robber, spoiler.

†airidhe, s.f. Spectres, visions. 2 Preparations.

airidheachd, *s.f.* Worthiness.

†airigh, see àiridh, s.f. Sheiling.

†airigh, *v.a.* Observe.

†airigheachd, *s.f.* Speciality, sovereignty.

†airlichthe, *past. pt.* Lent.

airm, *Sutherland* for ainm, *s.m.* Name.

†airmghean, *a.* Well-born.

air mheirean, (MS), *adv.* Bestraught.

airmidinn, see airmid, an obsolete word for honour.

†airmidneach, *a.* Venerable, respectable.

airmig, *Sutherland* for ainmig, *adv.* Seldom.

†airne, (DC), *s.f.* Steep, rough. 4 Wooded hill or rock. Bluff.

†airneachd, *s.f.* Deer forest.

†airneadha, see àirneach, *s.m.* Murrain in cattle.

†airneadhach, *a.* Shrubby.

airneir, (AF), *s.* Cattle.

airneist, (DC), *s.f.* Cattle stock of a farm.

air oir, *adv.* On edge.

airrdhea, *s.pl.* Implements of destruction

àirseachail, (MS), *a.* For àrsaidheach Archaeological.

airsear, (AF), *s.m.* Dog, snapper.

†airtneamh, -eimh, *s.f.* Soldier's whetstone.

airtneulach, (MS), *a.* Insipid.

aiseach, *a.* Cheap. 2 see athaiseach, *a.* Slow, tardy. D,p.50.

aisead-roimh-mhithich, (AH), *s.f.* Premature delivery, premature childbirth.

aiseagachd, (MS), *s.f.* Passability of a ferry *et cetera.*

†aisealbha, *s.m.* Restitution.

aisean, *s.f.* 2 Joggled frame in a boat (C. in first column, D,p.73).

aisearranachd, (MS), *s.f.* Abjectness.

aisgeadh, *s.m.* Desire.

aisil an t-seic, *s.f.*, the same as dealgan na teic, spindle of the flyer of a spinning wheel. D,p.290, 23.

aisileag, (AH), *s.f.* see asaileag, *s.f.* Stormy-petrel, storm finch. D,p.49.

ais-imeachd, (MS), *s.f.* Counter-march.

ais-imeachd, *pr. pt.* of ais-imich, *v.n.* Go back.

aislingich, *v.n.* Dream.

aisne, *s.* Spoke of the driving-wheel of a spinning-wheel.

†aisneadh, for aisnean, *s.f.*, plural of aisean. Ribs.

aisridh, (CR), *s.f.* Axle-tree. *Arran.*

aisridh, *s.f.* 5 Pass, defile. 6 (G) Narrow step.

†aisteachan, *s:pl.* Sports, diversions.

aisthillteach, (MS), *a.* Repercussive.

†aistrioch, a. Inconstant.

†ait, *s.f.* Furze, gorse, whins.

àiteachaileachd, (MS), *s.f.* Habitableness

aiteal, (MS), *s.m.* A second of time.

aitealluidh, see itealaich, *s.f.* Flying, fluttering.

àitear, (MS), *s.m.* 2 Habitant.

àitfhear, see àitear, above.

†aithbhear, *s.m.* Blame, reproof.

aithchein, (MS), *v.a.* Recant.

aith-chiall, (MS), *s.m.* Alogy.

†aithdhreachadh, *s.m.* Reformation.

aitheach, (MS), *s.m.* 4 Cow.

aitheanach, (MS), *a.* Hepatical.

àitheanta, *n.pl* of àithne, *s.f.* Knowledge. 2 see athainte and aithnichte, past pt. of aithnich, Known.

†àitheantas, -ais, s.f. Acquaintance.

†aithearrach, see atharrach, *a.* Strange, curious, droll. Also obsolete.

†aitheasach, *a.* Impetuous.

†aitheasg, -eisg, *s.f.* Words, speech. 3 Commission, mandate.

†aithfear, *s.m.* Reproof.

†aithghe, *gen.* of aghaidh, *s.f.* Face.

aithghear, *a.* Very sharp.

aithghearan, *s.m.* Short-cut, foot-path.

aith-gheàrradh, *s.m.* 3 Aftermath.

aith-gheàrraich, *v.a.* see aith-gheàrr *v.a.* Cut again. D,p.23.

aithich, *pl.* of aitheach, *s.m.* False assertion. D,p.23.

aithinn, (DU), -inne, *s.f.* Remorse, vexation. 2 Difficulties. 'Tha aithinn orm', *I am sorry, vexed*; 'Tha a' chaora ann an aithinn', *the sheep is in difficulties*, e.g. caught in brambles *et cetera.*

†aithios, see aithis, *s.f.* Check. D,p.23.

aithir, see faithir, *s.* The shelving slope

between an old raised beach or other plateau, and the present beach. *West of Ross-shire.*

†aithir, see aighear, *s.m.* Gladness. 2 see faithir above. ' 'Se Coire Cheathaich an t-aithir prìseil'. Donn. Bàn.

aithis, (MS), *s.f.* 9 Fling.

aithle, -an, *s.f.* Old rag. Trace, vestige.

†àithn, *a.* See àin, *a.* Honourable. D, p. 14.

àithne, see aithinn, above.

aithneachdan, *Sutherland* form of *pr. pt.* of aithnich, instead of ag aithneachadh.

aithneanntach, *a.* Imposeable.

aithnich, *pr. pt.* in *Sutherland*, ag aith-neachdan.

aithn'teach, see aithneanntach, above.

†aithread, *s.m.* Patrimony.

†aithreas, s.m. Healing, curing.

aithrir, see oirthir, *s.f.* Coast D,p.708.

aithriseachd, *s.f.* 2 Imitatorship.

aitidh, *a.* 2 *Badenoch* for aiteamh.

aitir, *s.* Ebb, see oitir, *s.f.* Bank or ridge in the sea. D,p.708.

aitreabh, *s.m.* 4, (MS). Apartment.

aitreabh, s.f. in *Badenoch.*

àitreabhachd, (MS), s.f. Habitableness. 2 Architecture.

àl, (CR), *s.* 'Bò le a h-àl', cow with her progeny, including, according to the district, in addition to calf at foot, stirk, stirk and quey, or stirk, quey and 3-year-old heifer.

al, see all, *s.m.* Horse *et cetera* and *a.* White, foreign, great. See D,p.25.

†ala, *a.* Speckled, spotted.

ala s.m. 3 Nursing. 4 Wisdom. 5 Swan.

àlach, (DU), *s.m.* 8 Spell of any kind of activity, a "go". Thoir àlach air, *have a go at him.* 9 Brood. *pl.* àlaich, means a setting-on, attack with fists. Thug e àlaich air, *he gave him some rounds* (of boxing).

àlachadh, (MS), *s.m.* Seed.

àlachail, (MS), *a.* Alible, generative.

alachd, (CR), *s.f.* Carcase. *Sutherland.* 2 Sheep found dead (for falachd, from fuil, fala *blood.) West of Ross-shire.* D.U. gives *s.m.*

†alachda, s.m. Burial.

†aladh-ghorm, a. Speckled.

†aladhnach, *a.* Crafty. 2 Comical.

ala-gual, -uail, *s.m.* Pit-coal.

†alaich, *v.a.* Salute, hail. 2 Invade.

àlainnich, (MS), *v.a.* Grace.

alair, (DU), *s.m.* Funeral with special reference to the refreshment supplied to the mourners and carriers of the coffin.

alamh, see almha, below.

alanaine, (AF), *s.* Cattle.

alban, (AF), *s.* A small herd of cattle.

albannaich, (AF), s. Coulterner.

albh, (AF), *s.* Flock, herd, drove.

albhag, *Arran* for ailbheag, *s.f.* Ring D,p.12.

albhan-dubh, (DMK), s.m. Elephant *West coast of Ross-shire.*

albhinn, see ailbhinn, *s.f.* Flint.

alc, (AF), *s.m.* Auk. *Sutherland.* 2. Great auk. Also alca, (AF).

all, (DMK), *s.* 6 Heifer. 7 Elk (AF).

all, *a.* Another.

allabhair, (AF), *s.* See madadh-allaidh s.m. Wolf. D,p.380.

allabhi, *s.f.* Perforated St. John's Wort see eala-bhuidhe, *s.f.* D,p.380.

allabus, (AF), *s.m.* Great salmon.

allachaig, see ealachag, *s.f. Poolewe* for a block or hacking-stock.

allad, *a.* Old, of old.

†allan, *adv.* In former times.

†allanair, for a làimh an ear.

allan-fionn, *s.m.* Spinal marrow of man or beast. *Caithness.*

allibus, see allabus, *s.m.* Great salmon.

allmharrachd, *s.f.* †2 Barbarity.

allt, air, *adv.* So that, on account of. 'Air allt 's nach b'urrainn domh tighinn', *so that or for which reason I could not come.*

†alltuidh, *a.* See allaidh, *a.* Savage. D,p.25.

all'uair, (DMK), *s.* Hour or time of gasconade. *West coast of Ross-shire.*

†alma, *s.f.* Cattle.

alman, s.m. Aluminium.

almha, (AF), *s.* Cattle.

almsadh, *s.m.* Charity. Air almsadh, *out of charity. Dain I. Gobha.*

†alon, *s.m.* Stone.

alpach, (MS), *a.* Articular.

alpanach, *a.* Knotted.

alt. In *Arran* 'air alt' was a very common

expression and meant properly, rightly, perfectly. 'Thuig mi air alt', *I understood him perfectly*; cha'n 'eil fhios agam air alt, *I do not rightly know.*

alt, *s.m.* 3 Edifice. 4 Action, deed. Cha'n fhac iad alt deth, *did they not see an action of it? Celt. Rev.* II.

altaich, *v.* 9 Articulate. 10 Confess a fault to a superior.

altair, *s.* 'An uair a gheibh e fios gu'm bheil thu'm meas d'a altair', *when he will get knowledge that you are the fruit of his altar.* Duanaire, p.3.

altanach, (MS), *a.* Articular.

altar, (CR), *a.* Orderly, tidy. *Arran.*

alt-dubh, (MMcD), *s.m.* Neck-joint. *Lewis.*

alt-labhrach, (MS), *a.* Articulate.

†altraghadh, see altachadh, *s.m.* articulation of the joints. D,p.26.

alunn, (AF), *s.m.* Swan.

àm, *s.m.* An àm dol seachad amhaircidh e ortsa, *while going past he will look at you.* W.H., I.15.

†am, *s.m.* Circle.

ama-bhiorach, see ana-bhiorach, *s.m.* Centipede. D,p.31.

àmadair, *s.m.* Watch.

amadan, s.m. 2 Shaft or connecting rod between the treadle and crank of the driving-wheel, converting reciprocal into circular motion. Illustration 246, Cuidheall-shnìomha (MMcD) D,p.289. *Skye* and *West of Ross.*

amadan-Bealltuinn, *s.m.* Whimbrel, May-fowl. Very numerous in the Western Isles during the first fortnight in May, on their migration north. They are not distinguishable from the curlew to the uninitiated, but unlike that bird they will allow strangers to approach to well within gun-shot. Hence their name.

amadan-leithe, *s.m.* See dearbadan-dè. Butterfly. D,p.320.

amadan-mòintich, *s.m.* 2 Widgeon. 3 Snipe (AF) 4 Ringed plover (AF).

amadanachas, (MS), -ais, *s.m.* Apishness.

amadanaich, *v.a.* Besot.

a mach is employed both of motion and rest in *Perthshire* and 'a muigh' is not used there. (CR).

amaghar, Assynt pronunciation for àmhghar, *s.m.* Affliction. D,p.29.

amaideach, *s.m.* Dizziness from weakness.

amaideas, -eis. See amaideachd, *s.f.* Foolishness. D,p.27.

amail, *v.a.* 3 Infringe. 4 Choke (MS).

†amail, *a.* Broken, lost.

amailt, (MS), *s.f.* Hindrance.

amailteach, (MS), *a.* Barful.

amairt, *s.f.* Need, poverty. Dream a bha an amairt, *people that were in poverty.*

amaisgeil, *a.* Hitting, finding. R.7.

amal, *s.m.* Curl. 'na amlaibh. Conn Mac an Deirg. *Young's version.*

amaladh, *s.m.* 5 Destruction. 6 Ear mark on sheep, see under Illustration 185 and Names of Ear Marks on Sheep, 10. D,p.238. 7 (MS) Bar.

amalaich, (MS), *v.a.* Hinder.

amall, *s.m.* (Additional. See D,p.28). 5 Main swingle-tree, double tree. 6 See cuibh, *s.f.* D,p.287. Extra parts of a swingle-tree. 10 Lùb, *s.f.*, lùbach, *s.f.* Iron loop at the end and in the middle of the swingle-tree. 11 Cadhag, *s.f.* Swingle-tree wedge. 12 Gearrach, (CR), *s.m.* Rope from the harrow to the swingle-tree. 13 Gearraiseach, -eich, *s.m.* The chain or rope from the swingle-tree to the horses (CR) *West of Ross-shire.* 14 Geidh amaill, *s.* Iron band round the swingle-tree. 15 Amall beag, *s.m.* Small swingle-tree, "yolk". *West of Ross-shire.*

amar, *s.m.* 7 See amar-mine below.

†amar, s.m. 2 General.

amar-mine, (DMK), *s.m.* Part of a Highland mill into which the meal dropped as it was being ground, and into which it was generally sifted. *Caithness.*

amar-sìl, *s.m.* Manger.

amart, *prov., s.* Need.

amas, (MS), *s.m.* 4 Accident.

amasach, (MS), *a.* Accidental, adventive, adventitious.

amasaich, (MS), *v.a.* Aim.

amchannan, *Leabhar-nan-cnoc*, 261/9, for amhachannan.

†amh, *prep.* for maille ri, with, together with.

amhach, *s.f.* 2 Collar of bacon. 3 Part of a plough extending from the upper corner of the furrow-board to the muzzle-holder. D,p.261.

amhachail, -e, *a.* Necked.

†amhaich, *v.a.* Profess.

amhailt, -ean, *s.f.* Wile, stratagem. R.84.

amhalachd, (MS), *s.f.* Rawness.

†amhan, see †omhan, *s.m.* Fear and uamhann, *s.m.* Dread.

†amhanchall, *s.f.* The letter X.

àmharanach, *a.* Unapprehensive.

amharus, (MS), *s.m.* 2 Jealousy.

amharusach, (MS), *a.* Jealous.

†amhas, *s.m.* Man of quality.

amhasan, see amhsan, *s.m.* Gannet. D,p.30.

amhasg, see amhas, *s.m.* Wild, ungovernable man. D,p.29.

amchadh, see amcha, *s.f.* Cravat. D, p.29.

amh-dheoch, (DU), *s.f.* Drunkenness where the tippler is inactive and dull.

amhladh, *s.m.* 3 Distress, dismay. *Dàin I. Ghobha.*

amhlag, see amhlan. †2 see adhlac, *s.f.* Burial. D,p.8.

amhlag, (AF), *s.f.* Swallow, see gobhlan-gaoithe, *s.m.* & *f.*, D,p.512. 2 Storm-petrel.

amhlag-mhara, s.f. 2 Swallow.

†amhnar, *a.* Shameless.

†amhnas, *a.* Direful, formidable.

amhra, *a.* 3 Prosperous, lucky.

àmhradh, (MS), *s.m.* Ill.

amhraig, *Sutherland* for amhairc, *v.n.* Look. D,p.29.

†amhsan, -aine, *s.m.* Habitation.

†amhus, -uis, s.m. Hero.

†amhus, *a.* Restless.

amlach, -aiche, *a.* 3 Preventive.

†amm, *a.* Mischievous lad. 2 v. Refuse.

†amnus, *a.* Formidable.

amod, *s.m.* Green · plain almost encircled by the bend of a river or perhaps the meeting of two waters. It occurs twice in *Kintyre.*

†amodh, see air mhodh, *adv.* So that, in such a manner. D,p.21.

†amoileadh, see amladh, *s.m.* Copy, duplicate. D,p.29.

†amri, *s.f.* Kneading-trough.

amsgaoidh, (MS), *s.* Hare-brained, shatter-pated.

amsgaoith (MS) s. Affectation.

amasgaoitheachd, (MS), *s.f.* Headiness.

†amuich, *adv.* See muigh, *adv.* Out, without. D,p.676.

†amuid, *s.m.* Spectre, ghost.

amulaid, *s.* Unsteady person. *Sutherland.*

†amus *s.m.* †4 Noble youth. D,p.30.

amus (MS), *s.m.* Cast.

an, *prep.* In. In the *West* it still retains its double use like the Latin *in.* C'àite bheil thu fuireach? An taigh Aonghuis; c'àite bheil thu dol? 'Na bhùthaidh.

-an. Diminutive names of Saints ending in *an*, as Conan, Adhamhnan, etc. do not take an *i* in the genitive singular, as Caisteal Eilean Donan.

anabas, -ais, *s.m.* 3 Unripe cut stuff. D,p.30.

anabhiorach, *a.* 2 Ferocious, furious.

anacachd, *s.f.* Adversity, affliction.

ana-caitheinich, *prov.* for anacaitheamh, *s.m.* Extravagance, prodigality. D,p.31.

ana-caithteachd, *s.f.* See ana-caitheamh *s.m.* Extravagance, waste. D,p.31.

anacal, -ail, *s.m.* †3 Defence.

†anachd, s.f. Quiet.

ana-chuimheasachd, (MS), *s.f.* Prodigiousness.

ana-cleachdadh, *s.m.* 5 (MS) Abuse.

ana-cothrom, *s.f.* 4 (DU) Discomfort (the common meaning in *Wester Ross*).

ana-cothromach, *a.* 4 (DU) Uncomfortable *West coast of Ross-shire.*

ana-creideas, (MS), *s.m.* Incredulity.

ana-crìosdachd, *s.m.* 2 Pagan world.

ana-crìosdalachd, *s.f.* 2 Barbarity, cruelty.

ana-cudthromaich, *v.a.* Preponderate.

ana-cuibheasach, *a.* 2 Measureless.

ana-cuimheasach, see ana-cuimseach, *a.* Vast, immense.

ana-cuimseach, *a.* 3 (MS) Excessive, exorbitant.

ana-cùirtear, (MS), *s.m.* Anti-courtier.

†anacul, -uil, *s.m.* Defence.

ana-culachd, *s.f.* Leanness.

ana-ghlaodh, -aoidh, *s.m.* Loud shout.

anagladh tearnadh, *s.m.* Protection, *Sàr Obair*.

anagna, see ana-ghnàth, *s.m.* Bad custom, irregular habit D,p.32.

ana-gnèitheach, *a.* Dissimilar, heterogeneous.

an-aigneach, (MS), *a.* Sudden.

an-aigneachd, (MS), *s.f.* Curtness. 2 Harshness.

anaigneachd, *s.f.* Sullenness.

an-aignidh, (MS), *a.* Cursed (?Dwelly, 'Curst'). 2 Swart. 3 Incomposed.

anail, *s.f.* 4 Opinion, in *Arran*. Na'm faigheadh tu 'anail air, *if you would get his opinion on it* – evidently an adaptation of the Lowland "get his breath on it", probably derived from Gaelic *breith*, judgment.

an-airidh, -e, *a.* Illaudable.

anaisg, *s.f.* 2 (DMK), Nickname. Very common on *West coast of Ross*.

anaite, (DMK), *s.f.* Heifer. *Northern counties*.

analachadh, (MS), *s.m.* Inhalation.

analachd, *s.f.* Respiration.

analaiche, (MS), *s.m.* Breather.

an-altaich, (MS), *v.a.* Actuate.

anam (soul). *gen. sing.* anamain and an'main, *n.pl.* anamana. *Sutherland*.

anamaidibh, *pl.* of anam. *Assynt*.

anamain, genitive of anam. *Sutherland*.

anamaint, *s.f.* Lust, perversity. Ionad tàimhe gach anamaint, *the abiding place of every perversity. Dàin I. Ghobha*.

anamana. *n.pl.* of anam. *Sutherland*.

anamanach, (MS), *a.* Animable.

anamanaich, (MS), *v.a.* Animate.

anamanta, (MS), *a.* Animated.

ana-meas, *v.a.* Over-value.

†anamhla, *a.* Unlike, anomalous.

ana-miannachd, *s.f. ind.* Libidinousness.

ana-miannaich, *v.a.* Lust.

†an-annag, *a.* Impure.

ana-puinnseanach, -aiche, *a.* Antidotal.

anardolach, *a.* Intransitive in *grammar*.

anartach, -aiche, *a.* Linen.

anastachd, (CR), *s.f.* Hardiness, endurance of cold. *Arran*.

†an-athlomh, for an-ealamh *a*, indolent. D,p.34.

†anba, a. Prodigious.

†anbas, *s.m.* Deadly terror.

†anbfolta, *s.m.* Rage.

†anbhaine, *s.f.* Ecstasy.

†anbhainnigheadh, see anfhannaich, *v.a.* Enfeeble. D,p.34.

anbharrachadh, (MS), *s.m.* Amplification.

†anbhfhainne, *s.f.* Fainting, weakness.

†anbhfholtach, -aiche, *a.* Resentful, 2 Murderous.

†anbhodh, *s.m.* Falsehood.

†an-bhorb, *a.* Furious.

†anbhrith, *s.m.* Broth.

†anbhuain, *s.f.* Agony.

an ceartair, *adv.* (an ceart uair) *prov. pron.* "an gearduair". Immediately.

an-chleachdadh, see ana-cleachdadh *s.m.* Inexperience. D,p.31.

an-dàimh, -e, *s.m.* Inconnection.

an-dealbhachd, *s.f.* Inconcinnity.

an-deisealachd, (MS), *s.f.* Incommodiousness.

an-deisealaich, (MS), *v.a.* Incommode.

an-deurach, *a.* 5 (MS) Illachrymable.

an-dligheachas, see ain-dligheachd, *s.f. Ind.* Unlawfulness. D,p.15.

an-doimhneachd, (MS), *s.f.* Profoundness.

an eanar, Kintyre for an earar, the day after tomorrow.

†anfam, *v.n.* I stay, remain.

an-fheum, (MS), *s.* Abuse.

†anfhlath, -a, *s.m.* Tyrant.

†anfhobhrachd, *s.f.* Skeleton.

†anfholta, *s.m.* Affront, insult.

†anfhorasda, for an-fhurasda, *a.* Difficult. D,p.34.

an-fhuaimneach, -aiche, *a.* Inaudible.

†anfus, see anfam above.

†ang, a. Great.

†an-gairm, s.f. Appellation.

a niarraidh, (CR), *adv.* Middling in health. In reply to an enquiry about health, literally "in quest", *ann iarraidh*.

an-iarrtas, *s.m.* 3 Wrong desire.

an-iomadachd, *s.f. ind.* Superfluity.

†anius, *s.m.* Soothsayer. 2 Augur.

an-laghail, (MS), *a.* Anomalistic.

an-lainnirich, (MS), *v.n.* Dazzle.

an-luchd, -an, *s.m.* 4 Surcharge.

an-lus, (CK), *s.m.* Weed. *Sutherland*.

anmanach, *a.* 'Nuair 'thiginn dachaidh o'n bhuain, 's mi gu h-anmanach fuar', *when coming home from the reaping I was exceedingly cold. Duanaire*, 146.

†anmaois, *v.n.* We may stay.

†anmhoin, see fantuinn, *s.f. ind.* Staying. D,p.411.

†an'moiche, see an-mothachadh, *s.m.* Unfeeling.

†anmunnach, -aiche, *a.* Late in the evening.

ann. 'S e bh'ann gum b'èiginn mac an rìgh thabhairt do'n fhamhair, *this is what was in it, that it was necessary to give the prince to the giant.* W.H., I,41.

In Lochalsh and Wester Ross, *uime* is commonly used in composition with the first and second personal pronouns, singular and plural, where *ann* would be correct. "Cha'n 'eil umad ach amadan", *you are only a fool.* The 3rd person plural used is *annta.*

†annaid, s.f. Year.

annalaiche, (MS), s.m. Analyst.

†annamach, -aich, see ainmeachadh, *s.m.* Naming. D,p.16.

annas, *s.m.* 4 Darling. 5 (MS) Sight.

ann-deurach, *a*, see an-deurach above.

annos, *s.m.*, see annas, *s.m.* 4 (MS) maidenhead.

anns, in. Used before place names in *Sutherland.* Anns Raghart, *in Rogart.* Anns Bun-uillidh, *in Helmsdale.*

annsail, (G), *a.* Gleeful.

†anntar, *s.m.* Conflict of death.

ànrachd, *s.m.* Diminutive, ill-looking person.

ànradh, *s.m.* 3 Hardship. 4 Wandering, sojourning. 5 Degree of poetry.

†anradh, *s.m.* Boon, petition.

ànradhach, -aiche, *a.* 6 Disastrous, unfortunate.

an-riochd, *s.* Figment.

an-riochdaich, (MS), *v.a.* Besmirch.

an-riochdaichte,)MS), *a.* Affected.

†ansadhail, *a.* Miserable.

an-samhluichte, *a.* Incomparable.

an-sannt, *s.m. ind.* See an-shannt, *s.m.* Greed, covetousness. D,p.36.

an seo, *adv.* 2 Hither.

ansgoch, *s.* See ceann ruadh, An, *s.m.* Celandine. D,p.179.

an sin, *adv.* There. 2 Thither. 3 Then.

an-stèibheadh, *s.m.* Indetermination.

anstocaich, (MS), *v.a.* Overstock.

an-suidheachadh, *s.m.* Indetermination.

†antan (An t-ansoin), *adv.* In the time.

†antarruing, *s.f.* Strife.

an-tlachd, *s.m.* 4 (MS) Anger.

antoil, *s.f.* Gun a h-antoil thoirt dha, *without being disinclined to him.* R. 16.

an-toileach, *a.* 4 (MS) Arbitrarious.

an-toileachadh, *s.m.* Grumbling.

†an-toilidheachd, *s.f.* Concupiscence.

†an toirdhear. See an ear, *s.f.* The East. D,p.383.

an-uair, *s.f.* 3 Evil hour.

†an-uallaich, *v.a.* Overburden.

aobard, -an, (DMK), *s.m.* Ankle. *West Coast of Ross-shire.*

aobart See aobard, above.

aobhar, *s.m.* Aobhar taighe, *materials for making a house*; aobhar ministeir, *the prospective or probationary minister*; tha aobhar rìgh an Naoise, *Naoise has the makings of a king in him.*

aobharach, *a.* 4 (MS) Ascribable.

aobharaich, (MS), *v.a.* Ascribe.

aobhar-dùsguidh, *s.m.* Excitement.

aobharrach, *s.m.* 5 Hobbledehoy.

†aobhdha, *a.* See aobhach, *a.* Joyous, glad, cheerful. 2 Beautiful. D,p.37.

aobrann, *s.m.* Ankle. *Aobard* and *aobart* are variations in *Wester Ross.* Plural, aobardan.

aobrannach, *a.* Ankled.

aodach-oidhche, (DMK), *s.* Bedclothes. *West coast of Ross-shire.*

aodann, alternative plural aoidnean.

aodann, *s.f.* 4 Façade.

aodann-fuadair, *s.m.* Mask.

†aodhar. See athar, s.m. Sky. D. p. 51.

†ao-fhuathmhor, *a.* Detestable.

aog-dhruidheachd, *s.f.* Necromancy.

aoghaireil, -e, *a.* Pastoral.

aoghaist, (CR), *s.* the *gh* is sounded. Fishing-line. *Strathtay.*

aogharachd, *s.f.* Pastorship.

aognachail, (MS), *a.* Abominable.

aognachd, (MS), *s.f.* Abominableness. 2

Gloominess.

aognaich, v.a. 4 (MS), Abhor.

aognaidh, a. 2 (MS) Gloomy. 3 Of deathly hue.

†aoi, s.m. & f. 18 (AF) Cow, cattle.

aoibh, -e, s.f. 4 Aspect. 5 Affability. 6 Murmur. 7 Resort.

aoibheach, -eiche, a. Affable, courteous. 2 Hospitable.

aoideach, (AF), s.f. Cow.

†aoideanach, a. Well behaved.

aoideogam, v. I bind the hair.

aoidhich, v.a. House.

aoidnean, n.pl. of aodann, s.f. Face.

aoifi, a. Sweet.

aoigheach, (MS), a. Kindly.

aoileis, (MS), s.f. Truantship. 2 Vacancy.

aoileisich, (MS), v.n. While.

aoilfeog. See ailseag, s.f. Caterpillar D,p.13.

aoineadh, s.m. 2 Very steep hillside. 3 Stretch of steep brae surmounted by rocks. W & S, ii, 86.

aoineagaich. See aonagaich, v.n. Wallow, welter. D,p.40.

aoineagraich. See aonagaich above.

†aoinfheachd, adv. At once.

†aoinghein, for aon ghin, s.m. Only begotten one. D,p.41.

†aoire. See aoghair, s.m. Shepherd. D,p.38.

†aoireachdainn, s.f. Exclaiming against, blaming.

aoirean, s.m. See airean, s.m. Ploughman, Goadsman.

aoireann, gen. aoireann. dat. aoirinn. Ferry in place names. Celtic Rev. 3, 92.

†aoireil, a. Invective.

aoirneadh. See fuasgladh.

aoisich (MS) v.a. Antiquate.

aolaisde, (MS), s. After-wit.

aol-taigh. See oil-thaigh, s.m. School, seminary, college. D,p.706.

aoltair Gu'm biodh aoltair an fhuarain. Duanaire, 62.

aomad, (DU), s.m. Repairs effected on a worn plough-share or peat-knife, by welding a piece of new iron on to the worn part. Gairloch, Lochbroom et cetera.

aomaid, (DU), v.a. Repair by welding a piece of new iron on old.

aon. In Northern Arran, 'Cha'n 'eil aon duine an siod', is used for 'cha'n 'eil duine an siod', there is no one there. 'Chaidh steud an t-aon fhaotainn daibh', a horse each was got for them.

aonach, s.m. 12 Market place. 13 High moor, high uncultivated land. West of Ross-shire.

aona-chasach, (MMcD), s.f. Serrated seaweed used as manure.

aona-ghnàthach, (MS), s. Kindred.

aonagraich, (CR), s.f. ind. An alternative for aonagail. Rolling, as of a horse rolling on its back. West of Ross-shire.

aonagraich, v.a. Cause to wallow.

aonaig, -ean, s.f. Boulder of stone, Lewis. 'Dè tha thu dol a dhèanamh leis na h-aonaigean sin?', What are you going to do with those big boulders?

aon bheag, Very little. Arran.

aon chosach, An., s.f. Raoine's banner.

aon mhòr. Not a bit. Arran.

aon-mhunadh, (PJM), s.m. Only child.

aon-talamh, (DU), s.m. One (kind of) evil. 'Rinn e aon-talamh', he has become indifferent.

aorannachadh, from Cuairtear nan Gleann (Caipt Ruadh Gl. dubha).

aosachadh, (MS), s.m. Antiquatedness.

aosair, s.m. Senior.

aosdàna, (MS), s.m. Antiquary (aois dàna).

aotroman, -ain, s.m. Bearing-gear of a quern-wedge or screw that lightens pressure of stones on the grain.

apachadh, s.m. for abachadh, s.m. Ripening. D,p.2. Celt. Rev. III 166.

apar, (DMK), s.m. Haste, quickness.

àr,-àir, s. Death. Taigh-àir, house of death, used in the sense of lyke wake.

arabocan, s.m. Door lintel. North Uist. JGC.S.204.

arach, (AF), s. Dragon.

àraidh, a. 6 (DU) Friendly, consonant.

àraidich, (MS), v.a. Particularize, particulate.

arainn, s.f. Hearth. 'Aig arainn an taigh', at the hearth. Sutherland.

àrainn, "Air àrainn na beinne", *All around the hill*. Beinn Doran, p.93.

aran-buntàta, (DMK), *s.m.* Bread made of barley meal and potatoes, kneaded together. *Sutherland*.

aran-còinnich, (DMK), *s.m.* Loaf-bread. *Sutherland*.

aranach, (G), *a.* Vexing. *Perthshire*.

àranta, (MS), *a.* Arable.

àrantach, (MS), *a.* Aratory.

arasaid, see earasaid, *s.f.* Square of cloth, usually tartan, worn over the shoulders of females and fastened before with a brooch. Female robe. Ill. 290, D,p.383.

arbhar, *s.m.* Corn. Includes grain and straw, but ceases to be applied to either when separated by threshing.

ar leis, *v. def.* He thought.

arc-crannach, (AF), *s.* Young of sow.

arc-fhadmhuinealach, *s.f.* Plesiosaurus.

archoicid, (AF), *s.* Staghound.

arc-iasg, *s.f.* Ichthyosaurus.

arc-mhara, *s.f.* Enalisaurus.

àrdaigheachd, (MS), *s.f.* Arduousness.

àrd-cheannardach, (MS), *a.* Participial passing.

àrd-cheannardachd, (MS), *s.f.* Peerlessness.

àrd-chumhachd, *s.f.* 6 (MS) Armipotence.

àrd-chumhachdach, *a.* 2 (MS) Armipotent.

'àrd-èisg an droch fhilidh, *o thou prince of bad satirists*.

àrd-fheallsanach, (MS), *s.m.* Arch-philosopher.

àrd-sgoileach, *a.* Academic.

àrd-sheòladair, *s.m.* Admiral.

àrd-uaisle, (MS), *s.* A peer. 2 Prince. 3 Gentleman.

àrd-uaisleachd, (MS), *s.f.* Aristocraticalness.

arloch, see arlogh, cartage of corn, D,p.46.

armachadh, *s.m.* Armoury.

armaidh, *a.* Greasy.

armanach, *a.* Armorial.

àr-meadhonach, (CR), *s.m.* Second ploughing. *Islay*.

arm-ghille, *s.m.* 2 (MS) Armourer.

arm-stad, (MS), *s.* Armistice.

armunnach, (MS), *a.* Brave 2 Warrior-like. *R,7*.

arralach, *a.* 2 (DC) Easily annoyed. *Barra*.

arrchogaid, (AF), *s.* Hunting-dog.

àrsaideach, (MS), *a.* Original.

àrsaidhich, (MS), *v.a.* Outdate.

arsonaic, *s.f.* Arsenic.

arspag, *s.f.* 2 (DMK), The gull in its first year, before it has attained its full plumage, when it is known as faoileag-mhòr-an-sgadain.

arth, (AF), See † art, *s.m.* Bear D,p.48.

art-luachra. See dearc-luachrach, *s.f.* Lizard. Ill. 266 D,p.322.

asach (asbhuain), *s.* Place where corn has been newly cut. *Arran*.

àsainn, *s.f.* See àsuing, *s.f.* Apparatus, implements, instruments, tools, utensils D,p.40. In *The Songs of Duncan Bàn Macintyre*, àsainn is translated as 'equipment' in line 90; as 'appliance' in line 1353; but as 'secret' in line 2866." 'S i 'n àsainn a' mhuime tha cumail na cìche, means *the secret is the nurse who suckles the calves*. The *'nurse'* being the mountain pastures. *Beinn Doran*, p.86.

asair, *s.m.* 3 Girth-saddle.

as a nodha. Arran for *as ùr*. Anew, afresh.

ascaraid, *s.m.* See eascaraid, *s.m.* Adversary, enemy, literally 'non-friend.' "B'ann 'an sid a bha'n spàirn gun ascaraid, *the weather was conflict enough without enemies*. *Duanaire* 188.

asdail, *s.f.* 2 see fasdail, *s.f.* Dwelling. 2 Dome. D,p.418.

asg, (CR), *s.* Circular wooden frame of a riddle, corn fan or corn basket. *West of Ross-shire*.

asg, see asc, *s.m.* Snake, adder. 2 Newt (Obsolete) D,p.49.

as leth, *prep.* 2 On the side of. As leth an rìgh a's na còrach, *on the side of the king and the right*. MacI., 18, 24.

asnaichean, *s.pl.* Ribs.

aspic, See asc, above.

àsradh, *s.m.* (CR) Pining, a disease of sheep. *Sutherland*. 2 (DMK) A wasting disease in young cattle. *Caithness*.

asrann, see àsran, *s.m.* Forlorn object. 2 Destitute wanderer. D,p.50.

àsruidh, *a.* Dejected. Gu h-àsruidh tioma-chasach tinn, *dejectedly and with timid tread. Rob Donn.*

a staigh is employed both of motion and rest in *Perthshire*, a steach not being used there at all. (CR).

a stan, *adv.* Up. In Breadalbane used as the opposite of *a bhàn* down. Thoir a stan an rud sin, *Bring up that thing*; Thig a stan a dhuine, *Come up, O man.*

astar, *s.m.* Chaill e astar, *he lost speed.*

astar-sgrìobhaiche, *s.m.* Cinematograph.

as-thabhartach, *a.* Abstractive.

asuig-labhraidh, (MS), *a.* Labra.

àth, *s.f.* Kiln. D,p.50.
Parts of a kiln.

1. Builg, *s.* Receptacle.
2. Casaid, *s.f.* Receptacle.
3. Cealach, *s.m.* Fireplace and up to the eye of a kiln.
4. Coileach, *s.m.* As 3, above.
5. Crotag, *s.f.* Stone for making barley ready for broth (eòrn-crotaig) 18 inches high and 15 inches in diameter, with a round opening in the centre about 1 foot deep, by 7 or 8 inches wide. In the natural order of things the mill is merely an adjunct of the kiln.
6. Fiodhrach-tarsuing, *s.m.* Cross-sticks of the kiln.
7. Leac-a'-chealaich, *s.f.* Flag-stone of a kiln.
8. Leac-an-tealaich, *s.f.* Another name for the flag-stone of a kiln. The stone is laid over the mouth of the *cealach*, see above, to prevent straw or wind getting to the fire.
9. Maide-sùirn, *s.m.* Stick over the flue or eye, which supports the fiodhrach-tarsuing, or cross-sticks. It got its name because both ends were placed on stones (dà-shòrnach).
10. Poll-suathaidh, (AF), *s.m.* The rubbing-pool of a kiln. A slab 3 feet in height and 4 inches thick, where dried corn was trodden out to separate the "bristles" from the corn.
11. Sinridean, (AF), *s.pl.* or sìrnearan (AF), *s.pl.* Pieces of wood placed

across the *slugan* (see below).
12. Slugan, *s.m.* (AF) Opening of the kiln whereon the corn to be dried is laid.
13. Sràbhag, *s.f.* diminutive of sràbh, straw. Straw laid on wood under the grain.
14. Surrag, *s.f.* The *eye* or *vent* of a kiln.
15. Tioradh, *s.m.* Drying on a kiln.
16. Uchd-làr, *s.* The floor of a kiln round the eye.

athach, *s.m.* 4 (AF) Fierce boar. 5 (DC) Generic name for a monster, applied to all fabulous supernatural apparitions.

àthadh, (DMU), *s.* Quarter of an animal. Athadh feòla, *a quarter of flesh. West coast of Ross.*

athaich, 5 (DMK), *s.* Growing corn damaged by fowls or other animals. 2 Corn so damaged. *Caithness.*

athainn, (CR), *s.* Vexation, annoyance 'Chuir e athainn orm', he *annoyed me. West of Ross-shire.*

athais, *s.f.* 4 (DU) Shame, Diffidence, modesty.

athaiseach, *a.* 2 (DU) Diffident, modest.

athaisich, (MS), *v.a.* 4 Banter, *v.n.* 5 Simmer.

athann, see àthan, *s.m.* Little ford, shallow part of river, reaching from bank to bank. D,p.51.

ath-aodach. The following is said to a person who has got on a new suit or article of clothing 'Meal is caith e, pàigh an t-annsa 's tilg a nall an t-ath-aodach', *enjoy and wear it, pay the beverage, and throw over the cast off clothes.* The "*annsa*", means a dram from a married woman and a kiss from a young woman. It was considered unlucky for the above greeting to be first uttered by a woman, but a woman might say it if a man has said it first. (JM).

athaonach, (DC), *s.m.* Second opinion, doubt.

athar-dhaicinn, *s.* Aeroscopy.

atharnach, 2 Masculine in *West of Ross-shire.* 'An do chuir sibh an t-atharnach?' *Have you sown the "red" land?* (CR).

atharraich. 'Nach faiceadh call an atharraich' (Call Ghàdhaig), *who would not see a stranger lose.* Atharrach, *s.m.* means a stranger, alien as well as an alteration or change.

atharrais, *s.* 2 (MS) Play.

atharrais, *v.a.* 2 (MS) Play.

ath-atodhar, (CR), *s.* Second crop after a field has been manured by the folding of cattle or sheep.

ath-bhliadhnach, *s.* (CR) Two year old sheep.

ath-cheapach, *s.m.* Land from which two crops of corn *et cetera* have been taken. *Lochalsh.*

ath-cheo, (CR), *s.* Henbane. *Arran.*

ath-chinneachadh, (MS), *s.m.* After-crop.

ath-chonaich, (MS), *v.a.* Ask.

ath-chur, (DU), *s.m.* Second application e.g. of an argument. 'Ath-chur an t-soisgeil', *bringing home the gospel to the minds of the hearers.*

ath-dhìonag, (CR), *s.f.* 2 shear ewe, maiden ewe, "twinter".

ath-eo, *s.* Hemlock. *Arran.*

ath-ghamhnach, *s.f.* 2 Cow that has been two years without a calf and still gives milk. D,p.53.

ath-lìobaid, (MS), *s.* After-cart.

ath-mhugach, (CR), *s.* Mole. *Sutherland.*

ath-riochd, (MS), *s.* Alternateness.

ath-sgioblaich, (MS), *v.a.* Reprune.

ath-sgoladh, (MS), *s.m.* Leavings.

ath-teo, (CR), *s.* Henbane. *Lewis.*

ath-thal(mh)ainn, *s.* Mole. *Badenoch.*

ath-theiridh, (MMcD), *s.f.* Corn-kiln where corn was dried and hardened before being sent to the miller. *Lewis.*

ath-uanach, (AF), *s.* Lambless sheep.

at-reum, (CR), *s.m.* Swelling in the back of the mouth. *West of Ross-shire.*

aultan, (R), Sutherland for annlan, *s.m.* Condiment. D,p.36.

B

babag, *s.f.* Ermine (fur) Ill. shield.

babhdair, (CR), *s.m.* Good-for-nothing person. *West of Ross-shire.*

babhsgudh, *s.m.* Start, fright, shock.

babhuinn, *Sutherland* for bàghan, *s.m.* A church-yard.

bac, *s.m.* 16 (DMK), Terrace on the side of a hill, brink of a bank or brae. 17 Bank, ridge. *West of Ross-shire.* 18 Stake. 19 Stall-tree of a cattle house. 'Bac na bruaich', *the brink of the brae*; bac na tòine, *the rump*; aisridh 'na bac cho caol, *a path which was such a narrow ledge*; bac na h-uinneige, *the window sill.*

baca-bhràghad, *s.* The fore cleats of a boat. D,p.39 on p.76.

baca-h-amar, *s.* The quarter cleats. D,p.76.

bacaid, see bagaid, *s.f.* Cluster. 2 Gaelic spelling of the Scots word *backet*, see bucaid, *s.f.* 4 Gaelic spelling of *bucket.*

baca-meadhon, *s.* The middle cleats of a boat. D,p.76, 39.

bacan, s.m. 11 Stake of a byre, see D,p.79. 12 (DU) Bunch of articles strung together as fish on a withe, cluster of fruit, *et cetera.* 13 (MS) Hold. Bacan sgadain, *a string of herrings.*

bacan àrd, *s.m.* Ear-mark on sheep, see under comharradh-cluais, Ill. 185. D,p.238.

bacan ceàrr, (AH), *s.m.* Turbot, *rhombus maximus.*

bacan èisg, (CR), *s.m.* String of fish, or a twig with fish strung on it. *West of Ross-shire.*

bacan ìosal, *s.m.* Ear-mark on sheep, see under comharradh-cluais. Ill. 185. D,p.238.

bac-cliath, (DC), *s.m.* Small creel fit to be carried in the '*bac*' or oxter, and not necessarily on the back like the cliath or large creel.

bachailleag, (DU), *s.f.* Bud.

bachall, *s.m.* 7 Dolt, one deficient in smartness. *West of Ross-shire.*

bachullachd, *s.f.* Crispness.

bachullaich, (MS), *v.a.* Crisp.

bacraineach, (CK), *s.m.* The larger ferns as distinguished from the bracken, *Strathtay.*

bad, *a.* Many. *Arran.*

bad, *s.m.* Usually means a place or spot, although it may also mean a tuft, cluster, bunch and thicket. In the idiom 'Chaidh e 'na bhad', the meaning is 'he confronted or tackled him', either physically or metaphorically in the sense of verbally opposing him. Hence 'Na bhad gum bi Dòmhnull Mac Dhòmhnuill 's na Gàidheil 'an ordugh r'a chùl', means *getting to grips with him will be Donald MacDonald, with the Gaels in battle array behind him.*

bad, *s.m.* 12 (DMy). Sheaf. Bad coirce, *a sheaf of oats.*

badadh, (Cr), *s.m.* Drawing straw for the kiln. *West of Ross-shire.*

badan, *s.m.* 3 (MS) Lock. 4 Tuft of wool. 5 Square of flannel in which babies are wrapped.

badarais, (AF), *s.* Monster, literally *'clump in the path.'*

badaroisean, *s.* Has the same meaning as badarais.

badh-catha, (AF), *s.* Crow.

†baedh, (AF), *s.* Boar.

bagaid, *s.f.* 5 Knot.

bagailais, *s.f.* Gaelic form of the English word baggage. *Argyll.*

bagair, (MS), *v.a.* Bluster. 2 Brandish.

bagair, *s.m.* Glutton, D,p.58. 2 pron bagaire.

bagairteach, (DU), *a.* Threatening.

baganach, (CK), *s.m.* Brisk, lively person. *West of Ross-shire.*

baganaich, (JM), *v.n.* Tidy. Baganaich thu fhèin agus bi falbh, *tidy thyself and begone.*

baghair, (JM), -ean, *s.m.* See bagair. Baghairean is cladhairean, *corpulent men and cowards.*

baghastair, (CR), *s.m.* Dolt, blockhead, see baothair, *s.m.* D,p.68. *West coast of Ross-shire.*

bagrach, a. 'Là bagrach agus daoine togarrach', *a threatening day and willing men.* (In harvest time much work must be done in these circumstances).

bagradair, (MS), *s.m.* Bully.

baid, *s.f.* Group, flock, especially of goats. *Uist.* 2 Gaelic spelling of bait. *Arran.*

baid, (CR), *v.a.* Entice, allure. *Arran.*

baide, *s.m.* Company.

baidealach, *a.* Flapping, as a sail.

bàidean, *s.m.* Little boat, yawl, pinnace. Also spelt baidean.

baidne, s. (AF) Animal. 2 (DC) Group, flock, as of goats. *Argyll.*

bàight, (CR), *s.f.* Earthworm used as bait for trout. *Sutherland.* See baoiteag. *s.f.* 2 Bait for fishing. D,p.68.

baigsleis, (CR), *s.f.* Baggage, lumber. 2 Person who gets in another's way. *West of Ross-shire.* 3 Luggage, lumber. *Perthshire.*

baile, *s.m.* 6 Grange. 7 Farm buildings.

baileach, (CR), *adv.* Very. *Perthshire.* It is evidently distinct in use from *buileach.* 'Tha e baileach math', means *it is very good.* Cha'n 'eil e buileach deas, *it is not quite ready.*

baile geamhraidh, *s.m.* The infield, the low grounds of a Highland farm, in contrast to *baile samhraidh, s.m.* which was the summer town for the herds, and the custom of going to the sheilings allowed the land of the winter town to rest.

bailg-fhionn, (AF), *s.* White-bellied cow.

b'àillidh? Literally, *what is your pleasure?* Eh? What?

baineach, (JM), *s.f.* Weaveress. The same as Ban-fhigheach, *s.f.* D,p.65.

bainndeal, (DC), *s.m.* Horsehair snare for little birds. *Uist.*

bàinneach, (CR), *s.m.* Factor. *Arran.*

bainne-bò-gamhnach, *s.m.* Lousewort. *Colonsay.*

bainne breun, (AF), *s.m* Soured milk.

bainne briste, *s.m.* Whipped cream with oatmeal. *Caithness, Lewis* and *Sutherland.* (*C. Rev.,* III, 187).

bainne clabar, (AF), *s.m.* Clotted milk.

bainne crodh-laoigh, *s.m.* Lousewort. *Colonsay.*

bainne lampan, (DMK), *s.m.* Milk that thickens spontaneously. *Caithness.*

bainne-nan-each, (CR), *s.m.* Wild clover. *West of Ross-shire.*

bainne pingichte, (AF), *s.m.* Curdled milk. (I wonder whether this name comes from Pinguicula, the Common Butterwort or Bog Violet, as one of this plant's names in Gaelic is lus-a'-

bhainne, milk-wort, as it is used to thicken and curdle milk. Editor). Also b.-plamach (AF).

bainne reamhar, (AF), *s.m.* 2 Unskimmed, literally "fat", milk.

bainne slaman, (AF), *s.m.* Milk that thickens spontaneously. *Lochaber.*

bàinnigh, (CR), s.m. Factor. *Arran.*

bainnseil, *a.* Spaniel.

baintighearna, *s.f.* Dr. Watson has not met *baintighearna* in the sense of Our Lady, except in Creag, tobar and port na baintighearna, at Hilton of Cadboll. *Place names of Ross & Cromarty.*

baintighearnail, *a.* Lady-like.

bàire, *s.f.* Given under bàir, *s.f. D,p.60. In many districts it means 'one hail' in shinty. Leth-bhàir, s.* means 'hail' or goal in shinty. In Morvern and Mull, leth-bhàir = 1 hail; bàire, 2 hails, bàire gu leth, 3 hails. Leth-chluich, *s.* also means a hail in shinty. In *Eigg* leth-chluich means 1 hail; cluich, 2 hails and cluich gu leth, 3 hails. D,p.584-5.

bàirleig, *v.a.* meaning to summon or warn, like bàrnaig, *v.a.* D,p.70.

bàirleigeadh, *s.m.* 2 (MS) Menace.

bairm, *s.f.* Barm, yeast, ferment, see beirm, *s.f.* D,p.87.

bàirneach, *s.f.* 2 (AF) Barnacle 3 Cunner.

bàirneag, *a.* Perverse, see †bàirneach, *a.* Perverse 2 Obstinate 3 Final D,p.61.

bàirneag-coidhean, *s.f.* See bàirneag-cathan, *s.f.* Barnacle or limpet. (AF) *Arran.*

bairneul, *s.m.* Hesitation.

bairneulachas, s.m. Hesitation.

bairneulaich, (MS), *v.n.* Hesitate.

bairneulaiche, (MS), *s.m.* Stargazer.

baisgeil, *a.* 2 Lively. 'Chuireadh torman a port baisgeil', *who would draw a thrilling power from a lively tune. (Brosnachadh nam fineachan).*

bàit, *pt. pt.* Drowned, see bàite. D,p.61.

bàitheal, (CR), *s.m. Arran* for †bàidheal, *s.m.* A cow stall.

balach, *s.m.* 5 (CR) Bachelor of any age. *Arran.* 6 (CR) Ploughman.

balagadan, *s.m.* Calf of the leg. *Arran.*

balair, *s.f.* Opinion, for barail, *s.f.* in *Badenoch, Perth* and *Strathspey.*

balg, *s.m.* Bag. Trì builg sìl dà bhalg gràin, aon bhalg mine, *3 bags of corn make 2 bags of kiln-dried grain and one bag of meal.* The *balg* was made of the skin of a sheep, taken off the carcase by means of a cut round the neck without being cut down the breast and belly, in the same way that the skins of dogs are taken off to be made into buoys by the fishermen of the East of Scotland. This mode of skinning is called *fionnadh-balgain*, s.m. D,p.347. For an accurate description of *balg* see Martin's account of North Rona.

balg-bhiast, (AF), *s.* Belly-worm.

balg-losgainn, *s.m.* See balgan-losgainn *s.m.* Truffle. D,p.62.

balgan-beisde, (DU), *s.m.* Cyst.

balgan-buidseachd, (DMK), *s.m.* Generally used with the article. A small bag containing miscellaneous odds and ends used by a witch in the practice of her art.

ball (G), *s.m.* Soum of cattle. 2 Weapon – *'Manus' MacNicol's Version.* Ball, like English spot, means both a mark and a place. 14 Kind of hair rope, see ribeag, *s.f.* Hair. D,pp.62 & 758.

ball, *s.m.* According to Dwelly's correspondent, Mr Alex Henderson of Ardnamurchan, *ball* is also used for cards as follows; an t-aona ball, Ace; an dithis ball, the 2; an triamh ball, the 3; an ceithir ball, the 4; an còig ball, the 5; an sia ball, the 6; an seachd ball, the 7; an t-ochd ball, the 8; an naoi ball, the 9; an deich ball, the 10.

ball-air-baodhan, (WC), *s.m.* A cormorant. *Gairloch.*

ball-bhiasd, (CR), *s.m.* An imp, a mischievous person. *W. Ross-shire.*

ball deiridh, *s.m.* Afterleech of a sail.

ball-dòbhrain, *s.m.* Mole on the skin. 2 (AF) White spot beneath the chin or under the forearm of a giant, once thought to be his only vulnerable places.

ball-iomanaiche, *s.m.* Football.

ball-stadha, *s.m.* Guy, see bàta. D,p.76.

ball toisich, *s.m.* Tack of a sail.

balla-bhreac, (-AF), *s.m.* A dappled horse.

balla-tarsuinn, *s.m.* Means the same as tallan, *s.m.* the partition in black houses about three feet high, for separating the portion used by the cattle.

ballach, *s.m.* See ballach-muir, *s.m.* (AF). Rock-fish.

ballachd, *s.f.* 2 (CR) Mockery, ridicule, derision. 'Nach iad a rinn a' bhallachd air!', *what sport they made of him! West of Ross-shire.*

ballaire-ballach, (DC), *s.m.* Great Cormorant.

ballan-buidhe, *s.m.* Ragwort, groundsel. *Colonsay.*

ballan-ìm, (MMcL), *s.m.* Milk or butter tub. 2 Any article in which butter is kept. *Lewis.*

balloch, *s.m.* Shell-fish.

ballsganta, (MS), *a.* Foppish.

ballsgantachd, (MS), *s.f.* Foppishness.

balt, *s.m.* 4 Moustache. 5 (CR) Man's collar. *Arran.*

bàn, *s.m.* 4 (DMK). Placenta of a cow. *Caithness.*

bàn, *a.* 4 Fallow.

banabh, *s.m.* Land unploughed for a year. See banbh, *s.m.* D,p.65.

banabhain, *s.m.* The same meaning as banbh and banabh above.

banachaig, *s.f.* Dairymaid. *Ross* and *Sutherland* for banachag, s.f. D,p.64.

banachocach, (G), *v.a.* Vaccinate.

bana-chrùbag, *s.f.* Female crab.

bànag, *s.f.* 5 (AF) Sea trout.

bànag-ghuaineiseach, (MS), *s.f.* Airling.

banair, (CR), *s.m.* Enclosure where sheep are milked, see mainnir, *s.f.* Fold for cattle, sheep or goats on the hillside. D,p.624.

banais-taighe, (WC), *s.f.* When a bachelor opens a new house with a party or dance – considered to be unlucky by the old Gaels.

banas, *s.m.* Wifehood. Carmina Gad. 206.

banasachd, *s.f.* Female modesty, see banalachd, *s.f.* D,p.65.

banban, *s.f.* Brood sow.

banbh, s.f. 3 Brood sow.

banbhradh, (AF), *s. coll.* Swine.

ban-chiosachd, (MS), *s.f.* Uxoriousness.

ban-chumhachdach, (A' bh.), (MS), *s.f.* Smallpox.

ban-fhuamhair, *s.f.* Giantess.

bangaidich, (MS), *v.a.* Banquet.

bann, *s.m.* 16 (CR) Ring securing heel of the blade of a scythe to the handle. 17 (CR) Band of a sheaf. 18 Driving band or cord of a spinning-wheel. 19 Boom of a boat. 20 Ferrule of a bagpipe. See D,p.722. 21 Hasp.

bannaban, *s.m.* Forehead bandage. *Sutherland.*

bann-airgid, *s.m.* Deposit receipt. *Sutherland.*

bannanban, (DMK(, *s.m.* See bannaban above. *Caithness.*

bannas, -ais, *s.m.* Gum of a quern. No. 9, D,p.112.

bann beag, *s.m.* Regulating band or cord to prevent the reel of a spinning-wheel from revolving. It is stretched between bann-nam-maighdeannan and the beairt-mheadhan, see D,p.289.

bann-bhràghaid, *s.m.* Horse-strap.

bann-cuidhteacha, *s.m.* Receipt.

bann-droma, *s.m.* Back strap of a cart.

bann-mòr, *s.m.* Driving band or cord of a spinning-wheel.

bann-nam-maighdeannan, *s.m.* Band or cord stretched between the tops of the supports of the flyers in a spinning-wheel.

ban-rìoghlaiche, (MS), *s.f.* An administratrix.

ban-searaiste, (CR), *s.f.* A headstrong ungovernable woman. *West of Ross-shire.*

baobach! *Int.* (Mild imprecation). Folly on him!

baodhann, *s.m.* See baodhannach, (AF) *s.m.* Elk, moose, deer.

baoghal, *s.m.* 6 (MS) Hazard. 7 Advantage or opportunity of escaping or doing harm.

baoghalaich, (MS), *v.a.* Hazard. 2 Endanger. 3 Run. 4 Advantage.

baoghalaiche, (MS), *s.m.* Hazarder. 2 Adventurer.

baoiseid, (MS), *s.f.* Budget.

baoisgneach, (MS), (gu), *adv.* Ahead.

baoit, *s.f.* See boiteag, *s.f.* Cauldron. 2 White worm in dung. 3 Earthworm.

D,p.108.

baosg, baosgan, *s.m.* Silly man or boy.

baosgaid, (DC), *s.f.* Loutish, silly woman.

baosgaideach, (DC), Silly, sumphish.

baoth, (MS), (gu), *adv.* Ahead.

baothailt, *s.* Fool. *Badenoch.*

baothaireachd, (MS), *s.f.* Flatulence.

baothair-oidhche, (DC), *s.m.* Snipe.

baotharlanachd, (MS), *s.f.* Caprice.

baoth-fhear, (MS), *s.* Blockhead.

baoth-shealltach, *a.* Agape.

barad, Am, (MMcD), *s.m.* First row of peat taken from a bank with the toirsgian (peat-spade, cutter or knife). See D,p.960. *Lewis.* (See also *barr-fhad*).

bàraisg, (CR), *s.m.* Half-witted person. *West of Ross-shire.*

bàraisgeach *a.* Idiotic. *Sàr Obair.*

bàraisgeach, *s.f.* Foolish woman. *Sàr-Obair.*

baralaiche, *s.m.* Guesser.

baralta, (MS), *a.* Affirmative.

barantachd, (MS), *s.f.* Authenticity.

bàrasglaich, (CR), *s.f.* Boasting. *Skye.*

barbarachd, (MS), *s.f.* Barbarism.

bàrca, *s.* Barque, see **bàrc,** *s.f.* Bark, boat, skiff, barque. D,p.69.

†barcne, (AF), *s.* Cat.

bàrc uisge, (CR), *s.m.* Downpour of rain, thunder-shower. *West of Ross-shire.*

bard, (CR), *s.m.* Meadow, land on the edge of a river. *Strathtummel* and *Badenoch.*

bardaig, (CR), *s.f.* Warning. *West of Perthshire.*

bàrdainn, *s.f.* Warning, is also used by natives of Lochearnhead and Breadalbane as well as by those of Islay. **Bàirlinn,** *s.f.* is used only by incomers from Argyll. See D,pp.61 and 69.

bàrnaidh mi, *v.* I'll warrant. W & S. ii 180.

bàrnaig, *v.a.* Advertise.

bàrr, *s.m.* 16 Pee of an anchor.

barra, *s.m.* See D,p.70. Spike. 2 Bar. 3 Court of Justice. 'An uchd barra no binne b'i t'fhìrinn a sheasadh', in a court or judgment it is your truth that would stand. McI, 49, 8.

bàrr (for barrachd), *s.f.* Superiority, pre-eminence. "S iomadh fear a bhàrr orm', many a one beside me. McI 41, 11.

barrach, *s.m.* 4 (CR) Loppings of birch *West of Ross-shire* 5 Croppings.

barrachdail, (MS), *a.* Additional.

barran, (DU), *s.m.* Rag. 2 *pl.* Swaddling clothes of a baby.

barra-gèill, (DMK), *s.m.* Emulation. 'Bha iad a' toirt barra-gèill air gach chèile', *each surpassing the other*, a common expression in *West of Ross-shire.*

barraidh, *s.m.* Baillie, magistrate, alderman. *Rob Donn.*

bàrraisg, *s.f.* Boasting.

barranach, *s.m.* Kind of grass growing in pools and lochs.

barra-seisein, (CR), *s.* Corn-yard, premises, belongings. 'Tha brad barra-seisein aige', *he has a well-filled stockyard*; 'cha'n 'eil a leithid a ni air mo bh.', *I have not such a thing in my possession. Sutherland.*

barrasgal, (DC), *a.* Proud, supercilious.

barraisgeal, (DC), *a.* Proud, supercilious.

barr-deubhaidh, *s.m.* MacLeod & Dewar give this as meaning *battlement* in the Gaelic-English section, but give it as a word for a *terrace* in the English-Gaelic section. As McL & D also give barr'-bhalla as meaning *bartizan* in the Gaelic-English section and as another word for terrace in the English-Gaelic section, they seem to equate terrace with battlement. In the Gaelic-English section, they give *deubhadh*, -aidh, *s.m.*, see **dèabhadh**, which means drying or draining as its first meanings. Does barr-deubhaidh, therefore, mean "the top drying place?" [*Ed.*]

barr-dhèasach, (MS), *a.* Culmiferous.

barr-fhad, (DC), *s.m.* Skye and Argyll for feannad, *s.m.* surface "peat", as opposed to "dubh-fhad", the second or lowest peat. D,p.422.

barrlaig, (DU), *v.a.* Issue a rough command, warn, admonish. See **bàrnaig**, *v.a.* Summon, warn. D,p.70.

barrlaigeadh, (DU), *s.m.* Warning, admonition. See bàrnaigeadh, *s.m.* Summoning, warning. D,p.70.

barr-sgaoilteach, *a.* 2 Light. 3 (MS) Giddy-paced.

barr-suime, *s.* Overplus, number of cattle over what the farm or pasture can feed.

barsaich, *a.* Vain, prating, gabbling. *Dàin I. Ghobha.*

bar-sgaoilteachd, *s.f.* Vagary, fancy. 2 Pedantry.

bar-sgaoiltich, (MS), *v.a.* Amplify.

bàruinn, *s.f.* See ban-righinn, *s.f.* Queen. D,p.66.

bàsaich, *v.n.* We have some interesting variations in the language employed in describing the transition *from life to death*. In Matthew xxvi., 35, for instance, we have Peter saying "Though I should die with thee." The English revised version renders the phrase, "Even if I must die with thee." Our authorised Gaelic version has 'ged b' èigin dhomh bàsachadh maille riut.' The revisers have 'ged b' èigin domh dol eadhon gu bàs maille riut.' The Irish has 'bás fhiulaing,' and the Manx 'goll gy-basse.' Again in Romans v, 6, 7 and 8 we are told Christ died for the ungodly; and our revisers render the three verses thus:–

'6.   Oir an uair bha sinn fathast gun neart, ann an àm iomchuidh bhàsaich Crìosd air son nan daoine neo-dhiadhaidh.

7.   Oir is gann a bhàsaicheas duine air son fìrein; ach theagamh gu'm bitheadh aig neach èigin de mhisnich eadhon bàsachadh air son an duine mhaith.

8.   Ach tha Dia a' moladh a ghràidh fèin duinne, do bhrìgh, an uair a bha sinn fathast 'n ar peacaich, gu'n do bhàsaich Crìosd air ar son.'

In the authorised version we have 'bhàsaich' in the 6th verse as above; but in the 7th verse we have "dh' fhuilingeas duine bàs", and the same form of expression is used in the 8th verse "that is to suffer death". The Irish and Manx have also that form. Bishop Grant has "dh'eug Crìosta" in the 6th verse, but follows the language of the other translations in the following verses.

The word '*bàsaich*' (to die) is not generally applied as above. In many districts its use is restricted to animals. 'Bhàsaich an t-each' (the horse died) is right and proper, but to say 'Bhàsaich Iain' (John died) would be considered an inappropriate use of the word. In other districts, particularly in some of the islands '*bhàsaich*' is applied indiscriminately to man and beast.

Along the *Western mainland* one would, as a rule, say 'Chaochail Iain' (John has changed', that is to say, John has changed from the natural to the spirit life) Again we hear '*dh'eug Iain*', where "eug" (death) is used as a verb.

In Mid-Inverness-shire they say 'Theirig Iain', or 'Chrìoch Iain', the one implying that life was exhausted and the other that it had ended.

Further, in some districts we hear the phrase 'dh'fhalbh i' or 'e' and 'shiubhail i' or 'e' (as the case may be), meaning that the person had departed. A Lochaber man who once rejoiced over the death of his old *cailleach* began his gaudeamus thus:–

"Mìle beannachd aig an Eug,
'S ioma fear do'n d'rinn e feum,
Thug e bhuam-s' a' chailleach bhrèan,
'S èibhinn leam gu'n shiubhail i,
Shiubhail i, 's gu'n shiubhail i,"

In districts where such expressions as we have mentioned are used, "bàsaich" would be applied to animals.

The condition of being dead is described by the phrase '*Tha e marbh*' both in the case of man and the lower animals: but in the former we have several other expressions such as '*Cha'n 'eil e maireann*' (he is not enduring, i.e. he is not alive) and '*Cha'n eil e a' làthair*' (he is not in the present i.e. in life.) In the Reay country the common expression is 'Cha'n eil e seachla' (He is not remaining, or surviving.)

bas-àrdaich, v.a. Applaud.

basdalach, a. 3 (MS) Nice.

basdalaich, (MS), v.a. Daub.

bas-druidheachd, (MS), s.f. Palmistry.

baslaguch, (MS), a. Ragged.

bas-uaill, v.a. Extol by the clapping of hands.

bàta, s.m. ADDITIONAL TERMS CONNECTED WITH BOATS

1. Beul-dion, s.m. (MMcN) Coaming.
2. Bràigh-chrann, s.m. Top-mast.
3. Bràigh-sheòil, s.m. Top-sail.
4. Bràigh-shlat, s.m. Top-sail yard.
5. Caisteal-deiridh, s.m. Quarter deck of a ship.
6. Caisteal-toisich, s.m. Fore-castle of a ship.
7. Calpa, s.m. Shrouds or standing rigging of a ship.
8. Ceann-caol, s.m. Prow of a ship. E 1 7.73. Stem (DMcL).
9. Ceann-fiodha, s.m. Head A 1, p.73 (DMcL).
10. Clàbhdain. Argyll for clàdain (AH), s.pl. Oar cleats. Sheaths of wood or leather placed on oars to prevent them from being worn by the thole-pins.
11. Claigeann, better claigionn s.m. (AH) Stem of a boat. E 1, p.73.
12. Clàmbar, s.m. Box or sheath round the oar to prevent wear. The same as clàdain.
13. Cliathaich, (DMY), s.f. See sliasaid. The part of a ship's side towards the stern. It also means bilge.
14. Clic and clìchd, s.f. Clip-hook. Nos. 14 & 15, p.75.
15. Cliob, (JGC.S), s.m. Boat-hook.
16. Cnag, s.f. Thole-pin of a rowing boat.
17. Cnòd, s.m. Spur (No. 5, p. 76).
18. Conardan-sileadh, s. Limber (F 7, p.73) (MMcN).
19. Conna ghlac, (MMcN), s. Rebat (A 3, p.73).
20. Crann-ailbheige, s.m. Ring-bolt (32, p.76).
21. Crann-bratach, (DMcL), s.m. Flag-staff.
22. Crann-sùla, s.m. Eye-bolt (33, p.76).
23. Crios-alabhuird, (MMcN), s.m. Rubbing-piece. (E 6, p.73).

24. Croinn-grith, s. Mast rigging of a ship.
25. Deireadh leathann, (DMcL), s.m. Stern in a broad-stemmed boat.
26. Duin' iaruinn, (DU), s.m. Windlass Gairloch.
27. Fàrradh, s.m. Litter, straw or brushwood laid on the bottom of a boat.
28. Fàsair, (DC), s.m. Boat plug.
29. Galla shubh, (MMcN), s. Garb (A 2, p.73).
30. Giar, (JGC.S., 239), s. Knife.
31. Ghlac bheòil, A', (MMcN), s. Inside wale (E 9, p.73).
32. Lunn ràimh, s.f. The round or square part of an oar as opposed to the blade (liagh).
33. Mainbh, s. Board next the fliuch-bhòrd; the wet board.
34. Fliùt, s.f. Fluke of an anchor (No. 7, p.77).
35. Reang, s.m. Rib of a boat (E, 3, p.73). Also means the joggled frame of a boat (C, p.73) and limber, see conardan-silidh above.
36. Reang dealbh bheairt, (MMcN), s. Joggled frame in a boat (C, p.73).
37. Reusbaid, (CR), s.f. The groove in the keel to receive the edge of the fliuch-bhòrd or cairlinn.
38. Seòl cinn, (MMcN), s.m. Jib.
39. Seòl tobhadh, (MMcN), s.m. Jib.
40. Sguit-thoisich, s.f. Board on the bottom of a boat at the fore end. The sguit-dheiridh, s.f. is the same at the other end. D, p.836.
41. Sguit chinn asgail, (DMcL), s.f. Board on the bottom of a boat at the fore end. See sguit-thoisich.
42. Sgòd an àrd-sheòil, (MMcN), s.m. Topsail sheet (N7, p.73).
43. Slat bheòil, s.f. Gunwale, not slat beòil (E7, p.73).
44. Sòla, (DU), s.m. Bottom thwart containing the mast-step of a boat.
45. Stiùireadair, see stiùradair, s.m. Steersman.
46. Strac beòil (MMcN), s.m. Saxboard of a boat or the gunwale strake. (E 8, p.73).
47. Sùil, s.f. Thimble of a boat.
48. Taobh an fhuaraidh, (DMcL), s.m.

Windward side.

49. Taobh-an-fhasgaidh, *s.m.* Lee side.

50. Taobh-shlat, (DMcL), s. Gunwale. Also inside wale under the gunwale. (*Argyll*).

51. Tarruing mhòr, (MMcN), *s.f.* Main halyard. (E 4, p.73).

52. Tobhta shilidh, (AC), *s.m.* Thwart next to the "sileadh" or stem platform in a boat.

53. Tobhta tilgte, (DMK), *s.m.* Moveable thwart or seat of a boat. *West coast of Ross.*

54. Tobhta thogalaich, *s.m.* The mast is fastened to the second beam from the stern and "*tobhta thogalaich*", is the second from the stern.

55. Tolladh-fàsair, *s.m.* Plug-hole of a boat.

56. Toll-pìne, *s.f.* Plug-hole of a boat, see fàsag, *s.f.*, which also means plughole.

57. Urracag, *s.f.* Belaying pin. The belaying pin, the pin of the gunwale of a boat to which the sheet was tied. Formerly it projected outside the gunwale, but now it is on the inside and projects downwards. See uracag, (AH), *s.f.* Thole pin, North Lochaber, see bàta. No. 39 b, p.76 2 Belaying pin.

bata, (CR), *s.m.* Abundance. *Gu bata* is a stronger expression than *gu leòir*.

batadh, (MS), *s.m.* Bastinade.

bàthaich, *s.m.* Byre. People from Harris and other parts of the Hebrides use this as a *feminine* noun, with *bàthcha* or *bàthchadh* as the genitive singular. e.g. doras na bàthchadh, *the door of the byre*; Am bàthaich Ruairidh Ghobha, in Rory the smith's byre that is to say *in the open air.*

ADDITIONAL NAMES OF PARTS OF A BYRE.

1. Bac, *s.m.* A stall-tree.

2. Calpa, *s.m.* The part of a tether between the stake and the swivel.

3. Ceangal, *s.m.* Tie-band. Stall-tie.

4. Cìpean, *s.m.* Stake (No. 8, p.79).

5. Corrthalan, *s.* Swivel of a tether.

6. Dornan, *s.m.* Part of the tether between the swivel and the animal.

7. Geinne, *s.m.* A wooden wedge for fastening the 'buarach' or cow-fetter.

8. Grob, s.m. Channel, gutter or sewer of a byre. *Arran.* No. 12, p.79.

9. Innidh, *s.f.* Byre channel. No. 12, p.79.

10. Inich, (CR), *s.f.* The paved floor of the byre, elevated above the *carcair.* No. 13, p.79.

11. Udalan, *s.m.* Swivel of a tether.

bathainn, *s.f.* See buthainn, *s.f.* Long straw used for thatching.

bathar, *s.m.* 4 (CR) Whisky. *Arran.* An robh bathar aca air a' ghiùlan?, *had they whisky at the funeral?* 5 (DC) The placenta of a cow.

bàthte, *pt. pt.* Drowned. See bàite. D, p.61.

bè, (MS), *s.* Bleating of a sheep.

bè, s. Work. Tha mi a' cumail o bhè thu, *I am keeping you from your work. Islay.*

beabham, *v.a.* Die.

beachann, (CR), *s.m.* Beehive (not beachan) *Arran.*

beach-chapuill, *s.m.* Gad-fly.

beachdaidh. In *Arran*, 'Is beachdaidh leam gu'; *or* 'tha mi beachdaidh gu', means *I know that, I am sure of that*; 'bheil thu beachdaidh?', *are you certain?*; 'tha mi glè bheachdaidh', *Yes, I am quite certain.*

beadachd, (MS), *s.f.* Alertness.

beadagan, *s.m.* 3 (AF) Yearling ram. Lads in their teens inclined to have intercourse with women are called *beadagan.* D, p.80.

beadaganach, *a.* 2 Petulant.

beadaganachd, *s.f.* 2 Petulancy.

beadarrachd, s.f. Foolery.

beagachas, (MS), *s.m.* Regret.

beag-a-nasguidh, (DC), *adv.* With small profit (literally; little for nothing) 'Tha beag-a-nasguidh aig' air an obair', *he has little profit out of the work. Uist.*

beagnachd, (MS), *s.f.* Parvity.

beairteachas, *s.m.* Riches, see beartas.

bealach, s.m. 5 Road.

beallaidh, (CR), *a.* Filthy. *Arran.*

Beannachd, *s.f.* Beannachd an Dàin 's an Dòmhnaich, a common ending for tales in Eigg – a shrewd man's wish, to have both Fate and Heaven, paganism and Christianity on his side. 'Beannachd na caoimhe 's na caime', *the blessing of friendship and the sanctuary* – a common form of farewell in some of the Northern Isles.

beannach-nimhe, (AF), *s.* Horned monster.

bean-dùthcha, *s.f.* Countrywoman. 'Ur bean-dùthcha dhìleas', *your faithful countrywoman*, as an ending to a letter.

bean-mhuinntir, *s.f.* Servant-lass.

beann, *s.f.* Old nominative singular, the present nominative *beinn*, mountain, is really an old dative or locative.

bearcasach, *a.* 'Na h-eich bhearcasach, chalma', *the horses, quick-footed, strong.* Donn Bàn, p.48.

bearnachas, (MS), *s.m.* Jaggedness.

bearradh, (CR), *s.m.* Top, summit. 2 Any point that appears as a summit or is on the sky-line from the spectator's position for the moment. *West of Ross-shire.* 3 Abrupt ascent. Bearradh eòin is amadain, *clipping the hair or beard off one side of the head.* The idea is taken from clipping one wing of a bird, and it was a punishment inflicted of old, being frequently mentioned in Gaelic folk-lore.

bearranan, (CR), *s.pl.* Scissors, shears. *Skye.*

beart, *s.f.* 15 (DC) As many sheaves as a rope one fathom long will suffice to bind together as a burden. Uist. 16 (CR) Plough. *Arran.* There is no S sound as in the north.

beartachadh, (DMK), *s.m.* 2 Rigging a net to the back-rope. *West coast of Ross-shire.*

beart-dheiridh, (CR), *s.f.* Breeching.

beart-fhigheadaireachd, *s.f.* A weaver's loom. Names of parts. 1 Lonachan, rope in uprights of loom. 2 Snàth-dlùthaidh, An. The warp (AC) Snàth. 3 Snàth-nan-dual. Thread of the plies. *Car. Gad.* 308.

Beart-mheadhan, *s.f.* Horizontal bar bearing supports of the flyers of a spinning-wheel.

bheart-sheisreach, (CR), *s.f.* Plough-harness. In parts of Western Scottish Gaeldom, plough-harness consisting of a straw collar, a back-band of cloth or matting and traces of rope, used to be used. In earlier times the traces were made of thongs or withes. Parts were: 1 Druman, *s.m.* The back-band of a cart horse. 2 Drumanach, *s.f.* The ridge-band of a cart. 3 Sìnte, *s.m.* Traces by which a horse draws a plough. 4 Sìnteach, *s.f.* Traces also. 5 Suanach, *s.f.* Plough rein.

beatha, (DU) *s.f.* Life, welcome. 'Is e làn dith do bheatha', *you are welcome to it. West coast of Ross-shire.*

beathach, *s.* 4 (AF) Cow.

beathag, *s.f.* 5 (DU) Birch-rod used in correction.

beic. *s.f.* 2 Beckoning, hob-nobbery. *Dàin Iain Ghobha.*

beiceartach(?) *Deò Grèine* II 84.

beidhidh, *s.* See beididh, *s.* Lamprey. (AF).

beill, (CR), *s.f.* Blubber-lip, a thick under-lip. 2 Pout. *West of Ross-shire.*

beinc, (DMK), *s.* Settle or long seat, high-backed, but generally without cushions. *West coast of Ross-shire.*

beinge, (DMK), *s.f.* Heap of undressed grain in a barn; mow of unthreshed corn. *West coast of Ross-shire.*

beinn, *oblique case* of beann. High hill. In Ireland it is applied only to medium-sized hills.

beir, *pr. pt.* a' beirsinn in *Badenoch.* 'Chaidh beirsinn air', *he was caught.*

beirtheadaireachd, *s.f.* Satire. See beurradaireachd, *s.f.* Satire. D, P.90.

bèisd, *s.f.* See bèist, *s.f.* Beast. D, p.87.

bèist, *v.a.* Make a beast of. 'Is ann a bhèist thu na cairtean', *you did make a beast of the cards. Mac. Mhaigh. Alasd. Celtic Review*, v. 123.

bèist dubh, *s.f.* Sea otter. A fresh-water otter is *dòbhran.*

beisteag, *s.f.* 2 (AF) Dung-beetle.

bèist-ghorm, (AH), *s.f.* Dolphin *Delphinus delphis.*

bèist mhaol, *s.f.* Seal. JGC-S, 239.

bèist-na-sgrogaig, (AF), *s.f.* Unicorn. *Skye.*

bèist-nimh, (AF), *s.f.* Scorpion.

beitein, *s.m.* 2 The withered decayed grass of the hills.

beiteir, *a.* Neat, clean, tidy, compact. *Sàr-Obair.*

beith(e)-dubh, *s.f.* Black birch. *Colonsay.*

beith(e)-gheal, *s.f.* Silver birch. *Colonsay.*

beithir, (AF), *s.m.* Viper, adder. 8 (DC) Strong gust of wind. *Uist.*

beitir, *a.* 2 Pretty. *Oran an-t-samhraidh.*

beò, *s.m.* 5 (CR) Air in gentle motion. 'Tha'm beò a' fàs fuar', *the air is growing cold*; cha'n 'eil beò ghaoith ann, *there is not a breath of air.* This is not used of vital breath. Dè am beò th'ort! How are you? That is, *How is your life?*

beò-chrodh, (AF), *s.m.* Livestock.

beodail, (AF), *s.* Cattle.

beò-dhealbh, *s.m.* Cinematograph.

beòlam, *s.m.* Scold. See beolum, *s.m.*

beòlan, *s.f.* Life-rent, livelihood. *Perthshire.* See beò-shlàinte, *s.f.* D, p.88.

beòthachan, (AF), *s.m.* 2 Jellyfish, medusa.

beòthadair, (MS), *s.m.* Animator.

beòthaichean, (AF), *s.m.* jellyfish, medusa.

beòthanta, (MS), *a.* Frisky.

beòthantach, (MS), *a.* Animative.

beòthantachd, (MS), *s.f.* Animation. 2 Mercury.

beothir, (AF), *s.* Cattle.

beothlan(?) *Celtic Review* v. 347.

beuc, *s.f.* Roar. *Badenoch.*

beucadh, (MS), *s.m.* Bluster.

beucaich, *s.f.* 3 Cry of the roebuck.

beul, *s.m.* 4 Rim of a cart. 5 Tide-mark. Aig beul an làin, *at high-water mark.*

beul-fhothraghadh, *s.m.* 2 (JGM) Overhanging clump of heather covering a recess in a moor.

beul-na-cartach, *s.m.* Rim of a cart.

beul-na-troidhe, *s.m.* Instep.

beum, *s.m.* Ear-mark on sheep, see under comharradh-cluais. D, p.238.

beum, *s.f.* *Badenoch.*

beumach, *a.* 8 (MS) Critical.

beumadair, (MS), *s.m.* Ripper.

beum eòrna, (DMy), *s.m.* Sheaf of barley.

beum mheirlich, *s.m.* Ear-mark on sheep, see under comharradh-cluais. D, p.238.

beum-nan-clag, (DMK), *s.m.* Ringing of the bells. Beagan roimh b.-nan-clag, *a little before bell-ringing.*

beum os cionn na cluaise, *s.m.* Ear-mark on sheep, see under comharradh-cluais.

beum-sgèithe, *s.m.* Challenge, literally *shield-blow.* Bhuail e beum-sgèithe agus fàd-còmhraig, *he struck a shield-blow and a fight sod.* Evidently a technical phrase, meaning a challenge to the other man to fight.

beur, *s.m.* 2 Gibe, jeer. *Dàin Iain Ghobha.*

bhàrr, *prep.* Bhàrr a ghuaile, *off-hand* (DU).

bhos. In *Sutherland* this is the local form for *o'n, bho'n.* 'Is fhada bhos nach fhac mi thu', *It is long since I have seen you*; bhos a thàinig e, *since he came*, used to be heard in Kiltarlity. 2 Used locally in *Sutherland* for o chionn (since). Cha d'thàinig e bhos mìos, *he has not come for* (literally since) *a month.*

biadhadh, *s.m.* Feeding. 'A' biadhadh na cuidhle', *feeding the spinning-wheel.*

biadh-ianain, *s.m.* Wood-sorrel, see biadh-eòinein, *s.m.* D, p.92.

biadh-seangan, *s.m.* Stonecrop. *Colonsay.*

biadh-ùr-eunachan, *s.m.* Wood-sorrel. *Colonsay. Oxalis acetosella.* See Seamrag.

biadhta, *a.* Fat. Crodh biadhta, *fat cattle.*

biadhtachd, *s.f.* 2 (MS) Generosity.

biait, *s.f.* Bribe. *Celtic Review*, v. 28.

bian, *s.m.* Hide, skin. 3 (DU) Hair on fur, rather than the skin or hide, but only *bian* when attached to the hide.

bianan, *s.m.* Phosphoric fire. *Sàr-Obair.*

biast, *s.f.* 6 (DC) Generic name for all creeping creatures. *Uist.*

biastalachd, (MS), *s.f.* Barbarity.

biastan-na-snèap, (DMy), Turnip-flea beetle. *Haltica nemorum.*

biast-ghorm, *s.f.* 1 (DU) Cabbage caterpillar. 2 Blackhead (pore of the skin blocked with sweat and dirt).

biast maol, (DC), *s.m.* Seal. *Uist.*

biast ròin, (DMy), *s.f.* Female seal.

biathta, *past. pt.* of biadh, *v.a.* Fed. See biadhta, D, p.93.

biathainn-tràghaid, *s.f.* Lob or lug worm. (AF).

biathairne, *s.f.* Earthworm. 2 Bait See biathainne, *s.f.* D, p.93.

bicheantas, *s.m.* Frequently happening, frequency. See bitheantas, *s.m.* D, p.98.

bìd, *s.m.* Shrill chirping sound. In *Badenoch*, *s.f.*

bidean, *s.m.* 3 (CR) Complaining, incessant pleading or urging. *Arran.*

bideanach, (MS), *a.* Rattle-headed.

bideineach, *a.* 3 (MS) Hooded, like a hood.

Bìdie, *s.m.* Satan in *Arran.* See biotaidh, a bad man, below.

bìgeach, *a.* Seòrsa bìgeach, a small thing. *Arran.*

bighear, (MS), *a.* Asphaltic.

bigein, *s.* 6 (DC) Generic name for any small bird (wild) *Uist.*

bile, *s.f.* Rim. s.m. in *Badenoch.*

bileag-chàil, (DMK), *s.f.* Kale-blade.

binneach, (AF), *s.m.* Deer.

binneach-nan-allt, (AF), pl.-ich, *s.m.* Roe-deer.

binneag, *s.f.* 2 (MS) Height.

binn-sgaraidh, *s.f.* Ruinous verdict.

biodaidh, (CR), *s.* Imp, pest, one who annoys. *Sutherland.*

biodalan, *s.m.* The name of a "gowf ba".

bioganta, a. 2 Lively, smart, apt to start. *Sàr-Obair.*

biogarrachd, *s.f.* 2 (MS) Quibble.

biolaichean, *s.pl.* 'Biolaichean nam bruach 's àite còmhnaidh dhi', *plantations of the banks were her dwelling place.* MacLeod, line 3056, has 'bilichean nam bruach', translated "plantations of the banks", with a note: "*bilichean, pl.* of *bileach*, a young, leafy tree (Dwelly). Plantations provide cover and food." He also indicates that previous editions of the poem had '*biolaichean*'. Beinn Doran, p.91.

bior, *s.f.* 9 *(AF)* see biorag-lodain, *s.f.* D, p.96. 10 Log. *West Highland Tales.*

biorach, *a.* 6 (MS) Barbed.

biorach, *s.m.* 8 Spotted dogfish. Scyllium canicula.

biorach-chòmhnard, (MS), a. Plano-conical.

bioradh *s.m.* 2 (MS) Compunction.

bioraich, *v.* 'Bhioraich an t-each a chluasan', *the horse pointed his ears forward,* or *was all attention.*

bioranach, *a.* 4 (MS) Braky.

bioranachd, (DU), *s.f.* Incessant poking, as of a fire.

bioran-cnotala, *s.m.* Knitting needle.

biorasg, *s.m.* See biorasg and bior-iasg, *s.m.* Bait for fishing D, pp.96 & 97. 2 (AF) Shellfish.

bior-bhuafan, *s.m.* Water serpent. 2 Conger eel. See † bior-bhuasach *s.m.* D, p.96.

bior-bhusan, *a.m.* As bior-bhuafan above.

bior-chruaidh (DU) *s.f.* Sharp-pointed piece of steel used when red hot for boring holes in wood.

bior-deimhnidh, (CR), *s.m.* Fish about 8 inches long, scaled and without fins like an eel but tapering from shoulders to tail like a sturgeon, found in trawling and the ebb, thought to be the bandstickle. *West of Ross-shire.*

biorgadh, *s.m.* 2 Pricking pain.

bior-iasg, *s.m.* 3 (AF) Sword-fish.

biorrabhag, (DC), *s.f. Uist* for pior-bhuic, *s.f.* Periwig, wig.

biorraideach, *a.* 6 (MS) Pyramidal.

bior-snaois, *s.f.* 3 Bowsprit of a sailing-boat. *North Lochaber.*

bior-teinn, (CR), Minnow, pink. Pronounced *bior-tìnn. Gairloch* for bioran-deimhnidh, *s.m.* D, p.96.

bior-uileann, *s.f.* Acute angle.

bios! *Int.* See bios thad! below.

biosgach, *a.* 2 Catching at morsels, greedy. *Sàr-Obair.*

bios thad! *Int.* Cry to incite a dog after any animal, tame or wild.

bìotag, (DMK), *s.f.* Bad woman. Sometimes, by way of emphasis it is bìotag-na-pìce. *Caithness.*

biotaidh, (DMK), *s.m.* Bad man. Thàinig biotaidh, *the bad man has come. Caithness.*

biothanna, (MS), *a.* Quick.

bireach, (MS), *s.m.* Horse.

bite, (MMcD), *s.f.* Churn. *Lewis.*

biteal, *s.m.* for bitealt (corn). Saidhe agus biteal, *hay and corn. Perthshire.*

bith, (CR), *s.m.* Malice, malignity, venom. *West of Ross-shire.*

bitheach, (AF), *s.m.* Creature.

bitheach, *a.* Gummy.

bitheachd, *s.f.* Gumminess.

biurtaig, (CR), *v.n.* Gaelic variation of burst.

biuthas, *s.m.* 4 (MS) Quality.

blabail, (MS), *s.* 5 Babble.

blabhd, *s.f.* Loud bark. *Sutherland & West of Ross-shire.* 2 Sudden burst of barking. Leig an cù blabhd às, *the dog barked loudly.*

bladach-nan-ronn, *a.* Slavers. *Arran.*

bladm(h)al, (AF), *s.* Sea monster. 2 Sea-louse.

bladnait (AF), *s.* Weasel.

blaideire, *s.m.* Flatterer, see bladair, *s.m.* D, p.98.

blainnteag, (DC), *s.f.* Lullaby to soothe children. 2 Crooning to cows by diary-maids to induce the flow of milk.

blaiseag, (DU), *s.f.* Noisy smacking of the lips. 'Tha blaiseag aig air', *he is evidently enjoying it.*

blalaoghan, (AF), *s.m.* Wrasse (fish).

blà-lìn, *s.* Winding sheet. JGC. W. 172.

blaomag, – aig, *s.f.* 2 (JM) Irrelevant remark. 'Thug e blaomag às', *he made a remark not relevant to the subject under discussion.*

blaomastair, *s.m.* 2 (JM) One who talks in an irrelevant and pompous way. The general idea expressed by this word in the *Western Isles* is one suffering from a mental defect.

blaomastaireachd, *s.f.* 2 Preposterousness. 3 (JM) Boisterous talking, vain boasting.

blaosgan, (AF), *s.m.* Shellfish.

blaothanaich, (MS), *v.a.* Blather.

blàradhan, (AF), *s.m.* White-faced horse.

blàrag, *s.f.* 3 (AF) Bee. *Tiree.*

blar-aoghan, (CR), *s.m.* Rockfish as long but not as thick as the *muc-ruadh*, *s.f.* The fish ballan wrasse–*Labrus*

maculatus. D. p.675. *West of Ross-shire.*

blar-doidheag, (DMK), *s.f.* Species of small cod marked with large blue spots. It occurs in Loch Torridon.

blàr-fèille, *s.m.* Market-stance. *Arran.*

blasachd, *s.f.* Taste. 'Blasachd air', a taste of it. *Arran.* 'Boit air', in *Badenoch.*

blas-bheumnaich, *v.a.* Gaelic form of blaspheme.

blasdaidh, *a.* Gustful.

blàthachadh, *s.m.* 4 Effervescence.

blàthan-buidhe-nam-bò, *s.m.* Bird's-foot trefoil. *Colonsay.*

blatnait, *s.* See bladnait, *s.* Weasel above.

bleach, *s.f.* See bleachd, *s.f.* which is an obsolete word for milk and cows.

bleagain, *s.* Peeled grain. *Arran.*

bleaghan, *s.* 2 (AF) Curds on thickened milk.

blearom, (CR), *s.m.* Nonsensical talker.

blè'ch, (blàthach?) Pretty. *Badenoch*

bleideachadh, (MS), *s.m.* Annoyance.

bleid-mhiol, *s.f.* See †bleidh-mhiol, *s.f.* Whale.

bleir, (MMcD), *s.* Caulking of a boat. *Lewis.*

bleitheas, *s.m.* Gaelic spelling of blaze. 2 small brushwood.

bleithteach, (CR), *s.m.* Kind of gruel. Bleith teò at *Loch Tay.*

bleodhannach, (AF), *s.m.* Full uddered milch cow.

bliadhnaiche, (MS), *s.m.* Annuitant.

bliochd laith, (AF), *s.* Milch cow.

blìod, (DMK), *s.* Weeping aloud. Chuir e suas am blìod, *he commenced to weep aloud. West coast of Ross-shire.*

bloach, (AF), *s.* Whale.

blobhad, *s.f.* Loud bark or sudden burst of barking. See blabhd, *s.f.* above. *Farr Sutherland.*

blonag, *s.f.* 2 Fat of fowls.

blonaigeach, *a.* Full of suet, see blonagach, *a.* D, p.102.

boar, (AF), *a. & s.f.* Deaf or a deaf person. See bodhar, *a. & s.f.* D, p.105.

bobh!, (DMK), *int.* A highly offensive interjection pointing the fore and middle fingers forked at another and saying, 'am bobh ort!'. Frequently leads to blows. *West of Ross-shire.*

bobhdaig, (CR), *s.f.* Beating.

bò-bheannach, (AF), *s.f.* Horned cow.

bobhta, (CR), *s.* Swathe or breadth cut by a scythe in one stroke. *West of Ross-shire.*

bocachadh, (MS), *s.m.* Rutting of goats.

bocanaich, (MS), *v.a.* Outfrown.

bochain, *s.m.* Cottage. *Arran* for bothain.

bò-chonadail, (DC), *s.f.* Stray cow.

bocsa. *s.m.* 3 Body of a cart, see D, p.152. 4 (CR) Cavity in a potato. *Arran.*

bocsaichean, *s.pl.* Arrangement of peats when being dried. See under mòine, *s.f.* Peat. D, p.668. Bocsaichean, means 12 peats placed crosswise.

bocsa na deilbhe, *s.m.* Box for holding clew.

bodach, *s.m.* A crofting community Rev. J. Sinton, *Celt. Mag.* xii 296, wrote "Bidh siol bidh fodar...bidh sud aig na bodaich", *there will be seed, there will be straw...there will be there at the community.*

bodachan, *s.m.* 3 (AF) Year-old hart. 4 Very small star riding on the back of the middle star in the handle of "the plough", in the constellation of the Great Bear. Also called *bodachan a' chroinn.* Called Jack on the middle horse in England, and Alcor (the test) by the Arabs, as it needs good sight to make it out.

bodachan an doille bhodaich, *s.m.* Uist game corresponding to "Blind man's buff".

bodach-baic, (DU), *s.* The first cut in the face of an old peat bank. It is impaired by being exposed to the weather and is much thicker than the other peats.

bodag, *s.f.* 5 Part of a hand-line. See under dorgh, *s.m.* D, p.353.

bodaidh, *s.f.* Chamber-pot. *Sutherland.*

bod-an-leanna, *s.m.* Discharge-cock of a still. See D, p.730.

bod-àtha, *s.m.* Sea bird. The "Dirty Allen".

bod-dà-bhioran, *s.m.* Year-old hart. 2 Spayed, three-year old stag.

bodhag, *s.f.* 4 (MS) Aspect.

bodhaig, (MS), *s.f.* Face. 2 Demean.

bodhar, (CR), *s.* Murrain in cattle.

bodhar-gheum, (DC), *s.m.* Bell, cry of the roebuck.

bodht, *s.* A soft place. *Badenoch.*

bofalan, (AF), *s.m.* Toad.

bogadaich, *s.f.* 6 (DC) Frisking, leaping, like lambs and kittens. *Uist.*

bogadh, *s.m.* 8 (DC) Floating. 'Tha'n eithear a' bogadh', *the boat is afloat. Uist.*

bogag, *s.f.* 2 (AH) Soft crab, crab after moulting and before the new shell hardens.

bogais, (MS), *s.f.* Bug.

bogaiseach, *a.* Buggy.

bogaiseachd, *s.f.* Bugginess.

boga-leò, *s.m.* Bumpkin, blockhead. *Arran.*

bogha-muc, *s.* Wood hyacinth. *Colonsay.*

bogamh, (AH), -aimh, -an, *s.m.* Raw youth. *Argyll.*

bog-fhonntan, *s.* Sow-thistle.

boghag, (DC), *s.f.* Shore pipit (bird) *Uist.*

boghlanach, (MS), *a.* Vaulted.

bogluinneach, *a.* Healing.

bòidean-reodhaidh, s.m. Icicle. *Arran.*

boighichead, (MS), *s.* Beauty. See bòidhichead, *s.f.* D, p.107.

boineid, *s.m.* in *Badenoch.* See a' bhoineid D.P.107, *s.f.*

boineid smagain, *s.f.* Correct form in Aberfeldy for mushroom, not boineid-smachain as in D, p.107.

boinneacheann, (AF), *s.m.* A leader among cattle.

boinnean, *s.m.* Lad. *Argyll.*

boinne-mear, (CR), *s.m.* Hemlock, see minmheur, *s.m.* D, p.659. *West of Ross-shire.*

bointe, (CR), *s.* Relationship, kinship (equal to daimh), *s.m.* 7 *f.* D, p.307 *Arran.*

†bò-ionmharbhta, *s.f.* A cow fit for killing.

boirche, *s.f.* 4 Bank. 'Do bhoirchean daite sgùmgheal', *thy coloured froth-spangled banks.* Allt an t-siùcair. 5 Large hind.

boireal, *s.m.* 3 (AF) Teredo. Sea borer.

boirionnach, *s.m.* Female. This is an indefinite term corresponding to *fear*, but restricted to adults. *West of Ross-shire.*

†boirr, *s.m.* See boir, *s.m.* Elephant.

bois, (AF), *s.* Wild cattle.

boiseal, (AF), *s.* Wild cattle.

boiscne, (AF), s. Wild cattle.

boisgeachd, *s.f.* 3 Éclat.

boit, *v.* Acquire a taste for. *Badenoch.*

boitidh!, *int.* Call to a pig. *Badenoch.*

bò-lacht, (AF), *s.* Milch cow.

bolaidheach, (MS), *a.* Odorate.

bollsair, *s.m.* 4 (MS) Blazer.

boltraich, *v.a.* 3 (MS) Bespice. 4 (MS) Fumigate.

bo-mhuc, (MM), *s.* Blue hyacinth.

bonn, *s.m.* 9 Foot of a sail. 10 Bottom of a plough. 11 (*pl.* buinn) beams or sole beams of a cart. 12 (G) Part lot. 'Thug e bonn di, thug e na buinn di', *he took to his heels. West of Ross-shire.* In *Perthshire*, 'thug e na buinn na buinn às'; in *Lewis* 'thug e na boinn às'. 'Am bonn a th'agad ri dhèanamh', *the part you have to do.*

bonnacha-bac, *s.* Position under the eaves where the weights are set. See D, p.923.

bonnach-coirce, *s.m.* Oat-cake.

bonnach-iomanach, (DU), *s.m.* Girdle cake given as a reward to the first person to see a newly-born calf or lamb.

bonnach-luirg, *s.m.* Bannock given as a reward to a boy who finds a new calf.

bonnair, *s.m.* Footman.

bonn an fheadain, *s.m.* Chanter-sole of a bagpipe. See D, p.722.

bonn dubh, Am, *s.m.* 2 Thick part of the heel, heel-sole.

bonnsag, (CR), -aig, -an, *s.f.* Stone, boulder. *Lochcarron.*

boradh, *s.m.* Swelling. See borradh, *s.m.* D, p.110. (Breacan Màiri Uisdein).

borbair, (MS), *s.m.* Barbarian. 2 Gaelic spelling of barber.

borbarrachd, (MS), *s.f.* Rudeness.

bòrd, (DC), s.m. 5 Edge, especially of the sea or a lake. 6 Shore.

bòrd-aoisich, *s.m.* Front board of a cart.

See D, p.151 & 152.

bòrd-coise, *s.m.* Footboard or treadle of a spinning-wheel.

bòrd-cùil, *s.m.* Tail board of a cart. See D, p.151 & 152.

bòrd-deiridh, *s.m.* Tail board of a cart.

bòrd nan gràisg, (CR), *s.m.* The table at which children sit after others have been served at a wedding, harvest home and so on.

bòrd-taobh, *s.m.* Side board of a cart.

bòrd-taoibh, *s.m.* Perpendicular piece to the left; left earth-board, "bosom plate".

bòrd-ùireach, *s.m.* Mould-board of crann-nan-gad, *s.m.* a type of plough.

bòrlum, *s.m.* 6 Gush of water. *Dàin Iain Ghobha.*

borr, (DC), *a.* Sulky. A tribe of MacArthurs in Lorn were known as Borr-a-ghèill or Borr-gheillich, the sulky, the dour.

borrachan, *s.pl.* Banks of a burn or river. *Sàr-Obair.*

borr-agh, (AF), *s.* A large hind.

bos, (G), *v.* Intending.

bosdan, *s.m.* 4 (MS) Bandbox.

bòsgail, *a.* Vaunting, boasting. See bòs-dail, *a.* D, p.111.

bò-shlamhraidh, (AF), *s.f.* Dower kine.

bot, (CR), *s.* Swathe or breadth cut by a scythe in one stroke. See bobhta, *s.* above.

bot, (G), *a.* Reedy bog, bend. *Celtic Magazine.* ix. 519.

bota, (CR), *s.* Bog channel. 2 Vein or streak of bog or morass. *West of Ross-shire.*

bota, (CR), *s. Torridon* for bobhta, *s.*, swathe or breadth cut by a scythe in one stroke. See above.

botag, *s.f.* Sun-dried crack. 2 Narrow channel. 3 Wet or soft channel in a peat-moss. Occurs in place names.

botaidh, *s.f.* Chamber-pot. *Sutherland.*

both, *s.m.* 5 (MMcD) Opening in the wall of a sheiling dwelling used for holding milk vessels.

bothaig, (MS), *s.f.* Mien.

bothan dubh, (DMK), *s.m.* Illicit distillery but concealed among the hills. *Sutherland.*

bouta na h-aisil, *s.m.* Axle bolt of a cart.

brà, *s.f.* 4 Turbot. *Lewis.*

brà, *s.f.* Quern.

ADDITIONAL PARTS OF A QUERN

17 Leamhan, (MMcD), *s.m.* Quern-wedge. See Leamhan, *s.m.* D, p.575.

18 Cibhinn, *s.* (Presumably for cibhrinn. See D, p.193 and cùrainn, *s.f.* D, p.302). 4 support prop on which the brà was raised to enable one to grind while standing. *Lochbroom, Harris* etc

bracairneach, *a.* 2 Roan.

braclach, *s.f.* Badger's den. See broclach, *s.f.* D, p.126.

bracsi, *s.* Gaelic form of braxy.

brad, (DMK), *s.f.* Laying goose. *Caithness.*

bradan-pacach, *s.m.* See bradan-bacach, *s.m.* (AC). Literally a halting salmon. Sturgeon.

bradan-sligeach, *s.m.* 2 (AF) Sturgeon.

bradhag, (CR), *s.f.* Huff, tantrum. 'Ghabh e bradhag', *he took a huff. West of Ross-shire.*

bràghad, *s.m.* 4 Shoulder of a still D, p.730.

†braicheam, *s.* 3 See †braich, *s.m.* Stag. 2 Buffalo. 3 (AF) Wolf. 4 (AF) Badger.

braid, (G), *s.f.* Hiding, concealment. 3 Charm. *Conn Mac an Deirg (MacNicol's version).*

braighd, *s.f.* Arran for bràid, *s.f.* Horse-collar *et cetera.* D, p.113.

braighdean, (AF), *s.m.* Rope round a sheep's neck. *Arran.*

braighe, (DMK), *s.m.* Boat-painter. Braigh-giubhais, painter of bog-fir; the fibres of the fir being taken apart and spun into rope. *Applecross.*

braigheann, *a.* Greenish.

braile, (CR), *s.f.* 4 Clap, peal, outburst of thunder or sudden rain. *Arran.*

brailich. *Arran* for braighlich, *v.a.* Make a noise and braighlich, *s.f.* Noise.

braing, genitive of brang, *s.m.* A horse's halter. But 'a chur braing 'san fhearmhillidh', means *in order to put a halt to the destroyer,* probably referring to Napoleon, as these words come from a Skye song from the time of the Napoleonic wars. *Duanaire,* 71.

bràithrean, Na, *s.pl.* 2 Two stars called *Castor* and *Pollux.*

bralag, *s.f.* Caterpillar. *Arran.*

brallach, *s.m.* Shellfish. *Lewis.*

bramach-inilt, (DC), *s.f.* Midwife. *St. Kilda.*

bramachan-roid, (DC), *s.m.* Landrail, see trèan-ri-trèan, *s.m.* D, p.968.

bramalach, *s.f.* See bramanach, *s.m.* A noisy or boorish fellow. This word probably means something like *'monster',* or may simply be another form for *bramanach.* Thus 'Chunnaic mi a' bhramalach agus urabal 'gam fhàgail', may mean *I saw the female monster and my heart was in my throat. Sgeulnan-caol,* p.69.

braman, *s.m.* 5 Rump of a horse, see D, p.376. 6 (DU) A wicked fellow.

bram-uan, (AF), *s.m.* Pet lamb.

†bran. *s.m.* Avalanche, landslip.

brang, *s.m.* Horse's halter. This consists of two bars of wood 12 inches long, connected at one end by a cord about 9 inches long and at the other by a rope fixed to the one bar and running free through a hole in the other bar, with a cord fixed to the middle of each bar to go over the top of the head. The same kind of halter is used in some districts, such as Sleat, for tethering cattle. (CR).

braodag, (CR), *s.f.* 'Ghabh e braodag', *he took offence, he took the huff.*

braodh, (DMK), *a.* Beautiful, elegant, showy. Boirionnach braodh, a good looking woman. *Sutherland.*

braodhaire, (MS), *s.m.* A bully or annoyer.

braoileag, *s.f.* 6 Bearberry. *Colonsay.*

braoisgeil, (MS), *s.* 3 Grin.

braonaich, (MS), *v.a.* Bedrop.

braonan-a'-mhadaidh-ruaidh, *s.m.* Tormentil. *Colonsay.*

braoran, *s.* Briar bud. *Glenlyon* for braonan, *s.m.* D, p.115.

braosgalach, *s.f.* See braoisgeil, *s.f.* Idiotic laughter or prattling. See D, p.115.

braothag, *s.f.* A huff, see braodag, *s.f.* See D, p.115.

brath, *s.m.* A bheil thu brath an crodh a

thoirt leat?, *are you going to take the cattle with you?* In *Arran*, tha e 'brath = *he intends*. Tha e 'brath falbh, *he intends to go.* Tha e 'brath sin a dhèanamh, *he intends to do that.*

brathaigh, *s.m.* *Arran* for braigh, *s.m.* Loud report, peal of thunder, blow, stroke. D, p.113.

brath-air-bhrath, *adv.* To be found, to the fore, extant. *Sàr-Obair.*

breabag, -aig, *s.f.* Diminutive of breab, *s.m.*, A kick. 2 Wince. 3 A wincing mare.

breabair, *s.m.* 2 One who kicks. 3 A brave man.

breabaireachd, *s.f.* Acting bravely, gallantly.

breabanachd, *s.f.* Continual stamping or kicking.

breabanaich, (MS), *v.a.* Clout.

breac, (AF), 6 Dog.

breac, *v.* 11 (DMK), Sharpen a gun flint. 12 (DU), Sharpen a sickle by filing parallel grooves on the edge (inclined at 75° or so).

breacadh, *s.m.* 9 (DMK). Sharpening of a gun-flint. 10 Act of sharpening a sickle by filing parallel grooves on the edge. Bha'n spor ùr an deis a breacadh, *the new gun flint had been sharpened. Donn. Bàn.*

breac-an-ianaidh, (DU), *s.* Freckles.

breaca-seanadh, *s.f.* *Arran* for breac-sheunain, *s.f.* Freckles. D, p.119.

breac-beididh, *s.m.* Loach. See breac-beadaidh, *s.m.* D, p.118.

breac eunan, *s.f.* *Badenoch* for breac-sheunain, *s.f.* Freckles.

breac-feusach, *s.m.* See breac-feusagach *s.m.* Barbel. D, p.119.

breac-lannach, *a.* Speckle-finned, of fishes like trout and salmon.

breac-mheanaidh, *s.f.* See breac-a'-mheanaidh, *s.f.* Freckles on the face. D, p.117.

breach, (AF), *s.* Wolf. 2 Badger. 3 Dog.

breachd, (AF), *s.m.* See breac, *s.m.* Trout. 2 Salmon-trout. 3 Salmon. 4 Rarely badger. 5 Wolf. D, p.117.

breaman, *s.m.* In the *Beauly* district the evil maker or evil one, the Devil. Breamas is generally used there for most of the mischief done.

breamhain, *s.* Barrow. *Sutherland* and *Easter Ross.*

breas, *s.m.* Chimney-piece. *Arran.*

breath, *s.f.* 5 (CR) Layer or course of sheaves in a stack.

breathadh, (CR), *s.m.* Disease or rottenness in potatoes. 'Thàinig am breathadh anns a' bhuntàta', *disease has appeared in the potatoes*; nach iad tha air breathadh! *How diseased they are!* Derived from breothadh *s.m.* putrefaction and breoth, *v.a.* & *n.* To rot or putrefy. D, p.121 *Sutherland.*

breathalachadh, *s.m.* Staggering, bewilderment, confusion. See breithealachadh, *s.m.* below.

brech, *s.* See breach above.

breimein, *s.m.* See braman, *s.m.* Misadventure. D, p.114.

breith, *v.n.* Calve.

breitheal, *s.m.* 6 Whim. 7 Dizziness, fit, swoon. 8 Enchantment, reverie. 9 Dotage.

breithealachadh, s.m. Staggering, bewilderment, confusion.

breithealaich, *v.a.* 3 Stagger, as with dizziness.

breitheanas, *s.f.* Judgment. D, p.121, line 3, for "breathanas" read "breitheanais".

breithneachadh, *s.m.* 6 (MS) Construction.

brennig, (AF), *s.* Limpet.

breochlaid, *s.f.* Tenderness.

breochlaideach, *a.* Tender. 2 Crazy.

breodhuinn, (CR), *s.* Wheelbarrow.

breodhuinn-cheapaig, (CR), *s.* Both these words for wheel-barrow are used in *Sutherland & Alness (Ross)* for bleodhan, *s.m.* Wheelbarrow. D, p.101.

breòillein, *s.m.* See breòillean, *s.m.* Darnel, rye grass. D, p.121.

breos, (CR), *s.m.* Mantlepiece, Scots, *brace.*

breugan, (CR), *s.pl.* 2 Unwoven space near the top of the creel. *West of Ross-shire.*

breugan a' chlèibh, *s.pl.* Has the same meaning as breugan, above.

breunaich, (MS), *v.a.* Bedung.

breus, see breuthas below.

breuthas, -ais, *s.m.* Madness.

briachaill-brochaill, A' bh-, *s.f.* The banner of Goll Mac Morna.

briagan, *s.pl.* See breugan above.

briantach, *s.m.* See briantadh, *s.m.* Bream. (Ill. 78) D, p.123.

Briathar, *s.m.* The Scriptures. *Arran.* 'Tha e anns a' Bhriathar' (not anns an Fhocal), *it is in the Scriptures. South end of Arran.*

briathrachas, -ais, *s.m.* Declamation.

brìd, s. Whisper. *Arran.* 'Tha mi air son brìd riut', *I wish to whisper to you.*

brìdeag, *s.* 3 Cranium.

brìdeagaidh, (DMK), *s.f.* The little finger. *Lochbroom.*

brìg, s. 2 Heap of peats or potatoes built up with boards in a corner of the house. *Skye.*

brighear, (MS), *a.* Asphaltic. 2 Compendious.

brighichle, (MS), *past pt.* Abstracted.

brim, *s.* Pickle. *Argyll.*

brimean, (DC), *s.m.* Young male seal. *West of Sutherland & Ross-shire.*

brìob, *s.m.* Any considerable sum of money. *Arran.*

brìobag, *s.f.* Any considerable sum of money. *Arran.*

briogais. 2 Breeching of harness. 3 (Fionn) Used in certain islands for the roe of a fish. *s.f.*

briomal, (DC), *s.m.* Male seal. *Uist.*

brionglaid, *s.f.* 4 (MS) Clog. 5 (MS) Meander.

brionglaideach, *a.* 4 (MS) Cloggy.

brionglaidich, *v.a.* 2 (MS) Clog.

brionnach, *a.* 6 (MS) Amorous.

brionnas, (MS), *s.m.* Nicety.

briosgalachd, (MS), *s.f.* Mercury. 2 Briskness.

bris a staigh/a steach, *v.* Break into a house.

brisgean, (G), *s.pl.* Roots.

brisgean-nan-caorach, *s.* Silverweed. *Argyll.*

brisgean-tràghad, Am, *s.m.* Thrift (plant).

broc, *s.m.* 2 (AF) Wolf.

brocair, (AF), *s.m.* Fox.

brochan bàn, *s.m.* Thin gruel. *Celt. Rev.* iv. 187.

brochan beag, *s.m.* Infant's porridge. *Celt. Rev.* iv. 187.

brochan càil, *s.m.* Kale broth. *Arran.*

brochd, (MS), *s.* Grey. 2 Refuse.

broch-fheur, *s.* Heath rush. *Colonsay.*

brodan, *s.m.* Bog.

brod balaich, *s.m.* Boy.

brog, (G), *s.* Broch.

bròg, *s.f.* 6 (CR) Spawn of cod, coal-fish and other large sea-fish. *West coast of Ross.* (Iuchair, *s.f.* is the spawn of herring and salmon.) 7 Clog of a cart.

brogh, *s.m.* Outbreaking.

broghaich, (MS), *s.f.* Abominableness.

broilean, *s.m.* is the more correct spelling than broilein, *s.m.*- *nom. sing.* Snout. *Badenoch.* D, p.127.

broilleach, *s.m.* 2 Brisket of beef.

broineagan, (MS), *s.pl.* Frippery.

broinn-fhionn, (AF), *s.* Salmon.

brolamas, *s.m.* 2 Mess.

brollach, *s.* 2 (AF) See breallach, *s.m.* Small hose-fish. D, p.119.

brollaich, *s.* Unintelligible, disjointed talk. Unpleasant sounds. Jargon. *Sàr-Obair.*

bronnaidh, (DMK), *s.m.* Swag-bellied man, *in derision.*

brosgail, (MS), *v.a.* Cajole.

brosgalaiche, (MS), *s.m.* Cogger.

brosleum, *s.f.* 2 Vigour. *Sàr-Obair.*

brotagach, *a.* Abounding in broth. *Oran a' gheamhraidh.*

brothach, *s.m.* Hairy, rough man. 2 Pimpled fellow. *Sàr-Obair.*

broud (Fionn), *s.m.* Chunk in *Lorn.* Broud arain, *a chunk of bread.*

bruaidhleònach, (MS), *a.* Mad.

bruaidleanach, *a.* "Le frasan blàtha, bruaidleanach", *with warm showers perturbed. Donn. Bàn.*

bruaghadair, *s.m.* Inhabitant of a '*brugh*' (large house), hence 2 One who does a silly action. JGC. S. 8.

bruailleanach, *a.* 5 Lethargic.

bruailleanachd, *s.f.* 5 (MS) Lethargy.

brù-àit, *s.m.* Abdomen.

bruanag, *s.f.* 4 (MS) Mouthful.

bruasgadh, *s.m.* Tearing in tatters, breaking asunder, confusion. *Sàr-Obair.*

brùban, (DMK), s.m. Girth or belly band of a horse. West coast of Ross.

bruc(h)ag, s.f. 8 (CR) Corner Arran.

bruchairreachd, s.f. Bruchairreachd a's cìob chuireadh sult air lòinneanaibh, heath rush and deer's hair grass would put comeliness on the meadows. Beinn Doran.

bruchd, s.m. Sudden rushing forth. D, p.130. Is s.f. in Badenoch.

bruchlais, s.f. See pruchlais, s.f. Den, cave. D, p.739.

bruic, s. Seaweed. Sutherland.

bruid, s. 7 (MS) Bond.

bruid, v. 9 Stab with the horns, like cattle.

brùideag, s.f. 3 Worm.

brùighteachd, (MS), s.f. Contrition.

bruinnean-beò, s.m. See buinnean-beò, s.m. Sea animalculae, phosphorescence. D, p.140.

brùiteachd, (MS), s.f. Aggrievance.

brùitich, (MS), v.a. Brutify.

brunsgal, s.f. Rumbling noise. 2 Mumbling. West of Ross-shire.

bruthainn, (DC), s.f. 2 The yielding time of the year, when the earth gives return for labour.

bruthan, s.m. 3 Lapful.

bu, past ind. of defective verb is. 'Cha bu leis bu mhath', it was not well with him. Bu does not aspirate a d following. (DC).

bua, (DC), s.m. Ashes, embers.

buab, s. A web of any kind of cloth. It is pronounced in Breadalbane with a sound somewhat similar to the 'uadh' in Stuadh and then ab or ap for the ending.

buabhall-an-eich, s.m. Horse-stall. Lewis. S. p.923.

buabhall-na-bà, s.m. Cow-stall. Lewis. D, p.923.

buabstair, s.m. Possibly this may correctly mean a cloth merchant or cloth wearer. In Breadalbane and elsewhere, however, it is used to denote an overbearing person, a bully.

buabstaireachd, s.m. Unruliness.

buachaille, Am, s.m. 5 The star called Arcturus, but not the Arcturus mentioned in the 38th chapter of Job.

buachaill-chaorach, s.m. Shepherd.

buachar, s.m. Cow-dung, s.f. in Badenoch.

buadhalachd, s.f. 7 (MS) Gallantry.

buadharlann, s.m. See buadhghallan, s.m. Ragweed, ragwort. D, p. 133.

bua-dhealt, (DC), s. Mildew.

buafan, (AF), s.m. Toad.

buag, s.f. White stone.

buaibh, (AF), s. Cattle.

buaic, s.m. 7 (MS) Buck.

buaicleach, (AF), s.m. Sheep's dung.

buaidheam, (DMy), s.f. Flattery. Lewis for foidheam, s.f. D, p.455.

buaidheanntach, (MS), a. Assailable.

buail-a'-chnag, s. Skip-jack insect. JGC. S. 228.

buaileadh-nam-boisean, s. An indoor Uist game in which the chosen person put his face on someone's knee and holds his hands behind his back, palms upward. Someone in the company then approaches and touches the hands (often with greater force than is necessary) and the "blind one" has to say who has touched him. Should he guess correctly, he is let up and the other has to take his place, but the first guesser is often down for a long time before being lucky enough to say who his opponent is. This game is also called "Ultaun altaun". Uist Games in Celtic Review. No. 16.

Buaileam ort! Int. I accept your challenge. Gaidheal II 172.

buaile-thadhair, s. An enclosure for cattle.

buailtean, s.m. 5 (DU) Gairloch. for buadh-ghallan, s.m. Ragweed, ragwort. D, p.133.

buailtean, s.pl. Nooks, private keeping places. Rob Donn.

buain, v.a. A' buain a' ghart, cutting corn. Arran. There is no S sound in gart.

buaireanta, a. 4 (MS) Giddy.

bualadair, s.m. Thresher. See buailtear, s.m. D, p.135.

buall, s.m. Stall of a byre. D, p.79.

bualtan, s.m. See buailtear above.

bualtan-buidhe, s.m. [This must be a

plant. Dwelly on page 135 of his Dictionary has 'buailtean, -ein, -einean, s.m. See bualan.' On page 136 he gives 'bualan, s.m. Groundsel, *Senecio vulgaris*' Thus the translation of] 'Agus cho guanach ri bualtan-buidhe an oidhche oiteagagach' [is, *and as giddy* – or *light-headed* – *as the yellow groundsel on a breezy night*].

buan-mhairtheanas, s.m. Abiding.

buanna, (DU), *s.m.* Boat-pole.

buannaidh, s. Bully. *Rob Donn.*

buanntaich, (MS), *v.a.* Earn.

buantaich, (MS), *v.a.* Arrive.

buarach, (DC), *s.f.* 5 Shackle on a chain.

buarpag, *s.f.* Receptacle for carded wool. *Skye.*

buathall, *s.m.* Stall properly for cattle but used as a horse stall also in *Ardnamurchan, Mull* and *Perth.*

buatham, (MS), s.m. 2 Crincum.

buathanta, a. Foolish, awkward, clumsy in conversation or action. *Sàr-Obair.*

buc, *s.m.* See buicean, *s.m.* Young buck or roe. D, p.137.

buchann, (DC), *a.* Swelling, rotund. Ian buchann, the long-tailed duck.

buchdach, (MS), *s.m.* Swain.

buclag, (DMK), *s.f.* Rounded stone about the size of a putting-stone. *Caithness.*

bucsach, *a.* See bocsach, *a.* Boxen. D, p.104.

bucas, *s.m.* Box. For bocsa, *s.m.* D, p.104.

buideal, *s.m.* 5 (MMcD) Vessel shaped like a barrel, 8 or 9 inches in diameter used for carrying water. It contained 7 Scots Pints.

buidh, *s.m.* Hero, champion. 2 Enemy. *Sar-Obair.*

buidhe, *a.* 5 Fallow.

buidheag, *s.f.* Buidheag mhòr na fèill Mìcheil, *the big yellow* (*moon*) *of Michaelmas.*

buidheam, *s.* Fits and starts. 'Mur breug a ruith le buidheam e', *if it is not a lie circulating by fits and starts.* W. Ross, 67.

buidhean, *s.m.* 3 Circular bag made of prepared skin. Formerly used to carry milk; but when kits of wood came into fashion, the name was transferred to vessels made of that material.

buidheann, *s.f.* Political parties.

Conservative Party – Buidheann nan Tearmann. A' Bhuidheann tearmannaich.

Labour Party – Buidheann nan Oibrichean. Na h-oibrichean.

Liberal Party – Buidheann nan Aghartach. Na h-Aghartaich.

Socialist Party – Buidheann nam Pàirtearan. A' bhuidheann Phàirteach. Na Pàirtearan.

Unionist Party – Buidheann na h-Aonachd. A' bhuidheann Aonachdach. Na h-Aonachdairean.

Irish National Party – Buidheann nan Eireannach dùthchasach. Na Dùthchasaich Eireannach. Na h-Eireannaich dhùthchasach. A' bhuidheann Eireannach dhùthchasach.

Irish Unionist Party – Buidheann Eireannach na h-Aonachd; A' bhuidheann Eireannach Aonachdach; Na h-Aonachdairean Eireannach.

Scottish Conservative Party. Buidheann nan Tearmann Albannach; Na Tearmannaich Albannach;

Scottish Labour Party – Buidheann nan Oibrichean Albannach. Na h-Oibrichean Albannach.

Scottish Liberal Party – Buidheann nan Aghartach Albannach. Na h-Aghartaich Albannach.

Scottish National Party – Buidheann nan Albannach dùthchasach. A' bhuidheann Albannach dhùthchasach. Na h-Albannaich dhùthchasach. Na Dùthcasaich Albannach.

Scottish Unionist Party – Buidheann Albannaich na h-Aonachd. Na h-Aonachdairean Albannach.

Welsh Conservative Party – Buidheann nan Tearmann Cuimreach.

Welsh Labour Party – Buidheann nan Oibrichean Cuimreach.

Welsh Liberal Party – Buidheann nan Aghartaich Cuimreach. Na h-Aghartaich Cuimreach.

Welsh National Party – Buidheann nan Cuimreach dùthchasach. A' bhuidheann Chuimreach dhùthchasach. Na

Cuimrich dhùthchasach. Na dùth-chasaich Chuimreach.

Welsh Unionist Party – Buidheann Chuimreach na h-Aonachd. Na h-Aonachdairean Cuimreach.

A Conservative – Tearmannach.

An Imperialist – Impireasach.

A Labour Party member – Oibriche.

A Liberal – Aghartach.

A Reactionary – Aischeumach.

A Socialist – Pàirtear.

A Tory – Tòiridh.

A Whig – Cuig.

A Unionist – Aonachdair.

Conservatism – Tearmannachd.

Imperialism – Impireas.

Labour Partyism – Oibreachas.

Liberalism – Aghartachd.

Reactionaryism – Aischeumachd.

Socialism – Pàirteachd.

Toryism – Tòiridheachd.

Whiggery – Cuigse.

Unionism – Aonachdas.

buidhe-ghlas, s. Yellow-drab (colour).

buidhreachd, (MS), s.f. Deafness.

buigealag, s.f. See buigileag, s.f. D, p.139.

buigean, (DC), s.m. dim. 2 Small quantity as of meal, sugar and so on. 3 As a name for a dwarf it gives a further diminutive "buigilean", usually applied in derision.

buige leò, s.m. Bumpkin, blockhead. Easdale.

buigeasg, genitive buigeuisg, Soft weather. JGC. W. 304.

buileag, (DC), s.f. Rash of measles or any other disease. Uist.

builgeannan-peasrach (DMK), s.pl. Pods of pease. West coast of Ross-shire.

builgean-peasrach, s.m. Pod of pease.

buille-bhàraich, s. First blow at shinty, given to a notability, JGC. W. 240.

buille-ghràinichidh, (DMK), s. An intentional offence. One who wishes to get rid of an unwelcome visitor says, 'bheir mi buille-ghràinichidh dha', I'll offend him. West coast of Ross-shire.

buillsgean, s.m. 4 Centre of commotion.

buineachadh, (MS), s.m. Appurtenance.

buineachas, (MS), s.m. Appurtenance.

buinneag, s.f. 10 Soft vegetable stem.

buinnealaich, (MS), v.a. Bedrop.

buinnig, (MS), v. Arrive.

buinnigeach, (MS), a. Available.

buinnseach, s.f. Big, strong, clumsy woman. W. H. Tales, iii 395.

buinntineachd, (MS), s.f. Respect.

buinte, s.f. Relationship, kindred. Sutherland & Arran.

buintineach, (MS), a. Appurtenant.

buintineachd, (MS), s.f. Appurtenance.

buirbeachd, (MS), s.f. Bloatedness.

buirbuich, (MS), v.a. Cancerate.

bùirich, s.f. 6 Bellowing of deer in the rutting season.

buisneachdail, (MS), a. Incantatory.

buisnich, v.a. See buitsich below.

buist, s. Stall of a byre. D, p.79.

buistireachd, s.f. See buitseachd, s.f. Witchcraft, sorcery. D, p.141.

buite, (AĊ), s.f. Puffin.

buiteach, s.f. 2 (CR). Scolding. 'Thug e buiteach air', he gave him a scolding. Sutherland.

bùitich, (CR), v.a. Scold, rate. Sutherland. Bùitich air falbh e, drive him away; bùitich air falbh am balgair sin, drive that dog away.

bùitichte, (CR), past pt. of bùitich v.a. Threaten. Sutherland. D, p.141 Ged a bhùitichte bàs orra, though they be threatened with death.

buitsich, v.a. Enchant, bewitch.

bulagan, s.pl. of bulag, s.f. See pulag, s.f. Round stone. MacLeod & Dewar in the English-Gaelic section give "Taw s. Cluiche air bhulagan, [a game with round stones, that is to say, marbles. A taw is a large, frequently streaked or variegated marble with which the player shoots.]

bulais, s. Suspender of a creel.

bulbach, (MS), a. Bulbous.

bullach, s. 2 (AF) Limpet.

bullaig, (MS), s. Bulk.

buluisg, s. The planted willow. The common willow is seileach, s.m. D, p.804 and the wild willow is gallanach, s. Beauly and elsewhere.

bunabhuachaille, (AF), s.m. Auk.

bunacha-bac, s.m. or bunnacha-bac, s.m. Horizon. See D, p.142.

bunacharach, a. Fundamental.

bunaitich, v.a. 6 (MS) Bottom.

bun-bac, s.m. Singular of bunnacha-bac. Portion of the horizon. 2 That portion of the roof of a house which is next to the wall. (The sky is, as it were, the roof of the earth) See D, p.922-3. Trans. Gael. Soc. Inverness. xiv. III.

buncharaich, (MS), v.a. Ground.

bun-cheangal, s. Part of a couple of a house. See D, p.922-3.

bun-dùirn, (DU), s.m. Wrist band of a shirt, blouse et cetera.

bun-fhaclachd, (MS), s.f. Etymology.

bungaid, (CR), s.f. Headstrong girl. West of Ross-shire. 2 Hussy. 3 Trash.

bunnan, s.m. 3 (AF) Heron.

bunnan buidhe, (AF), Heron.

bunntach, (DC), s.m. Refuse of wool, hemp, flax and so on.

buntach, (DC), a. Broken off short, truncated.

buntuinn, s.f. Feeling.

buraclach, (DC), s.m. The fabulous whelp of a water-monster.

burarus, s.m. Warbling or purling noise. Sàr-Obair.

burdaich, (MS), v.a. Scorn.

burdail, (MS), a. Antic.

bùrdan, s.m. Is mithich dhuinn...dàn bùrdain a chasgairt dut, Caismeachd Ailean nan Sop.

bùrn, s.m. Water. Nach e rinn am bùrn, how it has rained! Tha bùrn mòr anns an abhainn, there is much water in the river.

bùrn-èirigh, s.m. Spring water. Lewis.

bùrn-iaruinn, s.m. Mineral water. Lewis.

burra-bhuachaille, (AF), s.m. Great auk.

burrail, (DU), s.f. Bellowing of a bull or cow.

burt, s.m. See bùrt, s.m. Mockery. D, p.143.

bus. Gum bus bith. proverb, for ge b'e air bith. Whosoever.

bus, s.m. 10 Muzzle of a horse.

busachan, (DMK), s.m. Muzzle.

busag, s.f. 4 (DU) Piece put on the point of the sole of a boot or shoe.

butadh, (DU), s.m. Secret pampering.

butainneas. Misreading of 'buntainneis an fhreasdail. Leabhar nan cnoc 190.

buthaig, s.f. Long straw for thatching, drawn straw. West of Ross-shire. 2 (DU), Sheaf of corn, generally applied to threshed corn. A sheaf of corn in the ear is sguab, s.m. See D, p.835.

buthaige, see buthaig above.

buthair, s.m. "Booer" or "bouman", one who rents milch cows from a farmer. Arran. 2 (CR) Bumpkin. Arran. 3 See buaghair, s.m. Cow-herd. D, p.134.

buthtraidh, (CR), s.f. Elder-tree. West of Ross-shire.

butrais, s.f. 2 (DC). Unsettled weather, Lochcarron district.

C

cabairsich, (MS), v.a. Gabble.

cabar, s.m. 10 (DMK) Oar. Sutherland.

cabar-droma, s.m. Ridge-board.

cabar-naisg, s.m. Post to which cattle are tied in a byre.

cabar-slait, (AH), s.m. Stag's switch horn, horn without tines. 2 Stag with switch horns. 3 Stag's head with switch horns.

cabasdaireachd, (DU), s.f. Sharp caustic remarks.

cab-dubh, (CR), s.m. Small, dark-headed trout. West of Ross-shire.

cabhal, (MMcD), s.m. Bag-net in the form of a cone, used for catching salmon or trout in a river. Lewis.

cabhal, (DMK), s. Trap made of wicker for catching trout or salmon in a stream. West coast of Ross-shire.

cabhladh, s.m. Ship's tackle.

cablaid, s.f. 2 Hindrance.

cabrach-cròcach, (AF), s.m. Deer, stag.

cachaileith, s.f. 3 Hurdle. 4 Sticks or bars individually moveable to close a breach. 5 (MS) Sluice.

cachlaidh crò-snàthaid, (DMK), s. Turn-stile gate. Hebrides.

cadaisde, (CR), s.f. Catechism.

cadaidh, s. 'Cha'n 'eil suiridheach no cadaidh', there is neither wooer nor message-boy Rob Donn.

cadalan-tràghad, *s.m.* 2 (MMcD) Seaweed, cream coloured, something like a sponge or honeycomb in shape. On placing it under the pillow it was supposed to induce sleep. *Western Isles.*

cadal-ìnchean, *s.m. Sutherland.* for cadal-deilgneach, *s.m.* "Pins and needles" in a limb. Preceded by the article *an.*

cadal-ìneach. *Farr* for cadal-deilgneach, *s.m.* See above.

cadal-iongach, (DMK), *Sutherland* for cadal-deilgneach. See above.

cadal-ìonach, (DU), *s.m. Gairloch* for cadal-deilgneach, *s.m.* See above.

càdan, *s.m.* Egg-shell.

cadha, *s.m.* 5 Passage in a house between the "but" and "ben".

cadha-fairge, *s.m. Teachd. Gàidhealach.*

cadhag, *s.f.* 4 (CR) Double-hook, S-hook for linking "yokes" to the double swingle-tree. See under crann-nan-gad. D, p.263.

cadhlan, (AF), *s.m.* Goat, leader.

cadhlas, (AF), *s.m.* Goat, leader.

cadla, see cadhla, *s.f.* See D, p.146.

ca-doc, *s.m.* Gaelic name for "cat-dog", the game of rounders.

caernideacht, (AF), *s.f.* Cattle.

cagailt, (DMK), *s.f.* Hearth. Air cagailtean chàich, *at other people's firesides. West coast of Ross-shire.*

caglach or caglachan, (DU), *s.m.* Tangle of yarn or fishing line.

caglachan, (CR), *s.m.* Anything chewed, such as a piece of cloth that has been chewed by a cow. *West of Ross-shire.*

caibe-sìth, *s.m.* Fairy spade. A smooth slippery black stone, in shape rather like the sole of a shoe. It was put in water and given to sick people and cattle.

càich-mhine, *s.* Chaff. *Arran.*

caidreabh, *s.m.* 8 (MS) Inclination.

caidreabhachadh, (MS), *s.m.* Cherishment.

caig, *v.a.* 2 Contend, dispute, wrangle.

caigean, *s.m.* 2 Little parcel.

caigeann, *s.f.* 3 (CR) Two fish caught at the same time on one hand-line. 4 (CR) Two sheep with their heads tied together and also their tails, so as to be driven easily. *West of Ross-shire.* 5 (CR) Used of two things that have become interlocked or entangled. If, for example, two parts trying to pass did not clear one another, it would be said, "rinn iad caigeann".

cailcean, -ein, *s.m.* 3 (CR) A bald spot on the head. *West of Ross-shire.*

caile, *s.f.* 4 Maid servant who does more or less other work than housework.

caileach, *s.* 3 (AF) Sow.

caileag, *s.f.* 2 (AF) Lythe. 3 Circle of straw ropes placed round a heap of corn to keep it from spreading on the barn floor. Also "cat" in *Islay.*

caileachd, *s.f.* 5 (MS) Crasis.

caile-shearbhanta, *s.f.* Maid servant who does more or less other work than housework.

càil-ghuth, (CR), *s.f.* Voice. 2 Sweet or musical voice. 'Is brèagh a' chàil-ghuth a th'aige', *what a fine voice he has.*

cailich-fhodar, (DMK), *s.pl.* Fleas. *Lewis.*

cailleab-shìonain, *s.* Wild-fire.

cailleach, (DU), *s.f.* 2 Smoke cowl.

cailleachaileachd, *s.f.* Effeminacy.

cailleachalachd, (MS), *s.f.* Anility.

cailleach-chasach, (AF), *s.* Cheslip. 2 Millipede.

cailleach-fhasgnaidh, (DMK), *s.f.* Corn fanner. Until comparatively recently women winnowed and dressed corn in *Sutherland* and on the *West coast of Ross-shire,* hence the reason for this name there.

cailleach-fhraoich, (DMK), *s.f.* A large sheaf of heather tied tightly together with ropes of the same material, used as a door to a sheep cot or similar building. The same as cual-fhraoich, see below. *Caithness.*

cailleach-oidhche, *s.f.* Butterfly. (?Moth). *Arran.*

caille pianain, (DMY), *s.* Phosphorus, as seen in fish when it begins to decompose, or in the sea on a dark night.

cailm, (AH), *s.f.* Vigour, lusty health, strength, robustness, sturdiness (generally applied to persons). A bheil thu an cailm mhaith?, *do you enjoy lusty health?*

caimdeal, (G), *s.* Opposition.

caimeach, (AF), *s.m.* Small trout.

caimean, (DC), *s.m.* Spot of light, as when the sun shines through a cloud-rift on a wet day.

cainear, (CR), *s.m.* Salmon fisher. 2 Fisher for salmon in tidal waters. 3 (DMk), Water-bailiff. All *West of Ross-shire.*

cainneag, *s.f.* 3 (CR), Corn bag made of plaits or cloth or straw or rushes. [Such bags were in use in Skye well within Dwelly's living memory.]

cainneal, (DC), *s.m.* Cinnamon (Scots *cannel*), much used of old to perfume the breath.

cainneineach, *a.* Mìos chianail, chainneineach gheàrrt, *Rob Donn* (1899), 207.

cainnt, (a' cainnt), *pr. pt.* Talking. *Arran*, except in Shiskine where they say *a' bruthain.*

cainnteag, *s.f.* 3 see cainneag, *s.f.* Mote, small matter. D, p.150.

cainreach, (AF), *s.m.* Small trout.

caiplig, (DC), *pr. pt.* a' caipligeadh, *v.a.* Put ropes on thatch. *Uist.*

cairb, *s.f.* 7 (CR) Wooden arch of a saddle. The crook-saddle that was used in the Hebrides for carrying panniers or creels, consists of a piece of wood, initially curved or arched with hooks cut out of the solid wood on either side of the ridge to receive the suspenders of the creels. A sufficient thickness of sacking or straw matting – sumag, *s.f.*, – is put under this saddle on the horse's back. See D, p.916. 8 Carcase, provincial for cairb, *s.f.* See D, p.150 *Dàin Iain Ghobha.*

†**cairbheam**, *v.* Man a fleet *et cetera.*

cairbhean, *s.m.* See cairbean, s.m. A sailfish.

cairbhil-a'-choin, (DU), *s.m.* The herb Robert.

caireineachd, *s.f.* Lickerishness.

caireal, s.m. 7 Loud and continual speaking.

cairiche, *s.m.* Wrestler, tumbler. *Sàr-Obair.*

cairig, *v.a.* See caithrig, *v.a.* Take refuse

out of straw by hand. D, p.154.

cairig, (AF), *s.f.* Sheep.

cairim, *s.* Oidhche nollaig 's mi'm chairis, 'cur le cairim ri n-òl, (?caith-ream). *Duanaire*, 186.

cairiste, *s.m. & f.* See cairbhist, *s.m.*

cairbhist, (DC). *s.m.* 6 The extra rent, labour and kind paid to a tacksman by tenants. A common *cairbhist* was 7 days labour in spring; 7 days labour in harvest; a Lunasdan (Lammas) lamb; a "molt" Samhna (a hallowmas wether). These were over and above the stipulated rent paid in money.

cairbhre, *a.* Abounding in carcases. *West Highland Tales*, iii 344.

cairmeachd, *s.f.* B'anns leam cairmeachd mo rùin S. *nan caol.* p.17.

cairnean, (DC), *s.m.* Awn of barley.

cairr, (AC), *s.* Udder.

cairt, *s.f.* Bent ridge of a pack-saddle.

cairt, *s.f.* additional names of parts (See D, pp.151-152.).

1 Aisridh, *s.f.* Axle-tree.

2 Beul, *s.m.* Rim.

3 Bòrd-aoisich, *s.m.* Front-board (13).

4 Bòrd-cùil, *s.m.* Tail-board.

5 Bòrd-deiridh, s.m. Tail-board.

6 Bouta na h-aisil. Axle-bolt.

7 Cairt, (CR), *s.f.* Tumbrel on a coup-cart. *E. Ross-shire.*

8 Cas-cùirn, *s.f.* Shaft, tram (2).

9 Ceann-teannachaidh, *s.m.* Rack-pin.

10 Chathach, s.m. Side.

11 Crann-tarruing, *s.f.* Shaft, tram (2) 2 Axle-pin (10a).

12 Cromag-deiridh, *s.f.* Breeching-hook (6).

13 Cromag-guailne, *s.f.* Draught-hook (8).

14 Cromag-thoisich, *s.f.* Draught-hook (8).

15 Doras, *s.m.* Tail-board (9).

16 Pinne na h-aisil, *s.m.* Axle-pin (10a).

17 Speilear, *s.* Runner, runner hook.

18 Taobh, s.m. Side.

cairtear, s.m. 3 Tanner.

cairteir, See cairtear above.

cairt-gheal, *s.f.* Quinine.

cairt-locha, (DC), *s.f.* Produces a blue colour. The method of gathering it, is to wade into the water barefoot, and raise up the roots with one's toes. The roots are those of the water-lily. *Uist.* D, p.152.

cairt-phostachd, s.f. Post-card.

caiseannachd, *s.f.* 2 (MS) Quarrel. 3 Anger.

caisg, *v.* 3 Wean.

caisgdhleidh, *s.* Chaff. *Arran.*

caisineachd, *s.f.* See caiseannachd *s.f.* Fretfulness, peevishness. D, p.153.

caisionnach, (AF), *s.m.* Spotted cow.

caislich, *v.* Bed cattle.

caisreaganaich, *v.a.* Curl.

cait-chinn, (AF), *s.* Cow.

c'àite is used locally in *Sutherland* for *far am.* Bha mi c'àit 'an d'robh e, *I was where he was.*

càiteach, (CR), *s.* Cloth or skin on which corn is winnowed; winnowing sheet. 2 Vessel made of rushes for measuring corn.

caiteinich, (MS), *v.a.* Curl.

caith, *v.a.* Eat.

caitheachan, s.m. Jetsam.

caitheamh, *s.m.* Spending, consuming. May also be *s.f.*

caitheinich, (MS), *s.f.* Sumptuosity.

caithriseach, *a.* 3 (MS) Unsleeping.

caith-sgioladh, *s.* Chaff. *Arran.*

caithteachail, (MS), *a.* Corrodable.

caithtealachd, (MS), *s.* Corrosability.

càlag, *s.f.* Puffin.

calamand, *a.* Stout. *Sutherland.*

càl-deanntaig, (DMK), *s.m.* Leaves of the common nettle cooked and eaten as cabbage. *Caithness.*

càl-diolais, (DMK), *s.m.* Leaves of the mugwort – artemisia vulgaris – cooked and eaten as cabbage. *Caithness.*

callaid, *s.f.* 8 (MS) Hood.

callaideach, *a.* 6 Hooded.

callaidh, *a.* Stiff, benumbed. *Rob Donn.*

callaidh, *s.* See callaid, *s.f.* Fence D, p.156 *Leabhar-nan-Cnoc,* 47.

callanaich, ? Le fuaim na guirm a callanaich, [should read 'Le fuaim na gairme galanaich, *with the sound of the baying call.* So callanaich is a misquotation of *galanach,* bay. In Moladh Beinn Dòbhrain; Angus MacLeod (Editor). The Songs of Duncan Bàn Macintyre, Edinburgh, 1952, p.224, 1.3306.]

callan-gàraidh, (AH), *s.m.* Old dilapidated, grass-grown turf dyke.

calluinn, (DU), *s.m.* The part of the *caibe* which grips the inserted part of a *cas-chrom* or crooked foot-plough.

calman-codhail, *s.m.* God-sent or propitious omen. *Sàr-Obair.*

calpa, *s.m.* The walls of a house as distinct from the roof. 9 Part of a tether between the stake and the swivel.

càl-slapach, *s.m.* Wild goosefoot. *Colonsay.*

calumach, (MS), *a.* Tumorous.

camachraosan, (DMK), *s.m.* Act of making wry faces at another.

cam-allt, (DMK), *s.m.* Winding burn.

camanachd, *s.f.* Shinty. The national game of Gaeldom. Equal sides are picked, the object of the game being to score as many goals or *hails* as possible. Stones are used for goals. The ball may be of wood, hard wound worsted, or of hair, peat or other available material, while the *caman* is a bent stick of wood or a large tangle. In Uist, people have to be ingenious and to make the best of the materials they have. As Uist is barren of trees, a tangle *caman* is nearly as common as a wooden one. Another ingenious *caman* is made of a large piece of canvas bent with both ends caught in the hand. It is very effective. The Uist boys used to be, and in some places still are, very proficient at the game, the main qualities necessary for an ideal player being speed and dexterity.

The following is an invitation to shinty: 'Thugainn a dh'iomain. Dè'n iomain? Iomain chaman. Dè'n caman? Caman iubhair. Dè'n iubhar? Iubhar adhair. Dè'n adhar? Adhar ian. Dè'n t-ian? Ian air iteig. Dè'n iteag? Iteag fithich. Dè'm fitheach? Fitheach feòla. Dè'n fheòil? Feòil dhaoine. Dè na daoine? Daoine naomh. Dè naomh? Naomh eich'. The translation is as follows: Come to play a ball game. What ball game? Shinty. What club? A yew club.

What yew? Yew of the sky. What sky? Sky of the birds. What bird? Bird on the wing. What wing? Raven's wing. What raven? A raven of flesh. What flesh? Flesh of men. What men? Holy men. (Saints) What holy man? (Saint) Saint of horse.

cam-chòmhdhail, (G), s. Misadventure.

càmlachail, (MS), a. Culmiferous.

camhlaich, see cabhlach, *s.m.* Fleet. D, p.144.

camhtair, (MS), *s.m.* Rowel.

camlagaich, (MS), *v.a.* Curl.

campraid, (CR), *s.f.* A slight quarrel *West of Ross-shire.*

cam-strannd, (CR), *s.f.* Bickering, constant quarreling. *West of Ross-shire.*

camus, (G), *s.m.* In inland districts, the bend where a steep slope meets the level ground.

camus-fhliuch, (AF), *s.m.* Lythe.

cana, (AF), *s.* Puppy, whelp.

canabhalach (?) *Guth na bliadhna* II 360.

canabhlas, (DMK), *s.* Form of imprecation – canabhlas ort! *Caithness & Sutherland.*

canach an t-slèibhe, *s.f.* Moss cotton.

canaidh, (CR), *a.* Gaelic form of *canny.*

cànaimheach, (MS), *s.m.* Philologist.

canal, *s.m.* The bevel on the edge of a cutting tool.

canda, See †canna, *s.m.* Can. D, p.159.

candaraig, (AF), *s.f.* Foul salmon.

cannadh, s.m. Porpoise. *Arran.*

canntaireachd, *s.f.* 5 The ancient Highland manner of noting classical pipe-music by a combination of various syllables by which tunes could be more easily recollected by the learner. See D, p.159. It was evidently based on the composer's conception of the sounds of the notes, and this accounts for different words having been used by different pipers. Canntaireachd can hardly be looked upon as a complete system of notation if no means be employed to give the exact duration of each note. A teacher whose mother tongue was Gaelic, would have no difficulty at all in supplying this deficiency with his voice, and the system of canntaireachd would certainly in such cases, be of great assistance to the memory. When one is accustomed to the words of canntaireachd, it would be fairly easy to bring out a tune from them on the pipes, provided the air were known to the performer, but should he not be acquainted with the air, the correct performance thereof would not be so easy. Charles Bannatyne Esquire, M.B., C.M. of Salsburgh, Holytown, has worked out a complete key to canntaireachd as used by the Mac-Crimmons. It is the only detailed one that has ever been published, and as he has kindly placed it at our disposal, it is reproduced here in full. (See D, p.159) "The bagpipe scale from *ta* to d' in the key of A natural was formed by ancient musicians to give variety to modal tunes, in three pitches or keys, hence the confusion in the minds of many;. in other words piobaireachds are ancient modal tunes, played on an ancient instrument, whose compass is designed to allow the same modes to be rendered in three pitches, in order to give variety to the music. This is the secret of all pipe music as well as piobaireachds."

Three notations of canntaireachd were known to John Piper, the nurse of John Campbell of Islay.

1. The notation of MacCrimmon.
2. The notation of MacArthur.
3. The notation of Nether Lorn.

The first is given in the illustrated Gaelic-English Dictionary (p.159). The second has not yet been found and the third was discovered about 1912 and a table of the forms used in it is appended on page 42 of this Appendix.

caob, *v.a.* Tha e 'gam chaobadh, *he is nipping me.*

caocaire, *s.m.* A Quaker.

caocaireachd, *s.f.* Quakerism.

caoch, (AF), *s.m.* Grampus. 2 Mole. 3 Blind beast.

caoch, *a.* 6 One-eyed. *Arran.* Cnò chaoch, *an empty nut.*

caochail, *v.* 5 (MS) Abrogate.

caochan, (AF), s.m. Grampus. 2 Mole. 3

CANNTAIREACHD

KEY TO NETHER LORN CANNTAIREACHD

	Scale with high G grace note.	Scale with D grace note.	Scale with E Grace note.	Scale with no grace notes.	Siubhal.	Siubhal Sleamhuinn.	Leumluath to E.	Taorluath to low A.	Tripling or Taorluath Breabach.	Crunluath.
low G	him	dam or bam	em	em	himen	himem	himbare	himdarid	himbabem	himbandre
low A	hin	dan	en	en	hinen	hinen	hinbare	hindarid	hindaen	hinbandre
B	hio	to	eo	o	hioen	hioeo	hiobare	hiodarid	hiotoeo	hiobandre
C	ho	do	eo	o	hoen	hoeo	hobare	hodarid	hodoeo	hobandre
D	ha	—	ea	a or da	haen	haea	habare or harodde	hadarid	—	habandre or haroddre
E	che	—	—	e or de	che-hin	cheche	chebare	chedarid	—	chebandre
F	he	—	—	ve or dhe	hehin	hehe	hebare	hedarid	—	hebandre
G	hi or chi (high Ag-n.)	—	—	di	hihin	hihi	hibare	hidarid	—	hibandre
A	—	—	—	I	Ien	no example	Ibare	I darid	—	Ibandre

The nomenclature of most of the different movements has for convenience been taken from the Piobaireachd exercises in Logan's Tutor, price 1s., and the examples here given refer to the staff notation examples given there and should be compared with them.

Blind beast. See caochag. D, p.161.

caochan, *s.m.* See D, p.161. 9 A stream which is so small as to be almost covered by the heather. Common in *Gairloch.*

caochlaideachas, (MS), *s.m.* Giddiness.

caod, (AF), *s.m.* Cat.

caod Choluim Chille, see caod-Chaluim-Chille, *s.m.* For both of which see eala-bhuidhe, *s.f.* Perforated St. John's wort. D, p.380.

caoibhreachan, (AF), *s.m.* The herb ragfoot or marsh ragwort, a 'mystery' plant used by prudent housewives in byres, dairies and elsewhere to guard stock, milk and other commodities from the evil eye.

caoin, *s.f.* 5 (DU) Polished surface on a metal. 6 Sharpness of edge. "Bhris a chaoin air", *rust has attacked it.*

caoinealachd, (MS), *s.f.* Amicability.

caoin-shùil, (MS), *s.f.* Belgard.

caoir, *s.f.* 10 (DU) The sound of burning.

caoit, see †caoitein, *s.m.* The Gaelic spelling of kitten. D, p.163.

caoiteag, (AF), *s.f.* See cuiteag, *s.f.* Whiting. D, p.296.

caolaichte, (MS), *past pt.* of caolaich *v.a.* Make or grow small. Abstracted.

caolan, *s.m.* Small gut. D, p.164 The plural in *Gairloch* is caolanan, (DU), not caolain as it is elsewhere.

caolanaich, *v.a.* Gut.

caol-an-droma, *s.* Small of the back.

caol-dìreach, *s.m.* 'A' dèanamh orra caol-dìreach', *making a bee-line for them.*

caol-dubh, *s.m.* Black willow. CG, v. 252.

caol-duirn, *s.* Wrist.

caolruith, *pr. pt.* Closely pursuing. 'Chunna mi na caoirich a' caolruith a' bhalgaire', *I saw the sheep closely pursuing the fox.* From a sequence of 'Rannan Brèige' ('Lying Verses'), D. Macpherson, *An Duanaire*, Edinburgh 1868, p.48.

caonnagach, *a.* 3 (MS) Strenuous.

caonntag, (MS), *s.f.* Precipitancy. 2 Haste, hastiness.

caora, *s.f.* The Appendix gives this additional information to that given on D, p.165:

ath-bhliadhnach, 2 year-old sheep.

ath-dhìonag. 2 year-old sheep.

bliadhnach muilt. *Lewis* for bliadhnach mult. A yearling.

deathaid, for deata, an unshorn sheep.

dò-bhliadhnach muilt. *Lewis* for dà bhliadhnach mult, a two-year wether. (MMcL).

dò-bhliadhnach reithe. *Lewis* for dà-bhliadhnach reithe, a two-year sheep.

ruig, ruigleachan, rùta, rùda, rùd, a ridgling.

tiaraineach, An 18 months old sheep, derived from 'an t-sia-raidheach', *the six-quarter old*, the *t* of the article drowning the "*s*", hence tiaraineach.

uan leth aon, *a twin lamb.*

caora, *s.* 'A' mhuir 'na caora geala', *the sea in white foam. Arran.*

caora bheanan, *s.f.* 2 (AF) Ewe.

caora bhrogach, (CR), *s.f.* Black-faced sheep. *Arran.* [recte *bhrògach*?]

caora-caorthainn, *s.* Rowan. *Colonsay.*

caora-caothaich, *s.* St. John's wort. *Colonsay.*

caora-chàraidh, (AF), *s.f.* Sheep exacted from a tenant at Hallowmass. A heriot or herzeld sheep.

caora-chòsag, *s.* Ant or emmet. JGC. S. 228.

caora-chrom, *s.f.* Metaphorically, the worm of a still.

caoraigh-bhrocach, *s.f.* Black-faced sheep. *Arran.* See caora bhrogach, (MMcD), speckled or spotted sheep. D, p.166.

caoranach, *a.* Gulfy.

caora-mheanglain, *s.* Honeysuckle. *Colonsay.*

caora-mhòr, (CR), *s.f.* Black-faced sheep of old, in contrast to the smaller Highland sheep that preceded them, now applied to Cheviot sheep.

caorunnach, (DU), *s.m.* Large fire of red embers.

caora Shasunnach, *s.f.* Cheviot sheep.

caornan, *s.m.* Tufted vetch. *Colonsay.*

caorrthanan, (MS), *s.pl.* Heath-pease.

caorthann, see caorunn, *s.m.* Rowan or Mountain Ash. D, p.166.

caparaid, see càpraid below.

càpraid, s.f. Drunken riotousness.

car, (G), v.a. & n. Double upon, trick. 'Char a' mhaigheach sinn', the hare doubled upon us (tricked us) D. MacInnis (Editor) Folk and Hero. Waifs and Strays of Celtic Tradition, II Tales. London, 1890. p.80. (DU), v.a. Trick, cheat. 'An do char thu e?', did you cheat him? Ullapool.

car, adv. 'Car anmoch', somewhat late.

càr, s.m. 16 Screwing up of the face. Arran.

caradh, (G), s.m. Weir.

caraghaisd, s.f. Pronunciation of cairbhist, s. Carriage. Lochbroom.

càraideachadh, (MS), s.m. Conjugation. 2 Gemination.

caraidh, s.m. Grave-plot.

caraireachd, (MS), s.f. Cunning, art, artifice, guile, guilefulness, charlatanry, slyness, sleight. 2 Ambidexterity. 3 Gesticulation.

Caramhus, (MS), s.m. Quadragesima.

càra-lòbain, s. Low-set truck-like cart of wicker-work.

cara-meilidh, s. For carra-meille, s. Wild liquorice. Arran.

caran, s.f. See caran-creige, s.f. Sandeel, conger-eel. D, p.168.

càranach, s.m. Grumbling. Arran.

carathaisd, s.f. Statute-labour. Arran.

carathaist, s. See cairbhist, s.m. and f. Carriage. D, p.150.

carbad, s.f. 8 (DU) Back tooth, molar.

carbad-gluasadach, s.m. Motor-car.

carbhaich, v.a. Emboss.

carbhaidh, s.m. 2 (DU) Kind of sweet.

carbh-fheadh, (AF), s. See †cair-fhiadh, s.m. Hart. 2 Stag.

carcair, s.m. 4 Calk of a horse-shoe.

càrlach, (CR), s.m. Load of hay or straw. Arran. It is not obsolete, as stated on D, p.168.

carlum, (AF), s.m. Stoat.

car-mu-chnoc, s. The game of 'hide and seek'.

car-mu-shlios, adv. Upside down. Celtic Review, iv. 348.

càrn, s.m. 5 (DU) Gairloch for a cart. 6 (MS) Hold.

càrn-fianaidh, s.m. Peat-phaeton.

càrn-fiodha, (CR), s.m. Wood-cart. East Ross-shire.

càrn-lòbain, s.m. Low-set truck-like cart of wicker-work.

càrnag, s.f. Otter. JGC.S 240.

càrr, (AF), s.m. 13 Deer. 14 Stag. 15 (G) Sledge. South Hebrides.

carracaig, s.f. Pancake. Arran.

carrachan, s.m. 8 Place of stone circles. Urquhart & Glenmoriston, D, p.583. 9 (AF) Shell-fish.

carragan, (AF), s.m. Rock-fish.

carraiche, (MS), s. Scabrousness.

carraicheas, (MS), s.m. Prominence.

carraideach, (MS), a. 7 Debateful.

carraigeadh, (DMK), s.m. Process of separating the grain from the straw after threshing. Caithness.

carran, s.m. 3 (DC) Rough linen.

carran-brèige (creige?), s.m. Burbot (fish).

carran-gainmhich, s. See garrangaineamhaich, s.m. Angler (small fish).

carruicheachd, (MS), s.f. Scabrousness.

càrt 'Brod an àrd-leabaidh 's càrt os ar cinn' Rob Donn.

cartal, s.m. Mint. Colonsay.

cartal-uisge, s.m. Water-mint. Colonsay.

cas, s.f. 10 (CR) Hand-staff of a flail. 11 Support of stock of a spinning-wheel. In Arran 'air 'chois' = up, out of bed; air a chasan = standing or walking on his feet.

casachdaidh, s. Cough. A' casachdaidh, pr. pt. Coughing. Arran.

casaid, s. pl. Receptacles for corn used instead of sacks.

casaid-fhear, (MS), s.m. Accuser.

casair(e), (CR), s.m. Small hammer. Arran.

casan, s.m. 7 Footboard or treadle of a spinning-wheel.

casan-carbaid, (DU), s. pl. Gairloch. for casan-cairbe. Sun's rays. D, p.171.

casan-ceangail, s. pl. Joists of a house. D, p.923.

cas-arain, (AH), s.f. Toaster for drying and hardening oatmeal farls before the fire after being taken off the girdle.

casarmachd, (DMK), s.f. State of being bare-footed. Caithness.

cas-bhacain, The description of a wrestling feat given in *C. Rev.* III, 207, uses this expression.

cas-bhàrdachd, *s.f.* Certain kind of poetic metre. *C. Rev.* 116.

cas-bonnaich, (MS), *a.* Antipodal.

cas-bonnaich, (MS), *s. pl.* Antipodes.

cas-chaibe, *s.f.* Ear-mark on sheep, see under comharradh-cluais. D, p.238.

cas-cheangal, *s.m.* One of the joists of a house-couple. See D, p.922.

cas-cuipe, *s.f.* Whip-handle.

cas-ghaothach, *a.* Gusty.

cas-labhairt, (MS), *s.f.* Asperity. 2 Affront. 3 Stamping? *Gaidheal* III, 115.

caslachan, *s.m.* Foot-board or treadle of a spinning-wheel.

cas-mhaide, (DU), *s.f.* Wooden leg.

caspainn, (CR), *s.* Puce. *Arran.*

ca-speach, (AF), *s.m.* Hornet.

casragainn, *s.* Bindweed. *Colonsay.*

cat, (CR), *s.* Heap of potatoes, corn. cat eòrna, cat sìl, cat buntàta, *a heap of barley, corn, potatoes. Islay.*

càta'-chaorach, (CR), *s.m.* Cot or hut forming part of a sheep fold; a sheep-cote. 'Gum bu slàn do'n chàta chaorach as an d'thàinig a' chaora cheann-fhionn', *may that sheep-cote fare well from which came the white-faced ewe.* Angus MacLeod (Ed.) *The Songs of Duncan Bàn Macintyre,* Edinburgh, 1952, p.144, 1.2014.

cat-cothaich, *s.m.* See cat-cuthaich, (AF), *s.m.* Wild cat.

catan, *s.m.* Diminutive of cat. Little kitten.

cat draothaich, *s.m.* See cat-cuthaich, *s.m.* Wild cat.

cat grìosaich, (AF), *s.m.* Literally, *'fire-side cat',* a term applied to lazy men, who are too fond of the fireside.

cath, (DC), *s.m.* 5 Back-smoke. A' cathadh, *smoking, as from a down-draught in chimneys.*

catha, *s.m.* See cadha, *s.m.* A narrow pass at the side or foot of a mountain. D, p.146.

cathag fhirionn, (AF), *s.f.* Jackdaw.

cathaich, *v.a.* 6 (MS). Arm.

cathail, (MS), *a.* Gymnick.

cathair, *s.f.* 10 (CR) Knoll, hillock, fairy-knoll. Always the word in local lore for a fairy-knoll. *West of Ross-shire.*

cathair (A' chathair), *s.f.* The constellation *Cassiopeia.* It must be looked at in the W way in order to make out the 'chair'. It is difficult, even then, unless one can see a very small star which is nearer the Pole than the middle and largest stars of the group. This small star which is at the top of the front leg, forms with the middle star the very uncomfortable seat.

cathair-làir, *s.f.* Yarrow. JGC. W. 106.

cathair-shneadhan, (DU), *s.f.* Ant-hill.

cathair-thalanda, *s.f.* (JGC. W. 106) Yarrow.

cathair-thalmhainn, *s.f.* Yarrow. JGC. W. 106.

càthar, *s.m.* 3 Moss *in situ. Badenoch.* 4 Rough, broken surface (rarely).

cath-mhial, *s.m.* See cath-mheal (AF), *s.m.* Charger, warhorse.

cath-nan-coileach, (AF), *s.m.* Old Highland dance, literally 'the cock-fight'.

cathranas, -ais, *s.m.* 'S bhi blàth an àm cathranais is translated as *and when kindness was due, affectionate.* Mac-Leod, *The Songs of Duncan Bàn Macintyre,* 1.1228.

cealachd, (MS), *s.f.* Concealment. 2 Grimace.

cealaich, (MS), *v.a.* Bury.

cealair, *s.m.* 2 Virago. *Badenoch.*

cealcar, *s.m. Sutherland* for cearcall, *s.m.* Hoop, circle.

ceall, *s.f.* 2 Retired spot. *Dàin. I. Ghobha.*

ceallach, (DC), *s.m.* Flue of a kiln. Ceallach fada fiar 's a bheul 's an àirde deas, *a long bent flue with its exit towards the South.*

ceamp, (DC), *s.m.* Spinning darg. In order to help each other by sympathy of numbers, women in a township bring the spinning-wheels to one house and work together.

ceanabhag *Guth na bliadhna* II 361.

ceanaldar, (DMK), *s.m.* Winder, consisting of a piece of wood of a certain length with a cross piece at each end at right-angles to one another, used for winding and measuring yarn from the spinning-wheel. The hank thus measured was called 'iarna-shnàith' *Sutherland.*

ceanaltas, *s.m.* 4 (MS) Familiarity.

ceangail, na, *s. pl.* Couples of a house. See D, p.922.

ceangailte, *a.* 3 Married.

ceangal, *s.m.* 7 (DMK), Couple, the main support of a roof. 8 Tie-band, stall-tie.

ceangaldair, (CR), *s.m.* The double cross for winding yarn into hanks. See ceanaldar above.

ceangaltach, *a.* 4 (MS) Astringent.

ceanglag, *s.f.* Faggot.

ceanglaichean, *s. l.* Reef points of a sail.

ceanglaichean na stiùireach, *s. pl.* Rudder bands. See names of parts of a rudder. D, p.78, 2 & 4.

ceann, *s.m.* 15 (CR) Head of corn. Àrd mo chinn, *at the top of my voice;* air a cheann fhèin, *on his own account,* as one who is in business on his own account. *West of Ross-shire.* In compound words where *ceann* is the qualifier, the plural should not be *cinn* but *ceann;* where *ceann* is a noun, *cinn* is the plural.

ceannabha, *s.* Leader among cattle.

ceannabhoin, *s.* Leader among cattle.

ceannach-ruidil, *s.m.* Waste after sifting? *Gàidheal,* II 342.

ceannacha-simid, *n. pl.* of ceann-simid, *s.m.* Tadpole.

ceannag, *s.f.* 3 Truss or bottle of hay or straw.

ceannaiche-siubhail, (DU), *s.m.* Pedlar, packman.

ceannaidh, *s.f.* Headwind, contrary wind. *Dàin Iain Ghobha.*

ceannaidheachd, (DMK), *s.f.* Private parts of a woman. *Caithness.*

ceannaidh-teaghlaich. *Northern Highlands* for ceann-teaghlaich *s.m.* Head of a family, see below.

ceannair(e), *s.m.* See D, p.177. The driver or goadsman walked backwards before the horses. It must be remembered that 4 or 6 horses were the yoke. It survives in the word seisreach, *s.f.* which is still used for a plough-team although the number of horses is now

reduced to twò. (DC).

ceannaire, *s.m.* An alternative form of spelling for ceannair, a driver or goadsman, above.

ceannaire-cartach, *s.m.* Carter.

ceanaltachd, (MS), *s.f.* Comeliness.

ceannaldair, (DMK), *s.m.* Cylindrical pieces of wood with a cross-piece at each end, the planes of which are at right-angles to each other, used for winding and measuring yarn from the spinning-wheel.

ceannan, (AF), *s.m.* Small active animal.

ceann-an-duine-mhairbh, (DMK), *s.m.* The sea-urchin, *echinus esculeatus. Assynt.*

ceannan-sìolag. (AF), *s.* Sand eel.

ceanna-pholag, *s. pl.* Tadpole. *Arran.*

ceannarmachd, (DMK), *s.f.* Bareheadedness. *Caithness.*

ceannartachd, (MS), *s.f.* Ascendant.

ceannartaich, (MS), *v.a.* Preside.

ceannartas, (MS), *s.m.* Conduct.

ceann barr, *s.m.* Jack-fish, pike. See ceann-barrach, *s.m.* D, p.178.

ceann beag, *s.m.* 3 (DMK) Part of the old mill, fitted underneath the hopper, from which it received the grain and which regulated the quantity of it that entered the eye of the millstone.

ceann-bheartas, *s.m.* Ruling, governing.

ceann-carrach, (DC), *s.m.* Scabby head. 'Is beag an rud a bheir fuil air ceann-carrach', *'tis a little thing that brings blood out of a scabby head.*

ceann chruaidh-fhortain, (MMcD), *s.m.* Unfortunate fellow, blockhead. *Lewis.*

ceann-circe, (MMcD), *s.m.* Witless head. 'Ceann mòr air duine glic agus ceann circ' air amadan', *a large head on a wise man and a small head on a fool. Lewis.*

ceann-cnaip, (DMU), *s.m.* Leader of men, a man of light and leading. *Caithness.*

ceann-cnapaig, *s.m.* Fish's head stuffed with oatmeal et cetera. *Caithness. Sutherland* and *Lewis.*

ceann-craidh, (MMcD), *s.m.* Ship's rudder head.

ceann-cropaidh, (DMK), *s.m.* Head of a

cod or other fish stuffed with the liver of the fish, oatmeal and other seasoning. (Scots *crappit heids and stapped heids*) A favourite dish in the West coast of Ross and in the Hebrides.

ceann cula or cullach, (AF), *s.m.* Boar (leader).

ceann dubh, *s.m.* 4 (AF) Freshwater salmon. 5 (DC) Betony (plant) used for producing a black dye. *Uist.* 6 Wane, eclipse. 'Tha ceann dubh air a' ghealaich', *the moon is on the wane or is eclipsed.*

ceann fionn, (AF), *s.m.* Otter (literally hoary head).

ceann goibhre, (AF), *s.m.* Leader among goats.

ceann-gropaig, *s.m.* See ceann cropaidh above.

ceann-ianlainn, s.m. Leader of a flight of birds.

ceann iomair, *s.m.* Head ridge.

ceann iùil, *s.m.* 3 Grieve.

ceann mharc, *s.m.* See marc-cheann, (AF), *s.m.* Leader among horses.

ceann mòr, (DMK), *s.m.* Hopper of the old-fashioned mill.

ceann nith, (AF), *s.m.* Leader among cattle. May be *ceann-nì*.

ceann-phollag, (AF), *s.* See ceann phollan, *s.m.* Tadpole.

ceann-propaig, *s.m.* See ceann cnapaig, *s.m.* Fish heads stuffed with oatmeal. *Caithness, Lewis* and *Sutherland.*

ceannsachadh-chiad, *s.m.* See D, p.180 'Ghabh e mire-chath, 's an uair a ràinig e bha ceannsachadh-chiad aca air', *he was seized with battle frenzy, and when he arrived it took a hundred to subdue him. An Gàidheal,* III, p.72.

ceannsaich, *v.a.* 2 (DU) Restrain, repress.

ceann-snaoth, (AF), *s.m.* Salmon. 2 Leader among fish.

ceann-snaoth-nan-iasg, (AF), *s.m.* Salmon.

ceann-spreach, (MS), *a.* Proud.

ceannspreadhach, *a.* 2 (MS) Hardy.

ceanta, *s.m.* See cionta, *s.m.* Guilt, crime, sin, blame. D, p.197.

ceap, *s.m.* 2 (MS) Bilboes.

ceapag, *s.f.* Cheese. In the Beauly district this is applied to any wheel made of a solid block or without spokes or felloes. '*Cuile*' was always used if there were spokes or felloes.

ceapaire, (DC), *s.m.* Bread covered with butter fresh from the churn. A sheiling refreshment. *Argyll.*

ceapaire-taobhaidh, *s.m.* 'Love piece', given by a woman to a man, to conciliate or win his affections. *Reay.*

ceap-catha, *s.m.* See ceap, *s.m.* 6 D, p.180 A sign set up as a rallying point in time of battle corresponding to ceap-catha. *Conn Mac an Deirg (Mac-Nicol's version.)*

ceap-fuaraidh, (CR), *s.m.* First sod or spadeful of a furrow in digging. *West of Ross-shire.*

ceapsan, *s.m.* Gaelic form of capstan.

ceap sgiath, (DU), *s.m.* Winder. See liaghra. D, p.588.

ceap-snaidhidh, (DMK), *s.m.* See ealachag *s.f.* D, p.380 Used in *Poolewe* for a block or hacking-stock.

ceara, (DMK), *s.* Organ pertaining to the internal economy of a sheep. *West coast of Ross-shire.*

cearbach, *s.* 6 (MS) Artless. 7 (MS) Inattentive, inadvertent. 8 Unready.

cearbachd, *s.f.* 4 Bungle.

cearbaiche, *s.f.* 2 (MS) Inattention, inadvertence.

cearban, (MS), *s.m.* Bosvel.

cearcall-eàrraich, (DC), *s.m.* Bottom hoop of a cask. *Perthshire.*

cearc-choille, (DC), *s.f.* 2 Woodcock.

cearc-dhosach, (DC), *s.f.* Crested hen.

cearc-fearainn, (AF), *s.f.* Herzeld hen, fat hen once exacted as a tax from sub-tenants.

cearclachas, (MS), *s.m.* Rotundity.

cearclaich, (MS), *v.a.* Arch.

cearc-ribeach, *s.f.* See cearc-riobach *s.f. Argyll* for cearc-ghreannach, *s.f.* a rough-feathered hen.

cearc-thopach, *s.f.* 2 (DC) Coot.

ceardalan, *s.m.* See cèardabhan, *s.m.* Beetle.

ceardaman, *s.m.* See cèard-dubhan, *s.m.* Dung-beetle. D, p.182.

cèard-luaidh, (DMK), *s.m.* Plumber.

ceargan, (CR), *s.m.* Poor-house boy.

ceàrnachd, (MS), *s.f.* Angularity.

ceàrnaidh, *s.f. Northern Highlands* and *Lewis* for cèarn, *s.f.* Corner.

cearnallan, *s.m.* See cèard-dubhan, *s.m.* Dung-beetle.

cèarr, *a.* Wrong. "Cèarr 'sa cheann", *wrong in the head or mind. Arran.*

cèarraiche, (MS), *s.m.* Inaccuracy.

cearrail, (MS), *a.* Counter.

cearralan, *s.m.* See cèard-dubhan, *s.m.* Dung-beetle.

cearr-loman, (DC), *s.m.* Beetle (insect).

cearalach, *a.* See ceirsleach, *a.* Round.

ceart, *a.* Right. This has no S sound in *Arran.*

ceartachadh, *s.m.* 9 (DU) Correction, punishment.

ceartaich, *v.a.* 3 (DU) 3 Correct, punish. 4 (MS) Absolve.

ceathagach, (DC), *a.* Slightly misty. *s.m.* Autumn haze. *Argyll.*

ceathaichte, (MS), *a.* Cloud-capped.

ceathas, *s.* May mean a *fleck* or *speck of foam.* 'Maodhan maiseach d'an caoin cruth mar cheathas aige o shruth nan long'. *Lines on St. Modan.*

ceathraidh, (AF), *s.* Cattle.

ceathramh, *s.m.* A quarter of an ounce–land.

ceathramhachadh, (MS), *s.m.* Quartering.

ceathramh-dubh, (DMK), *s.m.* Disease in young cattle. *Caithness.*

ceideannach, *a.* See cèiteanach, *a.* Belonging to May or to the beginning of summer.

ceig, *v.* 3 Become matted or entangled, as in the case of wool, thread *et cetera.*

ceigich, (AF), *s. pl.* Goats.

ceileachd, (MS), *s.f.* Salve. 2 Disguise.

ceilearach, *a.* 3 Harmonical.

cèiliche, (DU) -an, *s.m.* & *f.* Visitor.

ceilig, *s.f.* Cod. *Sutherland.*

ceill, *s.f.* Boat. 'Is lìonmhor an ceill air an tràigh', *there are many boats on the shore*; maide na ceille, *the tiller of the boat.*

cèill, *s.f.* See gèill, *s.f.* Yielding. D, p.488. *Leabhar-nan-cnoc,* 33.

ceirean, (AF), *s.* See cirein-cròin, *s.m.* Sea-serpent. JGC. S. 220 below.

ceir'le, *Uist* for ceirsle, *s.f.* Clew.

ceirsleach, *a.* 3 Abounding in ringlets.

ceis, *s.f.* 2 Round belly. *Sutherland.* 'Is ann air a tha a' cheis!', *what a large belly he has!*

ceisdear, *s.m.* 2 Asker.

ceisin, (AF), *s.m.* See ceisean, *s.m.* Young pig.

ceiteag, *s.f.* Frame for holding reels of yarn. *Sutherland.* 2 (CR) *Farr* for ceitidh-suibhreag, (CR), *s.f.* Frame for holding filled reels of yarn. *Sutherland* below.

ceitean, (CR), *s.m.* Mood, humour. 'An d'robh ceitean math air?', *was he in good humour?*

cèitean, *s.m.* Month of May. 2 Beginning of summer. 3 Spring. 4 Fair weather. (Highland Society's Gaelic Dictionary) 5 Favourable season. (See D, p.187) There are four Cèiteans which are mentioned in *Carmina Gadelica* II 205, namely Cèitean Earraich (Spring), Cèitean Samhraidh (Summer), Cèitean na h-òinnsich (April 19th to May 12th) and Cèitean Geamhraidh (Winter).

ceithir-mheurach, (DC), *a.* Four-pronged. *Argyll.*

ceithir-ràmhach, *s.m.* Double-banked boat with four oars.

ceitidh-suibhreag, (CR), *s.f.* Frame for holding filled reels of yarn. *Sutherland.*

centeadh, *s.m.* Whipping. Deagh chenteadh, a good whipping. A phrase coined by soldiers serving under the Duke of Kent, who was a rigid disciplinarian. *Celtic Magazine.* xii. 99.

ceò, s.m. 4 (DU), Smoke of a fire, the word always heard round *Loch Ewe.* Ceò an teas de'n chuan, *heat-mist from the sea*; ceò 'n fhuachd dhe'n bheinn, *cold-mist from the hill.* Ceò is feminine in *Harris et cetera.*

ceògag, (CR), *s.f.* Heedless, silly woman. *Arran.*

ceòl, (DC), *s.m.* 3 Continuous theme in both a good and bad sense.

ceòl mòr, *s.m.* Generally speaking, ceòl mòr is made up of *grounds* which in many cases are doubled. Then follow the variations and then the *triluath,* singling and doubling and in several

instances *tripling*. Then comes the
ceithir luath or *crunluath* with its *singling* and *doubling* and in many cases
crunluath a mach. Marching with sing-
lings and standing with doublings was
the old way of playing. Now some
pipers maintain that marching should
be continued throughout the whole
performance. A. R. MacLeod, Edinburgh.
ceòlagraich, *s.f.* Crooning. *Celt. Rev.*
III, 175 [& *Sgrìobhaidhean Choinnich
Mhic Leòid*, T. M. Murchison (Ed).
Edin., 1988, 163].
ceòsan, (DC), *s.m.* This is the word in
Argyll for *cèasan*, *s.m.*, Coarse wool of
the flank.
ceòthachd, *s.f.* 2 (MS) Evaporation.
ceòthagraich, (MS), *s.f.* Fogginess.
ceth, (DC), *v.a.* Hand, fetch. 'Ceth
dhomh sin', *hand me that*. This word is
confined to *Uist* and the *Long Island*.
It is used in order to convey a clearer
meaning than the equivalent phrase
used in other places, namely 'thoir
dhomh sin', *give me that*.
ceud-chasach, (DU), *s.m.* Centipede.
ceud-shaoghalach, (MS), a. Antedilu-
vian.
ceum, *s.m.* 7 Stirrup.
ceusda-chrann, (DC), *int.* Crucifixion!
An interjectional malediction. May the
crucifixion agony be yours! It refers to
the agony of Mary at the cross. Heard
in *Uist*.
chaidh, *past aff.* of rach. Chaidh
'ghleidheadh, *he has died*.
char. *Lochbroom* & *Gairloch* pronunciation of chaidh.
chealg, *s.f.* *Arran* for shealg, *s.f.* Là
chealg (or cheal') na cubhaige, literally, *hunting-of-the-cuckoo day*.
chlios, *s.m.* *Arran* for shlios. 'Car mu
chlios', upside down (of clothes) for
'car mu shlios'.
chon, *adv.* For chun *adv.* To, toward.
chon an, *adv.* *Wester Ross* for far an,
adv. Where.
chonnaic, *past aff.* of faic. For chunnaic,
past aff. of faic. Saw.
chualaig. *Jura*, *North Argyll* and part of
West Ross-shire for chuala, *past aff.* of

cluinn. Heard. e.g. 'An cuala tu?',
'Chualaig', Did you hear? Yes.
chunna, *past. aff.* of faic. *North Argyll*
and *Skye* for chunnaic. Saw. Also in
Perthshire.
chunn, Another *Perthshire* localism for
chunnaic. Saw.
ciad-lomaidh, An, *s.f.* See ceud-
lomaidh, An, *s.f.* Breakfast. *Gàidheal*
III, 74.
ciall, *s.m.* in Badenoch, for ciall, *s.f.*
Reason, sense. D, p.192.
ciallairt, *s.m.* Sentence in *Grammar*.
cianail, *s.* 9 (MS) Anxious.
ciaran, *s.m.* 2 (AF) Brown or dusky bee.
ciar-dubh, (AF), *s.* Dark grey cow.
ciasan, *s.m.* Iron sole of crann-nan-gad,
s.m. A kind of plough. D, p.263.
ciath, *s.* Some sort of food. *Maol
Ruainidh Ghlinneachain*.
cibhinn. See under brà. D, p.112.
cich, *s.m.* & *f.* See ci, (AF), *s.m.* & *f.*
Animal, beast. D, p.191.
cidheach, *s.m.* See cigheach, (AF), *s.m.*
Fat lamb.
cidheach, *s.m.* See ceathach, *s.m.* Mist,
fog, vapour.
cigh-ceangach, (AF), *s.* Noble animal or
stag leader.
cigh-cingeach, (AF), *s.* Noble animal or
stag leader.
cighiall, (MS), *s.* Mandible.
cileag, *s.f.* 4 †Diminutive, weakly person. *Argyll*.
cilear, *s.m.* Modicum, = cillein, *s.m.* 4.
Small quantity. 'Bu mhaith cilear na
cèille', [*there was a good modicum of
sense, or*] *enough is better than a feast*.
Celtic Review, iv. 25.
cill, -e, *s.f.* Boat.
cill, *s.f.* The locative case of Old Irish
cell, a church, but in modern Gaelic, a
churchyard.
cìlleach, (MS), *a.* Cellular.
cilpean, *s.m.* See cipean, *s.m.* Stump,
stake.
cimeachd, (MS), *s.f.* Incarceration, cap-
tivation. 2 Arctation. See cimeachạs,
s.m. Captivity.
cimh, (AC), *s.* Speech. *Carmina Gad.*
138.
cinneabhar lomhail, *s.* 'Thig cinneabhar

lomhail banrìgh dhut', *the glittering headgear of a queen becomes you!* George Calder (editor), *Gaelic Songs by William Ross*, Edinburgh, 1937, p.134.

cinneachail, *a.* Generative.

cinneag, (DMK), *s.f.* Thread wound on a spindle as it is being spun. (This replaces: 2 Tuft of wool, especially wool on the spindle: D, p.195).

cinnteachadh, (MS), *s.m.* Ascertainment.

cinnteanach, (MS), *a.* Assertive.

cinntear, (MS), *s.m.* Ascertainer.

cinntinneach, (MS), *a.* Vegetative.

cintinneas, *s.m.* Vegetativeness.

cioba, *s.f.* See ciob, *s.f.* Tufted scirpus.

ciobach, *a.* 2 (MS) Pappous.

cioba-làir, (MS), *s.m.* Breast-plough.

cioch, *s.f.* 3 Bush or knob of wood between the frame of flyers and the stock of a spinning-wheel. D, p.290.

cìochag, *s.f.* Valve of a bagpipe. D, p.722.

cìochan-na-mnà-sìthe, (MS), *s. pl.* Canterbury bells.

cìocrach, See cìocar, *s.m.* A hungry creature.

ciogailteach, *a.* 2 (MS) Shy.

ciolarn, *s.m.* 2 (AF) Milk pitcher with a handle out of its side. A hand-can, hand-mother.

ciolchaireachd, (MS), *s.f.* Salvo.

ciolorn, *s.m.* See ciolarn, *s.m.* Vase.

ciolurn, *s.m.* See ciolarn, *s.m.* Vase.

cionaltachd, *s.f.* See ceanaltachd, *s.f.* Kindness, mildness.

ciopan Dochart, s.m. A trial of strength. Two men or boys sit on the floor opposite each other with the soles of their feet touching. They have a stout stick which they grasp with alternate hands. The one attempts to pull the other up on his feet. The game goes to the one who succeeds in this. Then they change hands and make another trial, so that neither shall have any advantage. *Uist Games in the Celtic Review* No. 16.

cìosaich, *v.a.* 2 (MS) Bind. 3 Sack.

ciosantachd, (MS), *s.f.* Appeaseableness.

ciothrom, *s.m.* See ciorram, *s.m.* Mischief, disaster.

cipean, *s.m.* 3 Pin of a watch-chain. 4 Block of wood tied to the neck of a cow or horse to keep them from running too fast. *Beauly.*

cìr an t-seic, *s.f.* Teeth of the flyers in a spinning-wheel.

cìr-chùil, (DU), *s.f.* Lady's back comb.

cireil, *a.* Managing. Duine ceannar cireil, a wise managing man. *Arran.*

cirein-cròin, s.m. Sea-serpent. (cròin or cròm?) JGC. S. 220.

ciseart, *s.* Light tweed. *Nether Lochaber.* See *cis-fheart* Mixed cloth. D, 198.

ciseag, *s.f. Guth-na-bliadhna* II 359.

cistidh, *s.f.* Coffin. *Gàidheal* II 360.

ciùbh, *s.m.* See cù, *s.m.* Dog.

ciùlach, *s.m. West Ross-shire* for ciùran, *s.m.* Drizzling rain.

ciùllacharan, (DU), s.m. Faint light.

claba dudaidh, *a.* Shellfish like cockles but with larger shells. *Arran.*

clabar-nasg, *s.m.* Clasp of a willow cow collar. *Argyll.*

clab-cìochran, (MS), *s.m.* Roach (fish).

clach-amail, *s.f.* Curb-stone of a byre. See D, p.79.

clacha-meilear, *s. pl.* Goatfell pebbles. *Arran.*

clachan, *s.m.* 6 † Pavement, 4 causeway.

clachan-buidseachd, (DMK), *s. pl.* Stones, generally three in number, possessed and used by witches in the practice of their art.

clach-bhalg, *s.f.* Term of contempt applied to one who goes about making a fuss without result. *Sutherland.*

clach-bheumnaich, *a.* Stamping, prancing.

clach-bhuadhach, *s.f.* 2 (MS) Amethyst.

clach-chopair, (MS), *s.f.* Lapis Lazuli.

clach-dhearbhaidh, *s.f.* Touchstone.

clach-fhaladair, *s.f.* Whetstone for sharpening a scythe.

clach-ghreimich, *s.f.* Gripe stone JGC. W. 93.

clach lasair, *s.f.* Carbuncle (stone).

clach-lèig, (G), *s.f.* Healing stone.

clach-luaidh, (DU, *s.f.* Weight of a hand fishing-line.

clach-maraidh, *s.f.* See clach-nearaidh,

s.f. Grinding stone.

clach-na-gilleadha-craigein, *s.f.* Frog-stone. JGC. W. 89.

clach-sgleata, *s.f.* Slate rock *Guth-na-bliadhna*, v. 126.

clach-shaichte, (DMK), *s.f.* Dressed or sculptured stone. *Caithness.*

clach-shìoman, (DMK), *s.f.* Stone that weights and keeps in its place the heather or other rope with which the thatch of houses is secured. *Caithness.*

clach-stoirm, *s.f.* JGC. W. 93.

clach-theine, *s.f.* 2 (MS) Agate.

clàd, -a, -an, *s.f.* †Wood hackle made specially for wool, about 10 inches long, with long iron teeth bent at the point.

cladhan, *s.m.* Foundation, cause, reason, heredity, atavism.

clagan, *s.m.* 3 Mill clapper. See D, p.677.

claidheamh a' choilich dhuibh, (G) *s.m.* Milkwort.

claidheamhan, *s.m.* See clàidhean, *s.m. dim.* of claidheamh. A little sword, scimitar, bilboe.

claigionn, *s.m.* Skull. In place names it is usually applied to a bare rounded knoll. When it is applied to a field or farm, it means the best arable land. 4 Head-stall of a bridle.

claigionn, *s.f.* This word means in the feminine, a field. *Celt. Rev.* III 90.

clair-shùl, *s. pl.* Blinders of a horse's harness.

clairsich, (MS), *s.* A quill.

clairsiche, (CR), *s.* The "off" or furrow horse in a ploughing-team.

clàmhdaiche, (MS), *s.m.* Claudication.

clampa, *s.* Oar-guard. *Sàr-Obair.*

clann, *s.* Young woman. *Uist. Uist Bards*, 17.

clann-fhalt, *s.* Luxuriant, waving hair. *Sàr-Obair.*

claoghan, *s.m.* See cladhan, *s.m.* Channel, very shallow stream.

claonachd, *s.f.* Aptitude.

claon-bhreithnich, (MS), *v.a.* Partialize.

claon-charachd, *s.f.* Prestidigitation.

claon-chlàr, *s.m.* Legerdemain.

claparach, (MS), *a.* Limy.

clàradh, (G), *s.m.* Screen, partition.

clàr-aghaidh, *s.m.* A footnote to the tale states that cùl-cinn (literally, back of head), means hill pasture. Here cùl-cinn and clàr-aghaidh mean very much the same as 'beinn' (hill pasture) and 'baile' (farm). *Trans. Gael. Soc. Inverness*, vol. xiv, p.111.

clàr-bhiodrail, *s.m.* Anything broken in pieces. 'Tha e 'na chlàr-bhiodrail', *it is in smithereens. Easter Ross.*

clàr-cioch, *s.m.* See clab, *s.m.*, open mouth.

clàr-càise, (DC), *s.m.* A slice of cheese.

clàr-coise, *s.m.* Footboard or treadle of a spinning-wheel.

clàrsach, *s.m.* Harp, is *s.f.* in some parts.

clarsaich, *v.a.* Harp, play the harp.

cleachdadhadh, *s.m.* See cleachdadh, *s.m.* Custom, practice.

cleachdadh, s.m. 3 Exercise in *Grammar.*

clearachd, (CR), *s.m.* Dawdling. *Arran.* Another form of cliarachd, *s.f.* See cliarachas, *s.m.* Singing, bardism.

clearaidh, (CR), *s.m.* dawdler. *Arran.*

cleas, *s.m.* Play, trick. 'Cleas a' chleiteam cleas an òigeam', *the cunning occult tricks of the ogham* in *Colonsay*, but 'cleasa cleiteam cleasach an ògam', in *Eigg.*

cleasach, *a.* 6 (MS) Ansated.

cleasachan, *s.m.* Footboard or treadle of a spinning-wheel.

cleasan, *s.m.* Shaft or connecting-rod between the treadle and the crank of a driving-wheel.

clèidhseam, (WC), *s.m.* 'Thàinig e fo'n chlèidhseam', *he came in a mad hurry.*

cleigh(e), *s.f. Arran* for creithleag, *s.f.* Gadfly, cleg.

clèireach, *s.m.* 7 (AH) Male crab.

clèireachas, (MS), *s.m.* Priesthood. 2 Secretaryship.

cleit, s.m. 16 (DC) Name given to the bee-hive shaped erections of stone by the St. Kildans, which are used by them as stores for corn, potatoes and so on.

cleitean, *s.m.* 4 See 16 (DC) above.

cleitheachd, *s.f.* 3 (MS) Reserve.

clèithean, Na, *s. pl.* Part of the roof of a house. See D, p.922.

clèithean-buinn, *s.* Strips of wood running upwards from the top of the wall, and resting on the *taobhanan ìosal.* (DMy) *Lewis.*

clèithean-mullaich, *s.* Strips of wood fixed to the ridge at the top and resting on the top rafters or *taobhanan àrda*, as opposed to the *c-buinn* resting on the lower rafters or *taobhanan ìosal.* (DMy).

cleuraidh, *s.f.* One who neglects work. *Arran.*

cliabh, s.m. Creel. *Parts of a creel* Faothaistean, (MMcL), *s.m.* An open space in a creel for lifting it.

cliabhan, *s.m.* 3 (MS) Wreath.

cliabhuinn, *s.m.* See cliamhuinn, *s.m.* Son-in-law.

cliaranach, *s.m.* 5 Wrestler. *Sàr-Obair.*

cliath, *s.f.* 18 Frame put on a cart for carrying hay or straw.

cliathach, (G), 5 Spòg-dheiridh, a three-quarter gammon or cushion.

cliathadair, (MS), *s.m.* Harrower.

cliathaich, *s.f.* Bilge. See D, p.76. Correct to cliathach, *s.f.*

clic, *s.f.* 7 Knavery.

clioc, *v.* Exhaust. When a fish is played on a line until it is exhausted, the fisherman says 'tha a 'n deidh cliocadh', *he is exhausted. West coast of Ross-shire.*

cliontach, (DMK), *a.* Clumsy, awkward. *West coast of Ross-shire.*

cliseach, *s.m.* Has the same meaning as cachaileith, *s.f.* See D, p.145 2 (DMK), *s.m.* Wall consisting mostly of wattle-work. Barns with such walls facilitate the seasoning of their contents, as they allow the air to circulate freely within them. *West coast of Ross-shire.*

clisgeanta, (MS), *a.* Alert.

clisgeartach, (MS), *a.* Airy.

clisneach, (DMK), *a.* See cliseach above.

clisteach, *s.* See cliste, *a.* Active, nimble, supple, swift, dexterous.

cliùcaireachd, *s.f.* 3 (MS) Netting, network.

cliùthachadh, *s.m.* 2 Admiration.

cliùthaich, *v.a.* 2 Admire.

clobhdach, *a.* 2 (DU) Ragged, untidy in dress.

clòidhteach, *s.f.* See clòimhteach, *s.f.* Down of feathers.

clòigheach, *a.* See clòimheach, *a.* Mangy, scabby, scorbutic.

clomhan, (DU), *pl.* -anan, *s.m.* Tatter, shred.

closd, (DU), *s.* Means the same as clos, *s.m.* 2 Quietness, silence, sudden silence.

clothaigh, genitive in *Gairloch* of clach, *s.f.* Stone.

clòthte, (CR), *a.* Fulled, thickened as cloth. *Arran.*

cluadain *s.f.* Care. *Arran.*

cluain, *s.f.* 9 Generally applied to sloping land. 10 Peace. 11 Slumber. *Sàr-Obair.*

cluainire, *s.m.* 3 (MS) Accomplice.

cluaisean, *s.f.* See cluas, *s.f.* Socket of leather.

cluas, *s.f.* 6 (DMK), Pan of a flintlock gun. 7 Socket of leather in which the spindle of flyers of a spinning-wheel revolves.

cluasag, (DU), *s.f.* 4 Shellfish of the genus *pecten-pecten opercularis.* 5 See cluas 7 above.

cluich an taighe, *s.m.* A game which is practically the same as rounders. Two sides of equal numbers are picked, one fielding and the other batting. The essentials are a bat or "driver", and a ball. Three circles are drawn in a triangle, the sides of the triangle being as nearly as possible 50 yards each. One side takes its stand inside the first circle, all the other side fielding round about with the exception of a bowler or as he is called, '*fear tha toirt nam faireag*', who stands in the centre of the triangle.

The batsman in circle No. 1 receives a *faireag* or bowl, and after striking the ball as hard as possible, runs immediately for circle No. 2 If the ball is caught fairly he is out. He is also out if while running, he is struck by the ball, or if the circle is struck. Another batsman then takes his place, receives a *faireag*, smites the ball and runs for circle No. 2, while the player in circle

No. 2 runs for circle No. 3. If either of them is struck or either circle is struck, or the player running in the circle that is struck, he is out.

Batsman No. 3 now stands forward, receives his *faireag*, the others running for the next circle. The boy in circle No. 3 runs to circle No. 1 this time, and this goes on until the whole side is out, when the opposing side takes its turn at batting, the erstwhile batsmen then fielding. Any number may be fixed, usually 50 to 100 to a side. For each time a player runs right round and back to circle No. 1, he earns one point. If neither side reaches the given number, the side which has the highest number of points is adjudged the winner. By the turn of the century, this game was practically dead in Uist, but at one time it was very popular. *Uist Games in Celtic Review* No. 16.

cluinntineach, (MS), *a.* Audible.

cluinntineachd, (MS), *s.f.* Audibleness.

cluith, *v. Badenoch* for cluich, *v.a.* Play, sport.

clumhachdadh, *s.m.* See cluthachadh, *s.m.* Clothing. 2 Chasing. D, p.216.

clùmhor, *a.* 2 (MS) Sleek.

cluth, *a.* Feathered.

clùth, *s.m.* Down of feathers. 2 Coat.

cluthadh, (MS), *s.m.* Apparel. 2 Accoutrement.

cluthmhor, *a.* Downy.

cnag, *s.f.* Locative *cnaigean.* 11 (DMK). Small pin or peg of wood sewn on articles of clothing for buttons. They were in use in Gairloch in the middle of the nineteenth century. 12 Stump to sit on. *Sutherland.* 13 Pin to which a harp string is attached. 14 Cog of a wheel.

cnag, *s.f.* 11 (DMK) Shinty ball. *Caithness.*

cnagadaich, (MS), *s.f.* Crepitation.

cnagag, (MS), *s.f.* Cog of a wheel.

cnagaich, (MS), *v.a.* Peg.

cnaideal, *a.* Scoffing, jeering, derision. *Sàr-Obair.*

cnàimh, *s.m.* Bone. Plurals in Sutherland are *cnainean*, (pronounced *cre-nan*, the *e* being nasal) and *cnànan.*

cnaimh-abruid, (MS), *s.m.* Ankle-bone.

cnaimh-an-uga, (DU), *s.m.* The collar bone or clavicle.

cnàimheach, (DC), *s.m.* Swarthy, thin man or boy. *Argyll.*

cnaimhseag, *s.f.* 4 (CR) Whortleberry. Is this the same as bearberry in the Dictionary? D, p.217.

cnainean, *s. pl.* of cnàimh. *Sutherland.*

cnaipean-seilcheig, *s. pl.* Snail heads. JGC. W. 88.

cnamh, *pr. pt.* a' cnamh (*pron. cramh*) *v.a.* Suck, as the young of animals. 'Tha 'n laogh a' cnamh a mhàthair', *the calf is sucking his mother, Caithness.*

cnamhag-tombaca, *s.f.* A quid of tobacco.

cnamhan-glasa, *s.m.* See cnaimhean-glas, *s.m.* A method of planting potatoes. D, p.217.

cnànan, *Sutherland* plural of cnàimh.

cnap (*pron.* crap) *s.m.* 10 Rope. *Caithness.* 11 (MS) Bang.

cnap, *s.m.* 10 (DU) Heel of a boot *et cetera.*

cnapach, *a.* 6 (MS) Articular. 2 Kneed.

cnapachas, (MS), *s.m.* Articulation. 2 Extuberance.

cnapag, (DC), *s.f.* Ball of worsted especially the first thread wound on the distaff, as the thread twined was gathered on this, it was put on criss-cross.

cnapaich, *v.a.* 6 (MS) Bang.

cnapalach balaich, (CR), *s.m.* Lump of a boy. *Arran.*

cneacalachd, (MS), *s.f.* Knack.

cnead, *s.m.* 5 Lament.

cneadaich, (MS), *s.m.* Blow.

cneapag, (DC), *s.f.* Ball of yarn when wound off the spinning-wheel. 2 (DMK) Swedish turnip. *Sutherland.*

cneasag, *s.f.* Shirt. *Stirlingshire.* Livingston's Poems, 204.

cneidhich, (MS), *v.a.* Gall.

cneutag, *s.f.* Ball for playing shinty tennis or football. See D, p.219 'A' cluich air a chneutag', playing at cricket or shinty.

cniomh chuileag na caoraid, *s.* Sheep-bot fly.

cniomh chuileag nan each, *s.* Horse bot.

cno, *s.f.* Gruffness. *Gàidheal* III 74.

cno-bhreac, *s.* Snail's shell.

cnocach, (MS), *a.* Abrupt.

cnocad, *s.m.* Barley hammered. *Arran.*

cnocaidh, in clach-chnocaidh, s. *Arran* for clach-chnotainn, *s.f.* Hollowed stone into which barley is put and beaten with a mallet. See D, p.200.

cnocan, *s.m.* 5 (DC) Ball of yarn when wound off the spinning-wheel *Lewis.*

cnò-chaoch (cnùdh), *s.f.* Empty nut. *Arran.*

cnochdach, *s.m.* Spayed 3-year old stag.

cnòdaidh, (DU), *a.* Well-clad.

cnoguisean, *s. pl.* Cogs on mill wheels.

cnoidear, *s.m.* Vamper.

cnoidich, (MS), *v.a.* Vamp.

cnomhan, *s.m.* Hazel. *Celt. Rev.* iv. 29.

cnotach, *s.m.* 2 (DMK) Slang term for a sixpence. *West coast of Ross.*

cnùacaich, (MS), *v.a.* Bang.

cnuachdachadh, (MS), *s.m.* Asperation.

cnuadhan a' chait, (G), *s.* Bird's-foot trefoil.

cnuasachd, *s.f.* Chewing. *Beinn Dorain.*

cnùdh, *s.f. Arran* for cnò, *s.f.* Nut.

cnuimheag, *s.f.* Maggot.

cnuimheag cruaidh dheud, *s.f.* The Ichneumon fly.

cnuimh neipe, (DMy), *s.* Turnip fly.

cnuimh shicein, (WC), *s.* A very bad wound, rupture or a wound from which a person is not likely to recover. This used to be a very common word in *Poolewe.*

coapag, (DMK), *s.f.* A short verse of an impromptu nature. *Rob Donn.*

cobh, *s.m.* A slanting water-worn channel in a rock-face.

cobhaireach, (MS), *a.* Comfortable.

cobharach, *s.m.* Field forget-me-not, *Myosotis arvensis, Colonsay.* This name relates to the plant.

cobharalachadh, (MS), *s.m.* Concurrence.

cobhartach, *a.* 2 Subject to. 'Gur cobhartach do'n bhàs gach feòil', that all flesh is subject to death.

cobhartas, *s.f.* See cobhartachd, *s.f. ind.* Prize, plunder. Highland Society's Dictionary, quoted by Dwelly.

cobhrach, *a.* 4 (MS) Protective.

cobhrachag, *s.f.* Pet name for a girl.

cobhrachan, (DC), *s.m.* Pet name for a boy.

cobhraichean, *s. pl.* Coffers, money drawers. *Sàr-Obair.*

còchaidh, (CR), *a.* Soft, spongy, as a decaying turnip. *Sutherland* and *Reay country.* Còthaidh in *Glen Moriston.*

co-chòrdadh, *s.m.* Concord, analogy.

cochull, *s.m.* 9 Envelope. *Arran.*

cochullach, *a.* 5 (MS) Membraneous.

cochullaich, (MS), *v.a.* Cod.

cocrach, *a.* See còrcach, *a.* Hempen.

coda-bàn, *s.m. Arran* for còta-bàn, *s.m.* 4 Groat or fourpenny piece.

codan, *s.m.* See cotan, *s.m.* Cotton.

coganta, (MS), *a.* Belligerent.

coghnadach, (MS), *a.* Auxiliary.

còghnaidheach, (MS), *a.* Auxiliary.

co-ghnìomhair, *s.* Adverb in grammar.

còib-a-làir, *s.m.* Instrument for cutting turf-divots. *Arran.*

coibhreach, *a.* See cobhaireach, *a.* Comfortable.

coidhichead, (MS), *s.m.* Seemliness.

còig-chearnach, *a.* Pentagonal, pentangular.

còig-chearnag, *s.f.* Pentagon.

còig-lagach, (MS), *a.* Pentacapsular.

còig-oiseanach, *a.* Pentangular.

coigridheachd, *s.f.* Strangeness.

còil, *s.* Cock of hay is a "tramp-coll", ten feet upwards in height. *Perthshire.*

coilchionn, -inn, (DC), *s.m.* Short corn, the result of drought on dry sandy soil as in *Uist.* On such occasions it is too short to cut and has to be pulled up, but even then the seed is good, hence a local saying 'Cha d'thug bliadhna coilchinn gorta riamh do dh'Uibhist', *a short-corn year never brought starvation to Uist.*

coileach-teth, *s.m.* See coileachteas, *s.m.* Mirage. *Sutherland.*

coileag, *s.f.* Goal at shinty. *Skye.*

coilig, (MS), *s.f.* Colic.

coilleag, *s.f.* Gulf.

coille-beanain, *s.m.* See coille-bionan, *s.m.* Sea animalculae. *Arran.*

coille-bhannain, *s.m.* See coille-bionan, *s.m.* Sea animalculae. *Argyll.*

coilleachan, *s.m.* Dryer. *Celt. Mag.,* 8.

coillteach, (MS), *s.m.* Brushwood.

coimbire, (MS), *s.m.* Boarder. 2 Compeer.

coimeadh, (MS), *s.m.* Compeer.

coimeasach, *a.* Comparative in *grammar.* 2 (MS) Drawn.

coimeasachadh, *s.m.* Comparison in *grammar.*

coimeasg, (MS), *v.a.* Beat.

coimeasgaich, (MS), *v.a.* Incorporate.

coimheadair, (MS), *s.m.* Guardian.

coimhearta, (MS), *s.* Enigma.

coimheasgaich, (MS), *v.a.* Intermeddle.

coimheis, 'Tha mi coimheis', *I don't care. Arran.*

coimhich, *v.a.* Disnaturalize.

coimhleasachadh, (MS), *s.m.* Gratification.

coimhleasaich, *v.a.* Gratify.

coimhreach, (MS), *a.* Favourable.

coimhreit, *s.* See comh-rèite, *s.f.* Agreement, reconciliation.

coimrig, (MS), *v.a.* Tangle.

coineibhinn, (DC), *s.m.* Extreme distress.

coingeall, (MS), *s.m.* Friendship.

coingeallach, (MS), *a.* Friendly.

coingeasach, (MS), *a.* Uninterested.

coingeiseachd, (MS), *s.f.* Skilfulness.

coinneach-dubh-a'-chaca, (DMK), *s.m.* The bird skua. He chases other birds until they disgorge their prey, when he adroitly seizes it in the air. The vulgar think that it is the droppings of the other bird that the skua has seized and devoured and hence the name by which it was wont to be known at *Poolewe* last century.

coinneal, s.m., in *Arran. s.f.* on D, p.227.

coinneal-buaic, (DC), *s.f.* Torch made of twisted cotton, hemp *et cetera* and dipped in grease or tar.

coinneamh, *s.f.* Meeting. *Lochalsh* and some other Wester Ross people use *a' choinneamh* (pronounced by them *a' choinnidh*) for the communion gathering. When others say *an comanachadh*, they say *a' choinneamh*. Bithidh a' choinneamh 's a Bhàighe 'n Iar an ath sheachdain *the Communion will be held at West Bay next week.*

coinneamhach, (MS), *a.* Congressive.

coinneanaich, (MS), *v.a.* Ascend.

coinnleag, (CR), *s.f.* Stalk, bud.

coinnlean-speic, *s.f.* Support for candles. *Celtic Magazine,* viii 558.

coinnteachail, (MS), *a.* Musty, rancid.

coir, *a.* Holy(?). In *Arran,* not liberal or hospitable. 'Cha'n 'eil a choir urad ann', *there is not nearly so much. Arran:* 'Dha'n neach dha 'n liugh' tha 'chòraichean', *to the man who has most vouchers.* R. 21.

coirce beag, *s.m.* Dwarf oats for light soil.

còire, *s.f.* 'Mo chòire, mo thruaighe', *My fault, my misery.* R. 3.

coireachan-beòtha, *s.m.* Thread not sufficiently twined in spinning.

Gu'n cual iad an Rudha Stòrr
A liuthad dath a bha 'sa chlò,
Plucanan is coireachan-beòtha
'S bu neònach leatha 'n dath a bh'ann. (Song by the brother of MacKenzie.) *Sàr-Obair.*

coireannach, (MS), *a.* Accusative.

còiriche, (MS), *s.m.* Accuser.

coiripeachd, (MS), *s.f.* Abuse.

coiripich, *v.a.* Defile.

coirmeagadh, (DMK), *s.m.* Trouble. 'Na cuir coirmeagadh air', *don't trouble him. Caithness.*

còir-sgoraidh, (AC), *s.f.* Cattle grazing right.

coise, An, *s.m.* Gaff of a sail.

coisgeil, (MS), *a.* Sleek.

coisirich, *v.a.* Aggroup.

coisrigeachd, *s.f.* Devotedness.

coit, *s.f.* Small fishing boat (See D, p.233) is *s.m.* also.

coitealan, (DC), *s.m.* diminutive of coit, a small boat. See above.

coitealag, (DC), *s.f.* Another diminutive of coit, a small boat.

còladh, *adv.* See còmhla, *adv.* D, p.244. Together.

colaisdeach, (MS), *s.m.* Academician.

còlamhaich, (MS), *s.m.* Partaker.

còlan, (MS), *s.m.* Comrade.

còlanaiche, *s.m.* Fellow.

colbhar, *s.m.* Greedy fellow. *Sutherland.*

colgaich, *v.a.* Irritate.

collagag, *s.f.* See colgag, *s.f.* Forefinger.

collaid, A', (CR), *pr. pt.* Arguing. *North*

end of Arran.

collarach, (DMK), *a.* Brave, active, efficient, effective. *West coast of Ross-shire.*

colmh, (MS), *s.* Column.

colmhach, (MS), *a.* Columnar.

colothanan, *s. pl.* Pebbles supposed to have been thrown by fairies.

com, *s.m.* 8 Base or stock of a spinning-wheel.

c'oma, *adv.* Why? *Arran* for c'ar son?

comaine, (MS), *s.f.* Gratefulness.

comaineachd, (MS), *s.f.* Beholdenness.

comairich, (MS), *v.a.* Prosper. 2 Protect.

commonta, *a.* Good.

comaraich, *s.f.* Direction or tendency forward. *Sàr-Obair.* 2 Petition, request, demand. *Sàr-Obair.*

comaraich, *Arran* for comanaich, v.a. communicate (take communion).

comasach, (MS), *a.* Absolute.

comasaich, (MS), *v.a.* Capacitate.

comhaid, *s.f.* Company.

comhaich, (MS), *v.a.* Earn.

comh-ailtich, (MS), *v.a.* Accompany.

comhaireach, *a.* Helpful.

comhairleachd, *s.f.* Agitation.

comhalaich (com-altaich), *s. pl.* Persons whom to meet brings good or bad fortune. JGC. W 239.

còmhant, "Mo sheobhag tha còmhant, cliùtach, bearraideach".

comharradh-cluaise, s.m. Additional ear-marks on sheep are:

1 Beum, (CR). Slit from the edge inwards. *West Ross-shire.*

2 Leacan-beòil, (CR), called "bacan àrd" (fore-quarter) in *Argyll* (12 on D, p.238) *West Ross-shire.*

3 Sgoradh, (CR), slit from the tip downwards. *West Ross-shire.*

Notches were also made in the ears of sheep to denote age. When a ewe has 6 notches, 3 in each edge, she is 6 years old (cast ewe or crock) Bacan-beòil = 12 bacan àrd (*Ross*) bacan-cùil = 13 bacan ìosal (*Ross*) (12 and 13 refer to the numbers on D, p.238). (AC) also gives cliopan, cliopadh, cluigean, corran, crocan, duile, meaghlan, meangan and slios. Under criomag, *An Deò Grèine* (I 97).

comharraichteachd, *s.f.* Remarkableness.

comh-bharalach, (MS), *a.* Coincident.

comh-bharalachadh, (MS), *s.m.* Coincidence.

comh-bhrigeadh, *s.m.* Group.

comh-charnadh, *s.m.* 2 Group.

comh-cheangailte, *a.* 3 Married.

comh-cheanglaiche, *s.m.* 3 (MS) Accompanier.

comh-chràthaich, *v.a.* Conquassate.

comh-chrith, (MS), *s.f.* Concussion.

comh-chritheach, (MS), *a.* Consussive.

comh-chruthachd, (MS), *s.f.* Conformation.

comh-chuideachdail, (MS), *a.* Concomitant.

comh-chuimhneachadh, (MS), *s.m.* Commemoration.

comh-chuimhnich, (MS), *v.a.* Commemorate.

comh-chuimseach, (MS), *a.* Reciprocally.

comh-chuimseachd, (MS), *s.f.* Reciprocalness.

comh-dhaingneachadh, *s.m.* 3 (MS) Consolidation.

comh-dhaingnich, *v.a* 2 (MS), consolidate.

comh-dhosgainn, *s.f.* common misfortune.

comh-fhailteachd, (MS), *s.f.* 3 Convoy.

comh-fhaithreach, (MS), *a.* Sympathetic.

comh-fhògair (MS) *v.n.* Co-migrate.

comh-fhreagarrachd, *s.f.* 2 (MS) Coherence.

comh-ghinealachd, (MS), *s.f.* Homogeny.

comh-ghleachd, *s.m.* 4 (MS) Shock.

comh-inbheachd, *s.f.* 2 Levelness.

comhlaideach, (MS), *a.* Indulgent.

comh-mheadhonach, (MS), a. Concentric.

còmhnardachd, *s.f.* 2 (MS), Slide. 3 (MS), Levelness.

còmhnardaich, *v.a.* 2 (MS) Level.

comh-neartach, (MS), *a.* Corroborative.

comh-neartachadh, (MS), *s.m.* 3 Corroboration.

comh-neartaich, (MS), *v.a.* 2 Corroborate.

còmh-nuidheachd, (MS), *s.f.* Habitableness.

còmhrag, *s.f.* Combat, on D, p.246. In *Badenoch* it is *s.m.*

comh-ragachadh, (MS), *s.m.* Concretion.

còmhraigich, *v.a.* See còmhraig, *v.a.* Fight.

comhrannach, *a.* Participial.

comh-rèitheachd, *s.f.* Levelness.

comh-shamhlachail, (MS), *a.* Assimilable.

comh-shamhlaich, (MS), *v.a.* Assimilate.

comh-shamhluidheachd, (MS) *s.f.* Semblance.

comh-sheasmhach, *a.* 2 (MS) Competent.

comh-smuineach, (MS), *a.* Abstract.

comh-steibheadh, (MS), *s.m.* Constitution.

comh-thabhair, (MS), *v.a.* Contribute.

comh-thàmhachd, (MS), *s.f.* Cohabitation.

comh-theamadh, (MS), *s.m.* Annexation.

comh-thiolaiceadh, *s.m.* Collation.

comunnachd, *s.f.* Socialism.

comunnair, *s.m.* Socialist.

con, (DC), *a.* Wild, unrestrained. *Uist.*

conail, *a.* Canine, doggish.

conalachd, (MS), *s.f.* Curship.

conathadh, (DC), *s.m.* Swelling, madness.

congaidh, *s.f.* See cungaidh, *s.f.* Cuir an congaidh air, *harness him (the horse).*

conghal, (G), *s.m.* Dog-collar.

còngnaich, (MS), *v.a.* Aid.

conoig, (DU), *s.f.* Fighting attitude or expression; crustiness exhibited in appearance.

conn, s.m. Reason, sense, meaning, see D, p.250. 'Gun chonn fo chèill', *without meaning or purpose.* (MS).

connbhail, *s.f.* Keeping. R 5.

connbhalach, *a.* Constant. R 11.

connlach, *s.f. North Uist* people use *connlach* for straw and *fodar* for fodder. *West of Ross, Harris people* and others use *connlach* for stubble and *fodar* for straw. See D, p.250.

connrag, *s.f.* Consonant in *grammar.*

connsachadh, *s.m.* 4 (MS) Nurture.

connspoidear, *s.m.* See connspoidiche, *s.m.* Wrangler, contentious person.

conspunnaiche, (MS), *s.m.* Attacker.

conuil, (DC), *s.f.* Rosary. *Uist.*

còp, (DC), *v.tr.* Charge with, "thriep". 'Rinn e chòpadh orm', *he charged me with...*

copaidh. Carn-copaidh, *s.m.* is a coup-cart.

copa, s.f. See cùb, *s.f.* Sledge. 2 Pannier. 3 Box-cart. 4 Coup-cart 5 Tumbril. 6 Gaelic spelling of coop. See D, p.286.

copach, (MS), *a.* Happy.

copan-cinn, (DU), s.m. Skill.

cor, s.m. In 'air chor's gun' = so that. Used negatively in Sutherland locally, as 'cor nach fhar mi do' n innseadh', *so that I cannot recount them.*

corachuill (?) Pìob chorachuill.

coraighear, (MS), *s.m.* Patentee.

coraigich, (MS), *v.a.* Arm.

corcach, (DC), *a.* 2 Short-eared. Applied to cows. In the Highlands of old, these were supposed to be 'sionn' or uncanny, as they were deemed to be the issue of a tarbh-uisge, or water-bull and an ordinary cow.

cordail, (MS), *a.* Agreeable.

cordalach, (MS), *a.* Agreeable.

cordalachd, (MS), *s.f.* Agreeableness.

cord-cuipe, *s.m.* Whip-cord.

cord-sgiùrsaidh, *s.m.* Whip-cord.

co-rèireachd, *s.f.* Mutuality.

còrn, *s.m.* Web of cloth. JGC. S. 173.

corpaich, (MS), *v.a.* Incorporate.

corp-ghearr, (MS), *v.a.* Anatomize.

corp-ghearradair, (MS), *s.m.* Anatomist.

corp-ghearradh, (MS) *s.m.* Anatomy.

corp-leigheas, (MS), *s.* and *a.* Anodyne.

corr, s. Shirt of armour, *W. H. Tales* ii 156.

còrr, *s.f.* Part of the roof of a house. See D, p.922.

corr-aodach, (MS), *s.m.* Flap.

corr-gheàrradh, (MS), *s.m.* Apstone.

corr-mhaileadhaich, (MS), *a.* Beetle-browed.

corr-shìomain, *s.m.* See cor-shìomain, *s.m.* Twist handle for making straw ropes.

corr-thollan, *s.* Swivel of a tether.

corra, (DC), *s.* Round-shaped, bent.

corra-bheinn, (DC), *s.f.* Hill with a rounded outline. 2 Place-name.

corra-chasach, (MS), *a.* Shambling.

corra-cheannach, *a.* 2 (MS) Beetle-headed, doltish.

corra-cnàmh, (DC), *s.f.* "Hunkering", that is to say when a dairy maid has no milking-stool, she bends her knees, thus tightening her skirt which she grips behind with her heels. "Hunkers". *Deo-Grèine* II 84.

corra-ghleus, *s.* 2 Battle-play.

corra-ghriothunn, (DC), *s.f.* See corra-ghritheach, *s.f.* See corra-ghritheach, *s.f.* Heron, stork.

corra-loigean, *a.* Malicious spirit frequenting places from which it is desirable to keep children after dark. JGC. W. 187.

corra-sgriach, *s.f.* See corra-sgritheach, *s.f.* Heron.

corra-spiod, (DMK), 'Air a corra-spiod air an togail', said of cattle that are so badly wintered that they have to be assisted to their feet in spring.

corrachan mhill a' choin, (G), *s.m.* Common Tormentil, *Potentilla erecta.*

corragan-an-duine-mhairbh, (DU), *s.m.* Dead man's fingers. *Alcifonium digitatum.* 2 Sea Campion.

corran, An, *s.m.* 10 Part of the constellation Leo. 11 See *Celtic Review* III 92.

corran-fiaclach, (CR), *s.m.* Serrated or toothed reaping-hook. This kind of sickle, like some other implements, is now known only by tradition in the Southern and Eastern Highlands, although still in common use in the North West.

còs, *s.m.* 4 (MS) Concavity.

còsach, (MS), *a.* 5 Rotten. 6 Concave.

còsachd, (MS), *s.f.* 2 Rottenness.

còsachadh, (MS), *s.m.* Excavation.

cosamhluidheachd, (MS), *s.f.* Resemblance.

cosannach, (MS), *s.m.* Mechanic.

cosannach-dùthcha, (MS), *s.m.* Peasant.

cosd, (DMK), *s.* 'Air cosd muigh', a *farm servant living in a bothy*: 'air cosd staigh', *a farm servant boarded in his employer's house.*

cosdas, *s.m.* Refreshments. JGC. W. 158.

còsgach, (MS), *a.* Antidotal.

cosgalachd, *s.f.* See cosdalachd, *s.f.* Costliness.

cosgaraich, *s. pl.* Conquerors, visitors. *Sàr-Obair.*

coslanach, (DU), *a.* Vesiculated, spongy

cosmhalachd, *s.f.* 7 Metaphor in *grammar.*

còta-bàn, (CR), *s.m.* Groat-land. In the Dictionary *ceithreamh* and *ochdamh* are given on the authority of MacAlpine as four and eight groat land respectively. In this case the mark should be the unit and the *ceithreamh* and *ochdamh* represent respectively 5 and 10 groats.

còta-gearr, (DU), *s.m.* Morning coat.

cotan-nan-uan, *s.m.* A kind of pen or enclosure to confine the lambs by themselves in the house in winter. *Lewis.* See D, p.923.

cothachadh, *s.m.* 7 (MS) Agitation 8 (DU) Overcoming, conquering, besting.

cothaich, *v.a.* 6 (DU) Overcome, conquer, get the better of. 7 Agitate.

cotharnach, (MS), *s.m.* Pumice.

cothlaim, *v.a.* 2 Mix different colours or quantities of wool.

cothoch, *a. West of Ross-shire* for còthaidh, *a.* Soft, spongy.

cothromaich, *v.a.* 7 (MS) Balance.

crabhaiche (MS), *s.m.* Ascetic.

crabhaidh, *a.* Hard, well tempered. *Sàr-Obair.*

crabharsaich, (MS), *s.* Job. *Hebrides.*

crachag, (G), *s.f.* Hard, unripe apple.

craiceannachd, *s.f.* Skinniness.

craicionn, *s.m.* This is the usual spelling for craiceann, *s.f.* Skin.

craicneach, (MS), *a.* Skinned, skinny.

craidhteach, (MS), *a.* Compunctious.

craithean, (DC), *s.m. pl.* Farm service roads.

crambag, (DU), *s.f.* Pan-cake.

cramh, (DU), *s.f.* Old Cow. *Coigeach.*

cramharsaich, (MS), *s.f.* Peddling.

cramhdaiche, (MS), *s.m.* Claudication.

crampadh, *s.m.* Versification, rhythm. *Rob Donn.*

crampag, *s.f.* 2 (DMK) Pancake. *West coast of Ross-shire.*

crann, *s.m.* Plough.

Additional names of parts (p.261).

3 Urchair, *s.f.* and bòrd-urchair *s.m.* Furrow-board, mould-board.

4 Druide-bòrd, *s.* Left earth-board.

7 Druim, (CR), *s.m.* Another name for the part extending from the upper corner of the furrow-board to the muzzle-holder.

8 Bonn, *s.m.* Bottom.

9 Bòrd-taoibh, *s.m.* Perpendicular piece to left, left earth-board, "bosom-plate".

10 Corragan, *s.f. pl.* Hafts.

11 Fuaidean, *s. pl.* Hands of plough.

12 Gearraiseach, *s.m.* Swingle-chain (1) between swingle-tree and horses. (2) between swingle-tree and plough or harrow.

13 Gobhal, *s.m.* Space between the stilts.

14 Gòbhlachan, *s.m.* Iron joining the furrow-board to the left-hand board of the plough.

15 Iaruinn amaill, *s.m.* Irons for swing-tree.

16 Iaruinn ghreallag, *s.m.* Irons for trestle-trees.

17 Muiseal, *s.m.* Muzzle.

18 Mullach, *s.m.* Main dorsal portion of a plough beam.

19 Slat, *s.f.* Stay.

20 Tarsanain, *s. pl.* Cross-bars. 'Chuir e car 'sa chrann', *he turned the plough upside down*, said of guest who put in a very long visit – signifying that he stayed from early evening when the *crann* (Plough in the constellation of the Great Bear) was "on even keel" below the pole until it was turned upside down in the morning – he must have stayed twelve hours.

crann-charaich, (MS), *v.a.* Allot.

crann-faladair, *s.m.* Wooden part or sned of a scythe. *Perthshire.*

crann-gleusaidh, *s.f.* The same as iuchair-na-cìche, *s.f.* A key to adjust the frame of flyers of a spinning-wheel to tighten the cord. See No. 16 on D, p.290.

crann-nan-gad, *s.m.* A kind of plough. Additional parts

6 Socach and socan, s.m. Sock.

8 Bòrd ur-chrainn, s.m. Mould-board.

crann-speala, *s.m.* Handle or shafting of a scythe.

crann-teine, (DU), *s.m.* Funnel of a steamboat.

cranna-phocan, (DMK), *s.m.* Sea-urchin.

crannach, *s.m.* Ploughman. *Rob Donn.*

crannag, *s.f.* See bàta, D, p.76. Round top of the mast and also the cross-trees of a ship. The semi-circular platform on the lower masts of square-rigged vessels. A full-rigged ship is known as 'long nan trì chrannag', having a top on the mizzen mast, which other 3-masted vessels do not have. *Crannag* was used in written Gaelic only.

crannaghail, *s. pl.* Implements, apparatus *Sàr-Obair.*

crannarachd, (CR), *s.f.* Ploughing, act of ploughing. *Perthshire.*

cranntachan-an-deamhain, *s.m.* Sun-spurge. *Colonsay.*

craobh, (CR), *s.f.* Any garden bush in *Arran*, where 'preas' is not used.

craobhaidh, *a.* Niggardly, mean. *Sàr-Obair.*

craobhail, (MS), *a.* Arboreous.

craobhannach, (MS), *a.* Arboreous.

craos, *s.m.* 6 Muzzle of a horse.

craosadh, (MS), *s.m.* Grin.

cràsg, *s.f.* 5 Crossing place over ridge.

cràsgach, *a.* Crispy.

cratachan, *s.m.* Churn-staff. *Maclagan's Evil Eye,* 95.

creachdach, *s.m.* Purple loosestrife. *Colonsay.*

creachadair, (DMK), *s.m.* Skua. *Caithness.*

creadhneach, *a.* Hurtful, painful, excruciating. *Sàr-Obair.*

creaga, (MMcL), *s.* Cluster of houses. Creaga an t-sìthein, *the group of houses at the eminence.*

creagach, (G), *s.m.* Rockfishing as opposed to *breacach* (troutfishing) and *iasgach* (angling).

creap, *s.* Lump of dough, as food on a journey. *Celtic Magazine* ix 316.

creapailid, *s.m. Skye* for creapull, *s.m.* Garter.

creapog, (MMcD), *s.m.* Ball of thread in the *dealgan* (spindle) of the *cuigeal* (distaff) of a spinning-wheel. It is wound in the form of a figure 8 and not in the usual manner.

crèbeilt, *s.f.* Garter. *Sutherland.*

creideasach, *a.* 3 Trustworthy.

creineastair, *s.m.* ? Skipper. *Gaidheal* III 72.

creiseim, *s.* These two pegs on the upper crossbar, as in the second illustration No. 236a (D, p.317), and two similar ones on the lower crossbar, explain the old form of *dealbh* (Warping-frame) formerly in use in Lewis, but the form shown in the first illustration is that generally used elsewhere. The form of winding thread on two top and bottom pegs in the lower illustration (236a) is called 'creiseim' in Lewis.

This is the modern method. In the upper *creiseim* Twelve threads are tied together and placed over the end peg as indicated, so that there are 6 threads above and 6 below. They are then crossed between the pegs so that the 6 threads that are below the first peg are on the upper side of the centre peg, and again they are brought below the third peg as indicated thus.

After rounding the third peg the twelve threads come together and are carried round the pegs in the side of the frame as indicated in the sketch. They then round the lower *creiseim* together, and are brought back round the side pegs to the top following in the same order as before until they come to the upper *creiseim.*

crèis na clòimhe, *s.* Natural oil of wool.

creitheach, (MS), *s.m.* Brushwood.

criarachan, (DMK), *s.m.* Nest of wild birds before it is lined or finished. *Caithness.*

criathar-garbh, *s.* Riddle, sieve.

cridhealaich, (MS), *v.a.* Rejoice.

crimeas, (MS), *s.m.* Mop.

crìochannach, (MS), *a.* Conclusive.

crìochanntach, (MS), *a.* Decretory.

criochdanach, *a.* Querimonious.

criochdanas, *s.m.* Querimoniousness.

crìod, (MMcL), *a.* Wise, old-fashioned.

crìod, *s.* Ball of hair or thread for playing shinty at night. JGC. W. 240.

criol, *s.m.* Creel. *Arran & Perthshire.* 2 (CR) Peat-cart. *Arran.* Formerly a peat creel.

criomag, *s.f.* 4 Notch made in the edge of a sheep's ear each year to indicate age. When a ewe has 6 notches, 3 in each edge, she is 6 years old and is then a cast ewe or crock.

crioplachail, *a.* Lame, crippled.

crios, *s.m.* 6 Belly band of a horse. 7 (CR) Band of a sheaf.

crìos, *s.m.* Grease. *Arran.*

criosfhuaim, *s.m.* Zonophone.

crioslaiche, *s.m.* Girdler.

criosnaiche, *s.m.* See crioslaiche, *a.m.* above.

criostaladh, (MS), *s.m.* Crystalization.

criostalaich, *v.a.* Crystalize.

criothnachd, *s.f.* Finitude.

crithearra, (MS), *a.* Afflicted by ague.

crithearrachd, (MS), *s.f.* Ague.

crith-thinn, (MS), *a.* Palsical.

criù. *Lochalsh* pronunciation of craobh, *s.f.* Tree.

crò *s.f.* Heel of a peat spade or 'torsgian', *s.f.*

crò *s.m.* 17 Pig-sty.

crò na fearsaid, *s.* or cnò an dealgain are alternative names for 'sùil na cuibhle', *s.f.*, the eye through which the wool enters a spinning-wheel. See D, p.290, No. 11.

crobhrsag, *s.f. Easter Ross* variation of groiseid, *s.f.* Gooseberry.

crocan, *s.m.* 3 (MS) Pot-hook. 4 (MMcD) Ball of wax and thread placed over the tips of the horns of cattle to prevent them from goring each other.

cròcan, *s.m.* 5 Fork-shaped twig for winding fishing line. 6 *North Argyll* winding fishing-line. 6 *North Argyll* for

cròcach, *s.m.* A spiked instrument to keep calves from suckling. 7 (DMK), Long handle of wood fitted with a grapnel for raising *barr-roc*, sea-weed or tangles from the bottom of the sea. *Lochalsh.*

crocas, *West of Ross-shire* for the English word cork.

cròchan, *s.m.* (MMcD) Wheezing in the throat. 2 (DMK) Broken and swampy ground in which rough grass grows. *Caithness.*

cròch-mhuir, *s.* 'Sid e tighinn 's cha'n ann righinn cròch-mhuir frithearr, basanach'. Iorram Chuain, v. 12.

cròdan, (DU), *s.m.* Soreness of the hoofs of cattle.

crodhan, *s.m. Arran* for crùbh, s.m. Horse's hoof.

crogagan, (WC), *s.m.* Kind of glove formerly worn by fishermen.

crogaig, *s.f.* Hook. *Sutherland.*

crogan, *s.m.* 7 Gnarled tree. *Argyll.*

crògan, *s.m.* Thorn-bush. *Argyll.*

cròic, *s.f.* Difficulty. See D, p.276. In *Arran*, 'Cha bu chròic sin a dhèanamh, cha bu chròic dha sin a dhèanamh', *that could easily be done, he could easily do that*; also 'dè is cròic sin a dhèanamh', *what is difficult about doing that?* And to anyone, for instance, leaving a *cèilidh* unusually early, 'Dè a' chròic a th'ort'; 'cha chròic', it is not difficult.

croileag, *s.f.* See craidhleag, *s.f.* and croidhleag, *s.f.* An egg-shaped wool-basket, about three feet in height, made of straw. The same as mùdag, *s.f.* Ill. 546 (D, p.675).

croileagaich, (MS), *v.a.* Encage.

croineachd, s.m. See cruithneachd, s.m. Wheat.

croineagan, *s. pl.* Small peat. *Badenoch.*

croiseag, (G), *s.f.* Crossing.

croisean Moire, *s.m.* Gossamer. *Uist.* Cho gòrach ris na croisean Moire, *as flimsy as gossamer.*

crois-na-loinid, *s.* Handle and cross of a churn-staff. HGC. W. 12.

crois-tara (A' chrois-tara), *s.f.* Part of the constellation Cygnus, the Swan.

crom-an-donais! *Int.* Blood and wounds!

crom-cruinnich, (MS), *v.a.* Arch.

crom-tòin, *s.m.* See croman-lòn, *s.m.* Snipe *Scolopax gallinaga.*

cromadh-dìreach, An, (DMK), *s.m.* Carpenter's square. *Ross-shire.*

cromag, *s.f.* 11 Gaff for landing fish, *West coast of Ross-shire.* 12 (DU) Boat-hook.

cromag-dheiridh, *s.f.* Breeching-hook of a cart.

cromag-ghuaille, *s.f.* Draught-hook of a cart.

cromag-thoisich, *s.f.* Draught-hook of a cart.

cromagach, (MS), *a.* Angular.

cromagaich, (MS), *v.a.* Accroach, clasp.

croman, *s.m.* 9 Buzzard. *Lorn.*

croman-cruinn, (MS), *s.m.* Arch.

croman-riabhach, *s.m.* See croman-lòin s.m. Snipe.

cròsgach, *a.* Big-boned. *W. H. Tales* iv 149.

crosgaileit, (DC), *s.f.* Linen band tied round an infant's head. *Barra.* In Argyll *barran*, s.m. is used. D, p.71.

crotag, *s.f.* 5 (CR), Curlew. *Arran.*

crotha, (MS), *a.* Stout.

cròthadh, (MS), *s.m.* Harvest-home.

cruachan, (G), *pl.* of cruach, *s.f.* Pile, heap. An alternative plural is cruachainnean.

cruachanach, (MS), *a.* Hilly.

cruadalaiche, (MS), *s.m.* Adventurer.

cruadalaich, (MS), *v.a.* Adventure.

cruadhachadh, (MS), *s.m.* Crystalization.

cruadhaich, *v.a.* 5 (MS) Swelter. 6 (MS) Bake.

cruaidh-bhior, (DMK), *s.* Steel punch, for punching holes in iron hoops. *Ross-shire.*

cruaidh-bhuilg, *s.* Corn on the foot? *Gàidheal* II 236.

cruaidh-imeachd, *s.f.* Walking very quietly.

†crùb, (DC), *s.f.* Obsolete name for the hand, usually applied to a child's hand, crùb an leinibh bhig, *hand of the little child.*

crùbag, *s.f.* 6 (WC), *s.m.* Not always so large in *Poolewe* as the size given.

crùbaich, (MS), *v.a.* Hamstring.

crùban-siùil, (WC), *s.m.* Full-reefed sail in a gale. 'Nach ann oirre tha'n crùban-siùil', *isn't her sail reefed to the last inch! Poolewe.* A well-known expression among fishermen.

crudhaiche, (WC), *s.m.* Horse-shoer.

crugais, (DMK), *s.* Frame of wood that enclosed the millstone and in which the hopper was set in the old mill. *Caithness.*

cruidheal, *s.m.* Perthshire for cliabh, *s.m.* Creel.

cruinn-chòsach, (MS), *a.* Convexo-concave.

cruinn-chulach, (MS), *s.* Gibbous.

cruinn-chumhachd, *s.f.* Gibbousness.

cruinneachadh, *s.m.* 4 (MS) Frequence.

cruinneagan, (MS), *s. pl.* Rondles.

cruinn-leum, *s.m.* Leap without a run, a standing jump. In *Poolewe* there is a well-known bridge called *Drochaid a' chruinn-lèim*, the Bridge of the Standing Jump, as before it was erected people used to leap the burn.

cruiseag, *s.f.* Cranberry. *Beauly.*

crùisle, *s.m.* 2 (MS) Church aisle. 3 (MS) Crucible.

cruislig, (WC), *s.f.* Untidy person. A' chruislig bhodaich, the untidy old man.

cruit, *s.f.* 6 (WC) Smart lassie. 'Nach b'e a' chruit i?', *isn't she a smart lassie?*

crùit-an-ùrlair, (WC), *s.f.* Best female dancer, belle of the ball. A very old expression.

crùn, (WC), *v.* Appear, as a rock or buoy coming in sight among the waves. 'Tha'n sgèir a' crùnadh', the rock is just in sight. A common phrase.

crunsgaoil, (MS), *v.a.* Rimple.

crùp, A' ch-, *s.f.* Part of a house couple. See D, p.922.

crùsach, *s.m.* Small fry, pigmy race. *Rob Donn.*

crùsgail, (MS), *v.a.* Crankle, crinkle, crumple.

crùsgladh, (MS), *s.m.* Crumple.

crùth, (DC), *s.m.* Wooden dish used to carry milk.

cruthail, (DC), *s.f.* Placenta of a mare.

cuagach, *a.* 6 (MS) Splay-footed.

cuagachadh, (MS), *s.m.* Incurvity.

cuagaich, (MS), *v.a.* Incurvate.

cuagraich, (MS), *v.a.* Belabour.

cuaicheineach, *s.* See cuaicheanach, *a.* Plaited, tight. See D, p.284.

cuairsgean, *s.m.* 5 (CR) A roller for land.

cuairt, *s.m.* 16 (DMK) Rounded piece of wood for strengthening the attachment of the gunwale of a boat to the stem and stern posts.

cuairteag, *s.f.* 9 (MS) Arch.

cuairtich, *v.a.* 6 (MS) Beguile.

cuairtichte, *a.* & *past pt.* 4 Arched.

cual-fhraoich, *s.f.* See cual, *s.f.* Faggot, burden. See D, p.285.

cuallaich, *v.a.* 2 (MS) Fagot.

cuanal, (DC), *s.m.* Herd, company. cuanal aidhean, *a herd of queys.*

cuartachd, (MS), *s.f.* Roundness.

cuartalan, *s.m.* 2 (MS) Gig.

cuartalanaich, *v.a.* Ramble.

cùbhraidh, *a.* 3 (MS) Grateful.

cùbhraidheachd, *s.f.* 2 (MS) Flavour.

cùbhraidhich, *v.a.* See cùbhraich, *v.a.* Aromatize.

cùbhraidhich, (MS), *v.a.* Perfume.

cudthromaich, *v.a.* Encumber.

cudum, *s.m.?* Variant of cudthrom, *s.m.* Weight, heaviness. A favourite word of Mac Mhaighstir Alasdair. 'Tilg sios le neart 's le cudum', *throw down with strength and with weight.*

cugainn, *s.m.* 2 Treasure.

cughainneach, *s.m.* 2 Mixture of different colours of wool. *Glenlyon.*

cuglach, (MS), *a.* Perilous. 2 Precarious.

cuibheall-iarna, *s.* Revolving hank-reel.

cuibh'n-an-fhèidh, *s. pl.* Deer's antlers. JGC. W. 78.

cuibhrinnich, (MS), *v.a.* Allot.

cuicheineach, *a.* Coquetting, secretly hobnobbing. *Argyll.*

cuideachdail, *a.* 3 (MS) Humourous.

cuideam, (MS), *s.m.* Sadness.

cuideamach, (MS), *a.* Sad.

cuideamachadh, (MS), *s.m.* Aggrievance.

cuideamaich, (MS), *v.a.* Balance. 2 Sag. 3 See cudthromaich, *v.a.* Poise. 4 (MS) Clog.

cuidheall-shnìomha, *s.f.* Spinning-wheel.

ADDITIONAL PARTS OF A SPINNING-WHEEL

Aisil, *s.f.* Axle of driving-wheel.

Aisil-an-t-seic, *s.f.*, see dealgan na teic, spindle of flyer.

Bann nam maighdeanan, *s.m.*, band or cord stretched between the top of the supports of the flyers.

Bòrd-coise, *s.m.* Foot-board.

Casan, *s.m.* Foot board or treadle.

Cìoch, *s.f.* Nave or hub of driving-wheel.

Cìr-an-t-seic, *s.f.* Teeth of the flyers.

Cleasan, *s.* Connecting rod. *Skye.*

Crangaid, *s.f.* Crank of driving-wheel.

Crann-gleusaidh, *s.m.* Nave or key. No. 16.

Crò an dealgain, *s.m.* Eye through which the wool enters.

Crò na fearsaid, *s.m.* Eye through which the wool enters also.

Cuilean, *s.m.* Spoke of the driving wheel. *Skye.*

Deil, *s.f.* Crank and axle.

Each, *s.* Frame bearing the flyers and standard or bearer of the driving wheel also.

Fearsaid an t-seic, *s.m.* Teeth of the flyers.

Fiaclan an t-seic, *s. pl.* Teeth of the flyers.

Gàirdeanan, *s. pl.* supporters of flyer, resting on beairt-mheadhon, No. 10.

Gruagach, *s.f.* Bar on which the maighdeanan rest. No. 14.

Iarunn-siubhal, *s.m.* Axle of driving wheel.

Iteachan, *s.m.* Reel or bobbin.

Maide-buinn, *s.m.* Stock.

Maighdean, *s.f.* Standard or bearer of the driving-wheel.

Maighdeag, *s.f.* Another name for maighdean, No. 10.

Marcach, *s.m.* Standard or bearer of the driving wheel also.

Rèim, *s.f.* Driving wheel. *Wester Ross.* 2 Grooved rim of the driving wheel.

Roithleagan, *s.m.* Wheel which turns the flyer. See rolan, *s.m.* No. 4, Ill. 245.

Roithlean, *s.m.* Wheel which turns the flyer also.

Seal-coise, *s.m.* Foot-board.

Seotal, *s.m.* Small receptacle in the stock. Shuttle hollow in the stock of a spinning-wheel, in which the first filled *pirn* or bobbin is kept until the other is ready for being reeled with it.

Snàthad an t-seic, *s.f.* Spindle of flyer. See dealgan na teic, *s.m.* No. 23.

Uilleadh-cuibhleach, *s.m.* Oil for spinning-wheels. *Arran.*

cuidheall-shnìomhaich, *s.f.* An alternative name for cuidheall-shnìomha.

cuidhle, (CR), *gen. sing.* of cuidheall used as a noun in *Arran.* Spinning-wheel, wheel of a ship. Any other wheel there was *roth, s.m.*

cuidimich, (MS), *v.a.* Cumber.

cuigealach-mhòine, *s.f.* Great mace weed. *Beauly* and elsewhere.

cuigealaich, *v.a.* Work with a distaff.

cùil, *s.f.* Private room or 'ben' of a highland house.

cuilc, *s.f.* 4 (DU) Pocket-knife.

cuilchionn, (DC), *a.* Crafty, cunning.

cuileaga-sneachda, (CR), *s. pl.* Flakes of snow. *Arran.*

cuilean, *s.m.* Small seed of oats. It was, at one time, hand picked for the purpose of using it as seed-corn, as a boll of it would go much further in sowing land, than its larger variety. *Lochearnhead.*

cuilean, *s.m.* 13 Spoke of the driving wheel of a spinning-wheel.

cuileanach, *a.* Having pups or whelps, having a large litter.

cuilse, *s.f. Kintyre* for cuisle, *s.f.* 8 Pulse.

cuiltig, (MS), *s.f.* The Gaelic form of quilt.

cuimh, (DU), *s.f.* Difficulty in breathing experienced by a person having asthma or consumption. 2 Rarely the appearance of such a person.

cuimheasachd, *s.f.* See cuimseachd, *s.f.* 2 (MS) Temperature.

cuimhsear, *s.m.* See cuinnsear, *s.m.* Dagger, sword, poniard. 2 Hanger.

cuimseach, (MS), *a.* 7 Abstinent. 8 (MS) Comprehensive.

cuimseachd, *s.f.* 2 Measureableness.

cùimteach, (MS), *a.* Plastic.

cuineag, *s.f.* 2 (DC) Distaff.

cuing-dhamh, (CR), *s.f.* Pair (literally yoke) of oxen. *West of Ross-shire.*

cuingeach-clèibh, (DMK), *s.m.* Pleurodynia. *Caithness.*

cuingeachd, (MS), *s.f.* Closeness.

cuingirich, (MA), *v.a.* Couple.

cuingnich, (MS), *v.a.* Restringe.

cuinlean, (DC), *s.m.* Stem of a boat 2 Nose. 3 Any projection, especially of corn cut from the stalk, hence a source of supply as in 'Is math a dh' fhuineas bean a' mhuilleir, Is math a dh' fhaodas – is math a cuinlean', Well bakes the miller's wife – well she may – plentiful is her source of supply.

cuinnsearaich, (MS), v.a. Indart, poignard.

cuir catha, s. Battle cry.

cuire, (MMcL), s.f. Lewis for curra, s.m. Woof.

cuirealdach, a. merry. R. 64.

cuiridhear, s.m. Inviter.

cuirteir, s.m. 2 Plaiding. Badenoch.

cuirteis, s.f. See cuirteas, s.f. Courtesy.

cùis, (DU), s.f. In compounds of this word the Gairloch plural is cùiseachan e.g. cùiseachan-truais, objects of pity, wretches.

cuiseachadh, (DMK), s.m. Proposing, intending. 'Tha mi a' cuiseachadh falbh', I intend to go. Caithness.

cuiseag-ruadh, s.f. Flower panicle of a dock. Colonsay.

cuislearachd, (MS), s.f. Venesection.

cuisle-shnìomhain, s. pl. Winding veins of trees. Sàr-Obair.

cuit, (DC), s.f. Disease. Uist. Cuit bhràghad, scrofula.

cuithir, s. Stronghold. The same as cuithe, s.f. 5 Stronghold.

cùl (air), adv. Aback.

cùl-chabag, (DU), s.f. Two species of bivalves, cyprina islandica and isocardia cor, genus cyprinidae. 2 Back tooth.

culaidh-uamhais, s. Terrifying. Beauly and elsewhere.

cùldaich, (MS), v.a. Absent.

cùlm, (DMK), s. Mill dust separated from the grain in the process of shelling. Caithness.

cùl-shleamhnachail, (MS), a. Apostatical

cùl-taigh, s.m. Out-house.

cumail-chas. 'Bha e gun chumail-chas', he couldn't stand on his feet. An Gaidheal III, p.74.

cumasgair, (MS), s.m. Mingler.

cumhachdach, (MS), a. Absolute.

cumhachdail, s.m. See cumhachdach, s.m. Mighty man, and cumhachdach, a. Powerful, mighty, strong.

cumhaideachd, s.f. See cubhaidheachd, s.f. Seemliness, decentness.

cumraig, v.a. Sutherland for cumraich, v.a. Cumber, encumber, impede, incommode.

cùngaichte, (MS), past pt. Abstracted.

cunglach, s.m. 2 Strait.

cunntas ùr, s.m. See fèill, s.f. Owing to the completion of the 19th century, there is now an additional day between the Old and New Styles, New Year's Day Old Style now being 14th January and in some parts of Gaeldom the dates of festivals continued to be kept according to 19th century Old Style reckoning, and in some districts three styles were in use. Cunntas ùr means New Style.

cunn-traigh, (DU), s.f. Neap-tide. See contraigh, s.f. Neap-tide.

cùp, s.f. See cùb, s.f. above. Sledge, pannier. D, p.286.

cupag, s.f. See cùb, s.f. above.

cupan, s.m. 2 Cup inside the ferrule of a bagpipe. See D, p.722.

cùr, v.a. Chastise, torture. 'Nach mise th'air mo chùradh', am I not chastened. Celtic Review, v.125.

curaisde, or cur-aisde, s.f. Quagmire.

curamach, (MS), a. 2 Stretch.

curamaichead, (MS), s.m. Seriousness.

curanta, a. 3 (MS) Magnanimous.

curantachd, s.f. 2 (MS) Magnanimity.

currach, s.m. 2 Level plain, marsh, bog or fen. Latterly applied to a racecourse on account of its levelness.

†currach, s.m. 3 (WC) Carcase of an animal.

currac-oidhche, s.f. Night-cap.

cùrrag, s.f. Chastisement. Celtic Review, v. 125.

curran cruaidh, (G), s.m. Common hemlock.

cursan, (G), s.m. Lapwing. Islay.

cuspaidheach, (MS), a. Choppy.

cuta, s. Cut, hank.

cù-uisge, s.m. 3 (WC) Dog-fish.

D

dà-chiallach, (MS), a. Ambiloguous.

dagan, (CR), s.m. A little thick-set man.

Arran.

daib, (MS), *a.* Poor.

dàicheil, *a.* Likely, probable. 'Tha 'daicheil gu'n tèid', *likely to go in Arran, not "peculiar".*

dàil, (CR), *s.f.* "Haugh", or low-lying land by a stream. 2 Lot. 'Cluain an domhain truagh an dàil', *the field of the world, hard the lot.* R. 1.

dàil, *s.f.* 'Thrèig an dàil mi gu là luain', *the tryst has left me for ever.* R. 18.

dailceanta, (CR), *a.* Strong, healthy. *Arran.*

daimheach, *s.m.* 4 Stranger *Sàr-Obair.*

daimheil, *a.* 5 Inward.

daimseir, *gen. sing.* of daimsear, *s.m.* rutting of deer. Ann am pollachaibh daimseir, *in the rutting holes. Beinn Dorain.*

dairb, *a.* Used in *Uist* preceeding its noun, to signify small or insignificant. It is applied to all animals, fowls and fishes. Dairb laoigh, *a small calf.*

daire, (MS), *s.* Brushwood.

daireach, *a.* See doireach, *a.* Woody, abounding in woods.

dairleanta, *a.* Strong, healthy. *Arran.*

dais, *s.f.* 4 Oblong stack.

daisean, (G), *s.m.* Heap of hay.

dallan, (CR), *s.m.* 7 Corn basket.

dallanach, (CR), *s.m.* 3 Corn basket of the usual size, about 2.5 feet in diameter. *West of Ross-shire.*

dallanaiche, (MS), *s.f.* Inebriation.

dallaranach, (MS), *a.* Purblind.

dallarag-deòir, s.f. Tear-blinded girl.

dallaran-deòir, s.m. Tear-blinded boy.

dall-eud, (MS), *s.m.* Bigotry.

dall-uinneag, (CR), *s.f.* Square cavity used as a shelf in the wall of a room. *Arran.*

dalta, *adv.* 'Is dalta sin', like that. *Arran.* Not dallta.

damh, *s.m.* 5 Also applies to the part of a rake to which the teeth are fixed.

damhair, *s.m.* 8 Cry of a deer. R. 84.

damh-cabrach, *s.m.* 3 5-year old stag.

damh-suirne, *s.m.* Corn kiln. *Arran.*

danaire, *a.* Dogged. *Arran.*

danarra, (MS), *a.* 6 Crabbed.

danarrachd, *s.f.* 5 Crabbedness.

dannaire, *a.* See danarra above.

dannsairean, *s. pl.* The Northern Lights or *Aurora Borealis. Caithness.*

daoirsnich, (MS), *v.a.* Outprize.

daolaireach, *a.* 2 Lousy.

daolaireachd, *s.f.* 5 Lousiness.

daolant, *adv. Perthshire* for daonnan, *adv.* Always, continually.

daornan, *adv. Kintyre* for daonnan.

dà-pheighinn, (DMK), *s.* The Scots bodle.

darag, *s.f.* 5 (CR). Big, stout woman *Arran.* 'Nach i an darag!', *isn't she stout!*

dà-sgillinn, *s.f.* One sixty-fourth of a davoch. See D, p.719.

dath, *s.m.* In *Arran* Cha'n 'eil e aon dath (fuar *et cetera*), *it is not the least* (cold *et cetera*).

deabh, (DU), *v.* To bleed to death.

deabhach, *a.* Leaky.

deacadh, *s.m.* Phonetic spelling of deachdadh, inditing. *Gaidheal* II 53.

deachdmhair, (MS), s.m. Caviller.

deachdmhaireach, *a.* Cavillous.

deachdmhaireachd, *s.f.* Cavil.

deagh-chainnteach, *a.* 2 (DC) Polite.

deagh-gheanail, (MS), *a.* Amicable.

deal, s. See deil below.

dealachan, *s.m.* Zeal, great glee, hilarity, earnestness. *Sàr-Obair.*

dealbh, (DU), 14 Small quantity. 15 Its semblance. Dealbh uisge, *a small quantity of water.* Thoir dealbh dheth sin, *give a small quantity of that. West coast of Ross.*

dealbh, *s.m.* 13 Warping-frame. In the old manner of warping the thread, the *creiseim* is formed in Lewis in the manner shown in Ill. 263a, D, p.316. In the modern method with the new looms now in use in Lewis, twelve threads are used and the *creiseim* is formed on 3 pegs in the upper bar and two pegs in the lower bar. Care must be taken when working the thread, that the same order is used when returning from the lower *creiseim* to the upper, otherwise the thread can never make the desired cloth. The posts or side sticks are about one and a half yards apart. (See also under *creiseim* above).

dealbhachd, (MS), *s.f.* Fantasy.

dealgach, (MS), *a.* 5 Braky.

dealgan an t-seic, *s.f.* See fearsaid an t-seic, *s.f.* Spindle of the flyer of a spinning-wheel.

dealtaich, (MS), *v.a.* Bedew.

dèan, v. irreg. Do, make, act, work, perform. In *Arran* the *fut. aff.* is deanaidh; the *fut. subj.*, ma dhèanas mi; *future pass.subj.*, deanar, ma dheanar. An toir mi da seo?, thoir (not bheir), *shall I give him this? Yes. Arran.*

deanaich, (CR), *pr. pt.* Working, see D, p.319. It is not essential that *obair* is understood in the first example, nor *mine* in the second. In *Perthshire dèan* is a distinctly intransitive verb.

deantair, *s.* (dheantair-yenter). [A Uist game called in the South "King", which was still played with great zest when Dwelly compiled his notes for the Appendix. In fact few other games could hold their own with it. Any number of players are allowed, one of whom is made the *rìgh* or King. Two lines are drawn facing each other at a distance of about 60 feet. All the players except the *rìgh* then take up their positions on one line, their object being to reach the other line without being crowned. The *rìgh* stands between these two lines and calls out 'a dheandair! a dheandair! Co 'n duine bhi 's agam bidh e air a chrùinidh!' Upon which all rush for the opposite side. The King then tries to catch someone and crown him, by laying his hand on his head. If the boy who has been caught can wriggle away before he is free, the boy who has been crowned then takes his stand with the *rìgh* and they again call out their challenge, both now attempting to catch somebody. This goes on until all are caught. Then the first to be crowned is king for the next time. Uist Games in *Celtic Review* No. 6.]

dearbadan-dè, *s.m.* Butterfly. See D, p.320, lines 39, 50 and 52; make the following correction, for *lycoena* read *lycaena*. On page 321, make the following corrections; on line 6 for *oethiope* read *aethiope*; on line 11, for *coenympha davus* read *coenonympha davus*; on line 16 for *matus corydon* read *polyommatus corydon*.

dearbh (gu), *adv.* Truly, really, certainly, indeed. This is pronounced in different ways. People in *Lochalsh* say *gu deara-u* and *gu dearathu*. *Harris* people and others say *gu dearra* and *gu dearbha*. *Gu dearra* (*dearbha*) *fhèine* is used in *Harris* and *Uist*.

dearcach, *a.* 4 (MS) Gazeful.

dearcadh, *s.m.* 4 (MS) Apprehension.

dearca-coille, *s.f.* 2 Blaeberry. *Colonsay.*

dearcadan, (MS), *s.m.* Gazer.

dearcan-dearg, *s.m.* Red currant, see raosar-dearg, *s.m. Colonsay.*

dearcan-dubh, *s.m.* Black currant, see raosar-dubh, *s.m. Colonsay.*

dearcan-geal, *s.m.* White currant, see raosar-geal, *s.m. Colonsay.*

dearcan-suiridhe, *s.m.* A weed good for the gravel. *Arran.*

dearg, *v.a.* 10 (CR) Delve.

dearg, *s.* 9 (AC) Dart. *Car. Gad* 2, 308.

deargachadh, (MS), *s.m.* Penetrability.

deargachd, (MS), *s.f.* Redness.

deargadh, *s.m.* 4 (DC), Impression of a coin. 10 used in *Gairloch* for dearg, red. 11 (M) Perceptibility, perception.

deargann-tràghad, *s.f.* Sand-hopper, skipper.

dearmad, *s.m.* 3 (MS) Vacancy.

dearmadach, *a.* 2 Vacant.

dearmaid, *v.a.* 2 (MS) Blanch.

dearmail *s.f.* 3 Earnestness.

dearmalach, *a.* 3 (MS) Intense, intensive

dearrasail, (DC), *v.a.* See diorrasail *v.n.* Spatter, hiss, crackle. 2 Nag peevishly.

dearsalachd, (MS), *s.f.* Brilliance.

deas, *a.* 12 (DC), Straight as a stick, erect.

deasag, *s.f.* Right hand. *Mac Talla* xi 201.

deas-àiteachadh, (MS), *s.m.* Agriculture

deasalachd, *s.f.* See deisealachd, *s.f.* Readiness, convenience.

deasbhartachadh, (MS), *s.m.* Artfulness.

deas-ghnàth, *s.* 3 (MS) Obsequies.

deas-labhair, (MS), *v.a.* Articulate.

deata, *s.f.* from diota. See diod, *s.f.*

drop. Hence *Arran* for dry.

deatachas, -ais, *s.m.* Effumability.

deathaid, *s.* See deata, `s.f. above.

deibh, (MS), *v.a.* Decant.

deibheadh, *s.m.* Decantation.

dèideag, *s.f.* 7 Conceit. *Sàr-Obair.*

deidheann, *s.* Horse-fetter.

dèidh-làimh, *adv.* 4 At need.

dèidh-leum, *s.* Horse-fetter.

deifreachd, s.f. Hastiness.

deigheannach, *s.m.* See eigheanach, *s.m.* Icicle.

deighionn, *s.f.* See deubhann, *s.f.* Horse-fetter.

deighreach, *s.m.* Dirling. *Badenoch.*

deighreachail, *a.* Chill.

deighreachd, *s.m.* See eighreachd, *s.f.* Glaciation. Frostiness below.

deil, *s.* Crank of the driving-wheel of a spinning-wheel. 2 Axle. *West of Ross-shire.*

deil, *s.* Heated, itchy feeling.

deilbhinn
   'deud   dhaithte   o'n   dheilbhinn chuireadh dreach air na h-armaibh 's na cùm chruaidh-each òn cheardaich 's deadh cholg orr'.

deile, (DC), *s.m.* Placenta of sheep, hind or goat.

deileachd, (MS), *s.f.* Quillet.

deileannachd, *s.f.* Humming of bees. 2 Barking of dogs. *Sàr-Obair.*

deile-trom, *s.m.* See eilitriom, *s.m.* Plank or board on which a dead body is placed.

deilleanachd, *s.f.* See deileannachd, *s.f.* above.

deil-tholl, (MS), *s.* See deala-tholl, *s.m.* Leech. 2 Lamprey.

deimhneachd, (MS), *s.f.* Cruelty.

deimheis, *s.m.* See deamhas, *s.m.* & *f.* Pair of sheep shears. 2 Scissors.

dèintheas, *s.m.* See dèineas, *s.m.* Eagerness.

dèintheasach, *a.* See dèineasach, *a.* and dèineachdach, *a.* Rude, rough.

deir-bhlèinn, (DC), *s. coll.* Orphans. *Barra.*

deir-buana, *s.f.* Skye for deireadh-buana, *s.f.* Harvest-home.

dèirc, (DMK), *s.f.* Alms, charity. Air an dèirce, depending upon alms or charity.

dèirceach, (DMK), *s.m.* Dirl or painful sensation caused in the hand by striking a stick against a stone or other hard substance. *West coast of Ross-shire.*

dèirceachd, *s.f.* Lowness.

dèircealachd, (MS), *s.f.* Beggarliness.

dèirceil, *a.* Kind.

dèireach, *s.* Gunfire. 'An spuir ghlas aig dlùths an dèirich', *their grey gunflints from their fire so close.* J. L. Campbell (Editor), *Highland Songs of the Forty-five,* Edinburgh, 1984, p.82, line 143.

deireadh, *s.m.* 6 (DC) Inferior or lighter grain blown away in the chaff when winnowing. 7 (DC) Death. *Western Isles.*

deireannan, *s. pl.* 2 (AH) Thirds or least valuable part of oats, barley or other grain, after being winnowed.

deirgnich, (DC), *s. pl.* A' deirgneachadh, *v.a.* Fester, inflame, swell.

deisbigil, *s.m. West of Ross-shire* for deisciobul, *s.m.* Disciple.

deisdeanach, (MS), *v.a.* Scribble.

deisdanachd, (MS), *s.f.* Antipathy.

deiseag, *s.f.* Velvet crab, *portunus puber.*

deiseag-thubaist, (DC), *s.f.* Mishap, e.g. illegitimacy, *Argyll.* Any evil unexpected stroke of fortune. When it comes on oneself it is a *trial*, but when it falls upon another it is a *judgment!*

deise-gleusta, (WC), *s.* Oilskin.

deisialas, (DMK), *s.m.* Euphemism for a chamber pot. *Gairloch.*

dèisinnich, *v.a.* Dirty, befoul.

deismear, (MS), *s.m.* Advocate. 2 Quibbler.

deithir, *s.f.* See deifir, *s.f.* Haste.

deithireachd, (MS), *s.f.* See deifreadh, *s.m.* Haste. 2 Difference.

deithirich, *v.a. & n.* See deifrich, *v.a. & n.* Hasten, hurry.

deithneas, *s.m.* 2 (MS) Rashness.

dèn, (DMK), *s.* Short deck in the bows of a boat, underneath which there is a cabin. *West coast of Ross-shire.*

deò, *s.f.* Breath. 2 Air, see D, p.329. *s.m.* in *Badenoch.*

deocail, (MS), *v.a.* Lick up, suck.

deoch, *s.f.* Drink. 3 (DU) State of intoxication (daorach) 'Tha 'n deoch air', *he is intoxicated.*

deoch-bhleith, *s.f.* See friochd, *s.m.* on page 456 of the Dictionary where Dwelly describes the drinks given to a guest in a house in Gaeldom to take when he is awakened. In the Appendix he gives a slightly modified description, based upon information from the Rev. Dr. Campbell of Broadford, Skye, which is as follows.

"A guest in a house in the Highlands might certainly have an appetite for breakfast. To a guest whom he is delighted to honour, the man of the house (fear-an-taighe) went with the *slapag* and wakened him; gave him the *gloc-nide* (nest gulp) and after he gave the *deoch air uilinn* (Drink on elbow), that is to say the guest would rise up in bed. After he got up and before he put on his clothes, he got the *deoch chas-ruisgte* (Barefoot drink). Before breakfast it was the duty of all to take another dram, the *clach-bhleith* (Sharpening or whet-stone). No wonder an increased tax on whisky is resented!

One presumes that *an sgaile-nide, am friochd uilinn* and *an deoch bhleith* correspond, respectively, with *an gloc nide, deoch air uilinn* and *a' chlach-bhleith.*

The statement that "the man of the house (fear-an-taighe) went with a *slapag* and wakened him", is rather curious as Dwelly gives *slapag, s.f.* as meaning slut, drab, slattern. Was this the Gaelic equivalent of the English word 'skivvy'?

deoch-chas-ruisgte, *s.f.* The barefoot drink described above.

deoch-chuimhneachain, (MS), *s.f.* Toast honoured at old Highland funerals to the memory of the deceased or other departed friends, usually drunk in silence.

deoch-gheal (DU) *s.f.* Drink for a cow made of oatmeal and warm water.

deonbhaidh, (MS), *s.f.* Inclination, bias.

detheodha, *s.m.* 2 (MS) Hemlock.

detiach † *s.* Accented on *iach.* Weasand, [an archaic name for the windpipe, oesophagus and throat generally.]

deudach, *s.m.* The teeth, see D, p.330

s.f. in *Badenoch.*

deuragach, *s.m.* Corn nettle. *Beauly.*

deuraich, *v.a.* Water.

dha, dha'n, dha'm, colloquial forms of do (to), do'n, do'm.

dheanadair, (G), *s.m.* A children's game, King or Willie Wawnie. See deantair above.

diabholaidh, *a.* See diabhlaidh, *a.* Devilish, diabolical.

Dia-ciadain, *s.m.* See Di-ciadaoin.

dialtag, (G), *s.f.* Sweet meadow-grass *Anthroxanthum odoratum.*

diamhaireach, (MS), *a.* Hermetical.

dian-leantail, (MS), *s.* Assiduity.

dian-thagairt, (MS), *s.* Animosity.

dianach, *s.m.* Steep place.

diasadach, *a.* See diasach, *a.* Of or belonging to ears of corn. 2 Luxuriant. 3 Bladed, as of corn.

diasagach, *a.* See diasadach above.

diasaich, *v.a.* 2 Ear.

diasg, (MS), *v.a.* Drain.

diasganaich, *v.a.* Thrum or strum.

diasradh, *s.m.* 2 The thing gleaned.

di-beatha, *s.* Welcome. Droch di-beatha, *poor welcome, equal to no welcome at all.*

dìbleachadh, *s.m.* Debilitation, debility.

dìblidheachd, *s.f.* Debilitation, debility.

dìblidhich, (MS), *v.a.* Debilitate.

Di-daoirn, *s.m.* Arran, *Islay* & *Jura* for Di-ardaoin.

didean, *s.f.* 5 (MS) Barracks.

di-dhraoidhich, *v.a.* De-charm.

Di-dòmhnaich, *s.f.* Sunday. 'Chaill iad sgeul air Di-dòmhnaich'; a way of saying, *they lost count of the days of the week.*

dil, (DC), *s.m.* Base, bottom. 'Treabh an fhiair gu dil', *plough the lea to its gravel.*

dilaoiris, (DMK), *s.* Poor, needful, helpless person, object of charity. May be equated with diol-dèirce, *s.m.* Beggar 2. Object of charity. *Caithness.*

dìleabaich, (MS), *v.a.* Bequeathe.

dileachd, (DU), *s.* Fluency of delivery "S ann ort tha'n dileachd', *how fluent you are!*

dìleagadh, *s.m.* Digesting.

dileidh, (MS), *v.a.* Concoct.

dìleigh, *v.a.* Digest.

dìlseachd, *s.f.* 9 (MS) Adherence.

di-moin, (DU), *a.* Not lasting, not durable. Opposite of buan.

dìobartan, (DU), *s.m.* Weak innocent person. 2 Infant.

dìobhail, *s.m.* 11 Decrement, decrease. 12 (MS) Invasion.

dìobhalachadh, (MS), *s.m.* Impairment.

dìobhalaich, *v.a.* 2 Denude. 3 Defalcate, embezzle.

diochnaich, *v.a.* See di-chuimhnich, *v.a.* Forget. 2 Neglect.

diocladh, (DC), *s.m.* 3 Assuaging, subsiding, especially of wind, flood. 'Tha diocladh air a' ghaoith', *the wind is subsiding.*

dioclaonadh, *s.m.* Inflection.

dioclaonaich, (MS), *v.a.* Inflect.

dioclaoineadh, (MS), *s.m.* Declension.

diogad, (DC), *s.m.* People. 2 Gathering of people. Diogad Dòmhnaich, *a congregation*; d. taighe, *household*; d. àth, *the tally of people necessary to work a kiln* et cetera.

dìoghaltach, (MS), *a.* Bloody.

dìoghlumachadh, *s.m.* See dìoghlumadh s.m. 'Gleaning' below.

dìoghlumadh, *s.m.* Gleaning.

diolan, *int.* A' dhiolan sinne! An exclamation. *Badenoch.*

diolanas, (MS), *s.m.* Uncleanness.

dioll, *s.m.* Diligence. *Arran.*

diolt, *a.* (DMK) Dìoltaidh Devilish. Diolt maith, *devilish good*; dìoltaidh dona, devilish bad. *Caithness* and *Sutherland.*

diombach, (MS), *s.m.* Anger.

diombuidheach, *s.m.* Disdain, despite.

dìomhaineachd, (MS), *s.f.* Vanity.

dìon, *s.m.* 6 (MS) Mound.

dìonadach, *a.* 2 Defensive.

dìon-cluaise, *s*, *Ear-covert* of a bird. Soft feathers covering the external organ of hearing. See under eun, D, p.398, No. 1.

diongmhailteach, (MS), *v.a.* Perfect.

diongmhalt, (DMK), *a.* Stubborn, self-willed. *Caithness.*

diongmhaltaich, (MS), *v.a.* Strengthen.

dìon-sgèith beag, *s.m.* Lesser wing coverts. See No. 4, D, p.398.

dìoraid, (DMK), *s.f.* Large worm that burrows in sound wood. *West coast of Ross.*

diosgain, *s.f.* See deasgainn, *s.f.* Rennet. 2 Yeast. 3 Lees, dregs, refuse.

dìosgan, *s.m.* 5 (DC) Creaking noise as of a ship labouring in a heavy sea. 6 (G) Rattling.

diost (diosd?), (MS), *v.a.* Verberate.

diostadh, (MS), *s.m.* Verberation.

dìpin, (DC), *s.* Properly the allotted length of a net made, as a day's work, by hand, at the time when nets were home-made. It was customary to meet in a house, in turn, so as to finish the train of nets required by each fisherman, as quickly as possible, the day's work being called 'dìpin'.

dìreachd, (MS), *s.f.* Straightness.

dìreanntail, (MS), *a.* Ascendable.

disbheagadh, (MS), *s.m.* Alloy.

dìseart, -eirt, *s.m.* Deserted place. Clachan-an-dìseirt, *the graveyard of the deserted place*, near Dalmally.

dìth-aireach, (MS), *a.* Absent.

dith-bheachdadh, (MS), *s.m.* Abstraction.

dith-bhinnich, (MS), *v.a.* Inlaw.

dith-chiallach, (MS), *a.* Absonant.

dith-dhearcadh, (MS), *a.* Absent.

dìtheachd, (MS), *s.f.* Annihilation.

dìtheadh, *s.m.* 5 Cramming, filling by force. *Sàr-Obair.*

dìtheairt, *s.m.* See dìobhairt, *s.m.* Vomiting, act of vomiting.

dìthean, *s.m.* 6 Tares.

dìtheanach, *a.* 3 Flowery.

dìtheannaich, (MS), *v.a.* Flower.

di-theodha, (CR), *s.* Henbane. *Skye.*

dith-faithriche, (MS), *s.* Apathy.

dith-ghnàthaich, (MS), *v.a.* Antiquate.

dìthich, *v.a.* 4 (MS) Spend. 5 (MS) Bereave. 6 (MS) Absorb.

dìthicheadh, *s.m.* See dìtheachadh, *s.m.* Abolition. 2 Destruction, destroying. 3 Causing to cease. 4 Failing.

dith-làthraich, (MS), *v.a.* Absent.

dith-mhothaiche, (MS), s.m. s.f. also ? Absence.

dith-riaghailt, (MS), *s.* Asymmetry.

dìù, *s.m.* 4 (DU) Sense of shame, modesty, worth. 'Duine gun dìù', *a worthless man.*

diùbhlach, (MS), *s.m.* Cock.

diùc, (DMK), *s.f. pl.* diùcach, Duck. *Caithness.*

diùcach, *s.m.* Duck. *Caithness.*

diù-chall. 'O'n chuir Finne 'n diù-chall mo shùgradh is mo bheusan.', *since the fair one has flouted my suit and my honour.* G. Calder (editor), *Gaelic Songs by William Ross,* Edinburgh, 1937, p.164.

diuchd, *int.* Come to me! Approach me!

diùdhlach, s.m. See diùlannach, *s.m.* Hero. D, p.342.

diuguidh!, *int.* Call to hens. *Badenoch.*

diùghachd, (MS), s.f. Inconsiderableness

diùghlach, *s.m.* See diùlannach.

diùlannach, *s.m.* 6 (DC) Champion. 'Diùlannach an dà eilein', *champion of the two Uists. Uist.*

diùltachas, (MS), *s.m.* Unobsequiousness.

diùnlach, *s.m.* See diunlaoch and diùlannach, s.m. Hero.

diùras, (DC), *s.f.* Confidence, secrets. 'B'fheàrr 'bhi breatas ri Seònaid, 's a bhi faotainn a diùras gun fhios', *better to be dallying with Janet and to be receiving her secrets unawares. Lochcarron.*

diurrasanaich (dearrasan), (G), *s.f.* Whispering.

dleasail, *a.* Governable.

dligheachas, *s.m.* 4 (MS) Appurtenance.

dlògh, *s.f.* See dlòth, *s.f.* below.

dlòth, *s.f.* 3 Handful of corn, *et cetera,* cut by one stroke of the scythe. 4 (*gen* dlòtha, *pl.* dlòthan) Handful of half-thrashed corn.

dloghainn, oblique case of dlogh.

dliùth, *v.a.* See dlùth, *v.a.* House corn.

dliùtheachd, *s.f.* 4 (MS) Strictness.

dlùthaichte, (MS), *a.* Brief.

dlùth-leantalach, (MS), *a.* Adjunct.

dobhran, *s.m.* 4 Wet place.

dobht, (DMK), *s.m.* Stupid man. 2 Partially demented man. *Sutherland.*

dòcha, *comp.* of dogh. More or most likely or probable. 'Tha cho dòcha', *it is as likely. Arran.*

dochair, *s.f.* 8 Aggrievance.

dochairich, (MS), *v.a.* Damage.

dochartas, *s.m.* 2 Agony.

do-cheannsaidheachd, (MS), s.f. Madness.

do-chlaiste, (MS), *a.* Inaudible.

do-chreidmhaidheachd, (MS), *s.f.* Incredibility.

dod, *s.m.* 2 Affront.

dòduman, *s.m.* Small four-sided spinning top. 2 Teetotum. JGC. S. 94 & 262.

do-fhreagrachail, (MS), *a.* Irrefragible.

do-fhuasgailte, (MS), *a.* Irresoluble.

do-fhuasgailteachd, *s.f.* Irresolubleness.

dogan, *s.m.* 2 (DMK) Short piece or cut of any cylindrical object. *West coast of Ross-shire.*

doichleach, (MS), *a.* See doicheallach. *a.* Churlish, inhospitable.

doichleach, (MS), *s.m.* Churl.

doich'neadh (dochainn) 'Nach d. am feur', *that would not injure the grass.* R. 14.

doideagan, *s. pl.* Falling snow flakes. JGC. W. 51.

dòigh, *s.f.* 10 Mood of a verb.

dòighealachd, (MS), *s.f.* Aptitude.

doilghein, (MS), s. Grief.

doilgheasaich, *v.a.* Curry 2 (MS) Aggrieve.

doilleir, *a.* 5 (MS) Blear-eyed.

dòimeach, *adv.* Sadly. R. 56.

doinid, *s.f.* Extreme cold, hoar frost, clemency. *Sàr-Obair.*

doinidh, *a.* Loathsome, contemptible, hateful. *Sàr-Obair.*

doinnead, *s.f.* See doinne, *s.f.* Brown colour, brownness.

doirbheachd, *s.f.* 9 (MS) Abstruseness.

doirbhidh, *a.* Bad, dreadful. *Arran.* Nach doirbhidh sin, *isn't that bad now.*

doire, (DMK), pl an, *s.m.* Corn, hardness of the skin. *West coast of Ross-shire.*

doirleanta, *a.* See dairleanta, a. Strong, healthy. *Arran.*

doitheadach, (MS), *a.* Cumbersome, cumbrous. 2 Perverse.

doitheadachd, (MS), *s.f.* Vexatiousness.

doitheadaich, (MS), *v.a.* Hatter, harass. 2 Vex.

doitheadas, (MS), *s.m.* Regret. 2 Heartburning. 3 Vexation.

dol, *s. ind.* Going, travelling, proceeding

1 Bha iad a' dol bàs le acras, *they were dying with hunger.*

2 Chaidh m'astar am maillead, *my pace became slower* (Idiom) Ross 71.

3 Chaidh mi m' iomrall, *I went astray. Duanaire* 12.

4 Chaidh mo shiubhal an lùgh'd, *my progress became slower.* Ross 71.

5 Chaidh slabhraidh òir a chur ma 'muineal, *a golden chain was placed on her neck.* W & S II 30.

6 Chaidh a toirt a staigh, *she was taken in.* W & S, p.30.

7 Dh'fheuch am faiceadh iad ciamar a rachadh dha, *to try if they would see how it would go with him.* W & S II 22.

8 Na chaidh 'dhìth oirnn do na daoine, *those of the men whom we lost.* W & S II 6.

9 Ma theid agad air a cheann a chur dheth, *if you succeed in beheading him.* W & S II 240.

10 Tha mi 'faicinn gu'n deachaidh agad air na h-ealachan a ghleidheadh, *I see you managed to keep the swans.* W & S II. 16.

dolaidh, *s.f.* 4 Aggrievance.

dolaidheach, (MS), *a.* Noxious.

doldach, s.m. See dorlach, *s.m.* 2 Number, quantity. *Strontian.*

do-licheinn, *a.* Stormy. 'Bheireadh iad a nìos ri àm do-licheinn', *that would pull them through in the stormy time.* [Angus MacLeod has dòilichean as being derived from dòlach, grievous. *Beinn Dorain*].

dol-ma-seach, (DMK), s. One who is in a state of inebriation beating the road from side to side. 2 Staggering *West coast of Ross-shire.*

do-lorgachail, (MS), *a.* Inscrutable.

domblasach, *a.* 6 (MS) Bilious.

domghlas, *s.m.* See domblas, *s.m.* Choler, gall, angèr. *Arran.*

domhainteachd, (MS), *s.f.* Abstruseness.

dòmhlaich, *v.a.* 5 Overstock. 6 Press, as a multitude.

dòmhrainnich, (MS), *v.a.* Cruciate.

dòmhruinneach, (MS), *a.* Bitter.

dòncaidh, *a.* See dongaidh, *a.* Moist, humid.

donn, An, *s.* Bile *Lochalsh* and elsewhere.

donnachadh-aotrom, *s.m.* The lungs of a sheep, "lights". *Gairloch.*

doracas, *s.m.* The Woodpecker.

dòrag, An, *s.* Expresses pity and some degree of disapprobation. *Arran.*

dòran, An, s. See an dòrag, *Arran*, above.

do-rannsalachd, *s.f.* Unsearchableness.

dorchadas, (MS), *s.m.* Blind, but in Badenoch it is *s.f.*

dornan, *s.m.* 10 The part of a tether between the swivel and the animal.

dorran, An, *s.m.* 4 Grumbling.

dòruinnich, *v.a.* Pinch.

dorus, *s.m.* 5 Tail-board of a cart.

dos, *s.m.* 17 Muzzle. Dos na gunna, muzzle of the gun. *West coast of Ross-shire.*

dos-fhuaimneach, (MS), *a.* Bass.

dosgach, *s.* Cattle disease. *Maclagan's Evil Eye,* 15.

dosgainn, *s.f.* 7 Adversity.

dota, *s.m.* Stupid fellow. *Sutherland.*

dotshag, *s.f.* Fat female. *Arran.*

drabalaich, (MS), *v.a.* Bespatter.

drabhag, *s.f.* 5 Faeces.

drabhas, *s.m.* 6 Faeces.

draghaich, (MS), *v.a.* Annoy.

draige, *gen. sing.* of draig, *s.f.* See dreige, *gen. sing.* of dreag, *s.f.* meteor. See D, p.357.

draighlichd, *s.f.* See draighilc, *s.f.* Trollop.

drammach, (DMK), *s.m.* A mixture of oatmeal and sea water. Prince Charles partook of this savoury dish one night when going to Benbecula and professed to relish it!

draodh, see drùidh, *v.a.* & *n* and *s.m.* Penetrate to the skin and druidh, *s.m.* Magician. See D, p.363.

draodhadair, *s.m.* See druidh, s.m. Druid, magician.

drann, *s.m.* See drannadh, *s.m.* Grinning.

dranndanach, (MS), *a.* 7 Cursed. 8 Cynical.

dranndanaich, *v.n.* 2 (MS) Grumble.

draoidhich, (MS), *v.a.* Spell.

dreachaich, (MS), *v.a.* Colour.

dreachmhor, *a.* 2 (MS) Colourable.

dreallsach, *s.m.* 3 (G) Tail of a meteor.

dreuchd, (MS), *s.* Art.

dreunasail, *s.m.* See dreamachadh, *s.m.* Grinning, snarling.

drilleagach, (DMK), *a.* Variability of temper and mood. *Lochbroom.*

driobaidich, (MS), *v.n.* Drip.

driogadh, (DU), *s.m.* Weak, ineffectual pulling or hauling, as at a rope.

dris, *s.f.* 2 (MS) Brake.

driseach, *a.* 4 (MS) Braky.

dritheanaich, *s. pl.* Spasms. *Arran.* 2 Fits. Chaidh e 's na dritheanaich ghàireachdaigh, *he went into fits of laughter. Arran.*

driuchaidean, (MS), *s.m.* Exorcism.

driuchdachadh, (MS), *s.m.* Rovation.

driùchdaich, (MS), *v.a.* Bedew.

drochard, (DU), *s.m.* Wicked person. 2 Mischief-loving person.

droch-chàradh, *s.m.* (or chàramh) Bad usage. 'Bhiodh an Diùc air droch-chàradh', *the Duke would be badly used.*

droch-choinneamh. An imprecation. Droch-choinneamh ort! *Bad luck to you.* Literally, bad meeting.

drog, *s.m.* Sea swell at its impact on a rock. *Argyll.*

dro'id, *s.f. North Inverness & Sutherland* for drochaid, *s.f.* a bridge.

droigheann, *s.m.* 3 Lumber. 4 Entanglement.

droighionnach, *s.m.* See droighneach, *s.m.* Thorns.

drois, *int. Arran* for truis! word by which dogs are silenced or driven away. Also said to a person in contempt. Drois a-mach, *get out!*

droiteachan, (DU), *s.m.* Loop made on clothes with thread to serve as an "eye" to receive a metal hook.

droman, (DMK), *s.m.* Peg for fastening heather thatch to the ridge of a roof. *West coast of Ross-shire.*

dromanach, *s.f.* See dromach, *s.f.* Back band of a horse.

dromlach suith, (CR), *s.m.* Gall. *Arran.*

drothaid, *s.f. Wester Ross* for drochaid, *s.f.* A bridge.

druaib, (MS), *s.* Residence.

druaip, *s.* 5 (MS) Mire.

druaipealachd, (MS), *s.f.* Muddiness. 2 Turbidity.

druideadh, *s.m.* 5 (MS) Barrier. 6 (MS) Hold.

druidseachd, (MS), *s.f.* Drudgery.

druim, (DMK), *s.* Back-rope of a net. 'Thàinig an lìon bho'n druim', *the net came from the back rope. West coast of Ross-shire.*

druim an t-saoghail, *s.* The Zenith.

druim an taighe, *s.* Ridge of a house.

druim beag, *s.* Short part of rope which steadies the *sròn*, the point of a plough.

druim-fuadan, (DMK), *s.f.* See forradhruim. A slip keel, a false keel A 4 on D, p.73 *Assynt & Ross.*

druim mòr, *s.m.* See D, p.263, No. 13. Long part of rope by which the plough is drawn.

druis, *s.f.* 3 (MS) Ooze.

druise, (AC), *s.f.* Bramble.

druiseach, *a.* 4 (MS) Oozy.

druman, *s.m.* 8 (MS) Wall-wort.

drumanach, *s.f.* 4 (MS) Wall-wort. [Both druman (6) and drumanach (3) are given on D, p.365 as the common elder, bore-tree or bourtree.]

drumlach-sithe, *s.m.* Gall. *Arran.*

drùsag, (DU), *s.f.* Small quantity.

drùthadh, (MS), *s.m.* Maculation.

drùthag, (MS), *s.f.* Sup. 2 Tuck.

dùad, (SMK), *s.m.* Blockhead. 2 Man having a "want". *Caithness and Sutherland.*

duaichneachd, *s.f.* 5 (MS) Gloominess.

duaineil, *a.* 2 Ridiculous, ludicrous, laughable, *Sàr-Obair.* 3 (DMK) Churlish, objectionable, not likeable. 'Cha 'n 'eil e duaineil idir', *he is not* at all a bad fellow. *Caithness & Sutherland.*

duainidheachd, *s.f.* Ugliness.

duairceas, *s.m.* 7 (MS), Obstinacy, 8 (MS) Boorishness.

duaiseachadh, *s.m.* Gratification. 2 Guerdon.

duaisich, *v.a.* Gratify.

duaithnidh, *a.* See duaichnidh, *a.* Deformed. See D, p.366.

dual, *s.m.* 6 Tuft of flax or wool on a

distaff.

dualart, *s.m.* Howl of a dog.

duba, (CR), *s.m.* Pool in a river. *Arran.*

dubaidh, *s.* Pool. *Arran.*

dùbailteachd, *s.f.* 3 (MS) Ambidexterity.

dubhain, *s.* Kidney.

dubhairich, (MS), *v.a.* Smirch.

dubhanach. *a.* 2 (MS) Barbed.

dubhanntachd, (MS), *s.f.* Haze. 2 Fogginess.

dubhar-lus, *s.m.* Water-cress.

dubharach, *a.* 2 (MS) Apocryphal.

dubh-bannach, *a.* Black-banded (of guns).

dubh-chlach, *s.f.* Flint. 2 Cabalistic stone. *Sàr-Obair.*

dubh-chlèith, *s.* Hock-bone of beef.

dubh-chridheach, (MS), *a.* Brokenhearted.

dùbhdan, *s.m.* 5 Beard of dried oats. See dùdan, *s.m.* D, p.370.

dubh-fhad, (DMK), *s.* The second peat in depth taken out of a bank or hag. *West coast of Ross-shire.*

dubh-ghamhnach, (DMK), *s.* Cow that is farr for two consecutive years. *West coast of Ross-shire.*

dùbhlanaich, (MS), *v.a.* Brave.

dùbhlanaiche, *s.m.* Defier.

dubhrach, *s.m.* Water-cress.

dùbhrachas, (MS), *s.m.* Cloudiness.

dùbhradan, (MS), *s.m.* Dùbhradan dubh-dallan àtha, the game of 'blind man's buff' or *folach-fead.*

dubh-sheileach, *s.* Sallow or goat willow. *Colonsay.*

dùcan dubh-threabha, *s.m.* Mole-hill. *Perthshire.*

dùchas, s.m. Ivy. *Colonsay.*

dùdaidh, *s.f.* Resembling in sound that of a horn. 2 Deep intonation. *Sàr-Obair.*

duchrach, (DU), *a.* Badly-off as regards nourishing food. Applied to a family that has no milk and hence no butter or cheese, a good supply of which makes a house rich.

dùdan, *s.m.* 4 (MS) Coom.

dudar C.G.T. xiv 106.

dùgan C.G.T. xiv 104.

duibh-lèabag, *s.f.* Uist for lèabag-mhòr, *s.f.* Plaice (fish).

dùibhreachd, (MS), *s.f.* Cloudiness.

duileachd, *s.f.* 3 Affliction, sorrow. *Sàr-Obair.*

dùilean, *s.f.* See dùileag *s.f.* Poor little girl, term of affection.

dùilean, An, (CR), pl. na dùileachan, s.m. Poor thing. *Arran.*

duil-fhear, *s.m.* Sulky fellow. *Sutherland.*

dùilidh, *s.m.* Creature. R. 64.

duille-chlaiseach, (G), *s.m.* Furrowed sword.

duilleag, *s.f.* 6 (CR) Blade of a scythe. 7 Breast-bone (prefixed by the article *An*) 8 Diaphragm.

duilleagaich, *v.a.* Infoliate.

duilleag-bhàite, *s.f.* 2 Pondweed. *Colonsay.*

dùin, *v.a.* 5 (MS) Lower the portcullis.

duinean-talmhaidh, *s.m.* Little cleft in a rock. *Arran.*

duinein, *s.m.* See duinean, *s.m.* Manikin.

dùinteachd, *s.f.* 2 Strangeness.

duirbhidh, *a.* See doirbhidh, *a.* above. Bad, dreadful in *Arran* generally, but in *Kilbrandon, Arran, duribhidh* in its place.

duirceall, *s.m.* 4 Half-worn knife or dirk. *Sàr-Obair.*

duitheaman, *s.m.* Laminaria digitata, type of seaweed. *Tiree.*

dul, (MS), *s.m.* Hanger.

dula, *s.* 2 Staple.

dula-cliabh, *s.* See dubh-chlèith, *s.* Hock-bone of beef, above.

dunach, *s.m.* Misfortune.

dùnaidh, *s.m.* 4 (MS) Deluge.

dunaigh, *s.f.* See dunaidh, *s.f.* Woe, disaster; misfortune.

dunaoileachd, *s.* See duinealachd, *s.f.* and duinealas, *s.m.* Manliness. D, p.372.

dùnan-fhamh, *s.* Mole-hill.

dùn-faimh, *s.* Mole-hill.

dùn-feòir, (DMK), *s.* Conical stack of hay. *Caithness.*

dùngachd, (MS), *s.f.* Poachiness.

dùngaidh, (MS), *a.* Damp, dank. 2 Fusty. 3 Poachy.

dùn-mùill, (DMK), *s.m.* Heap of undressed corn in a barn.

duntar, (MS), *s.m.* Mome.

dur, dur, *int.* Repeated several times as

a call to pigs. *Islay.*

durabhag, (G), *s.f.* Pig. *Islay.*

durabhaidh, (AH), *a.* Morose, sullen, sulky, ill-tempered, cantankerous, frumpish.

durach, (DMK), *s.* Craving for tobacco. 'Tha'n durach orm', *I'm craving for tobacco. West coast of Ross.*

duradh, Dwelly's note says simply – 'see durradh'; whether this refers to durradh! durradh!, *int.* A call to pigs in Argyll; or to durradh, *s.m.* see durraidh, *s.f.* Provincial for sow, pork is not clear.

dùr-cheannach, (MS), *a.* Blockish.

durradha, (MS), *a.* Currish. 2 Dogged.

durradhantachd, (MS), *s.f.* Pervicacity. 2 Gruffness.

duslann, *s.f.* 5 (MS) Arbour.

dusluing, *s.f.* See duslainn, *s.f.* Gloomy solitary place.

dusluinn, *s.f.* See duslainn, *s.f.* Gloomy solitary place.

duthan, (CR), *s.m. pl.*, duthain. Kidney. *Arran.*

E

eabaraich, (MS), *v.a.* Begrime.

each, *s.m.* Parts of a horse. Add to 8. Seirein, *s.* Pastern.

each, *s.m.* Standard or bearer of the driving-wheel of a spinning-wheel. 2 Frame bearing flyers of the spinning-wheel.

each-uisge, *s.m.* 2 (MS) Hippopotamus.

eadar, *prep.* 'Eadar dhà sgeul is eadar dhà bheul a' chlobha', *by the way and between ourselves.*

eadar-dhà-bhìth, *s.* Space between the outer door and the kitchen-door. See D, p.923.

eadar-dhà-linn, (DU), *adv.* for eadar-dhà-lionn, *adv.* Between sinking and swimming, floundering.

eadar-dhà-thràth, *s.m. Poolewe* and elsewhere for *an interval of time.*

eadarrach, *a.* 2 (MS) Indifferent. 3 (MS) Reciprocal.

eadhaich, (MS), *v.a.* Scrape.

eadraigich, (MS), *v.a.* Interpose.

eaga, *adv.* See theagamh, *adv.* Perhaps.

eagar, *adv.* See D, p.380. Ceann eagair, *s. pl.*, chief instructions. R. 50.

eaghadair, *s.m.* File maker. 2 Filer.

eaglachd, (MS), *s.f.* Cowardliness.

eaglaisich, (MS), *s. pl.* Priesthood.

eagnaich, (MS), *v.a.* Ascertain.

eagnaidh, *a.* 5 (MS) Curious.

eagnaidheachd, *s.f.* 5 (MS) Curiosity. 6 (MS) Adequateness.

eàl, (CR), *a.* Keen, zealous. *Arran.* 'Nach e tha eàl', *how earnest he is!*

eala, *s.* Ancient tombstone. *Celtic Review*, iv. 289.

eala-bhì, *s.f.* Perforated St. John's wort. Probably a corrupt spelling of eala-bhuidhe, *s.f. Hypericum perforatum.*

ealachag, (MS), *s.f.* Tache.

ealaidh, *s.f.* 6 Instrument.

ealainich, (MS), *v.a.* Address.

ealantachd, (MS), *s.f.* Address. 2 Genius.

ealbh, *s.* First ploughing. *Cameron's Aberfeldy Guide.*

ealpag, (DC). *s.f.* Knob or catch on iron, wood *et cetera Perthshire.*

eanadas, *s.m.* See aineadas, *s.m.* Vexation.

eang, *s.f.* 13 (MS) Blemish.

eapag, *s.f.* Trifling superstitious observance. JGC. S 229.

earalas, *s.m.* 6 (MS) Case.

earasaideach, *a.* Gowned.

earbadaraidh, (MS), *s.m.* Counsellor, confidant.

earnaidh, (DU), *s.f.* Romping, playing. Ag earnaidh, *playing.*

eàrr, *s.m.* 12 (MS) Botch.

earrach, *s.m.* Keel. *An Iorram Dharaich.*

earrachallach, (MS), *a.* Successless, unsuccessful.

earraid-mhial, (DMK), *s.f.* Small-toothed comb, louse-trap. *Skye.* Said to be inscribed "Death" on the one side and "No mercy" on the other.

earraideachd, *s.f.* Business of a police officer or messenger at arms.

earrail, *s.f.* Hortation, giving advice, behest.

earrlaid, (MS), *s.f.* Reliance.

earr-leigeadh, (MS), *s.m.* Need.

eascar, (DC), *s.f.* Storm, tempest of wind and rain. *Argyll.*

eas-creideamh, (MS), *s.m.* Incredulity, atheism.

eas-creidmheach, (MS), *s.m.* Atheist.

eas-creidmheach, (MS), *a.* Profane.

eas-corpachd, (MS), *s.f.* Incorporality.

èasgaidh, *a.* 7 (MS) Dapper.

easgann, *s.* See †easga, *s.f.* An obsolete word for the moon, with which it equates.

eas-òrdonaich, (MS), *v.a.* Confuse.

easpach, (MS), *s.m.* Hasp.

eathar màsach, (DMK), *s.m.* Boat with a square stern. *West coast of Ross.*

eibhreaireach, *s.m.* The soul of an unburied body, like Palinurus. In *Grimsay, North Uist,* is 'leab' an eibhreaireich', the grave of the (up to that time) unburied one, where was buried the body of an unknown person cast up on the shore, over more than fifty years previously. (DC).

eide, *s.m.* See oide, *s.m.* Foster father.

eidhrich, (MS), *v.a.* Conglaciate.

èididh, (DU), *a.* In want, need and miserable in consequence.

èifeachdas, *s.m.* Validity.

èigeannas, *s.m.* See èigeantas, *s.m.* Necessity.

eigear, (MS), *s.m.* Curmudgeon.

eigheanach, (MS), *a.* Glacially, icy.

eigheanach-shiubhail, (G), *s.* Glacier.

èighneach, (MS), *a.* Involuntary.

eighreachail, *a.* Chilled.

eighreachd, *s.f.* Glaciation. 2 Frostiness.

eighrich, *v.a.* Frostbite, freeze.

eighrichte, *past. pt.* Frostbitten.

èiginneachd, (MS), *s.f.* Compulsion.

eilchoirich, (MS), *v.a.* Alienate.

eileach, *s.m.* 6 Mill-race. 7 Embankment. 8 (G) Stone fort or hermit's cell.

eileachd, (MS), *s.f.* Arraignment. See †eileachadh, s.m. Accusing, accusation.

eileadrum, *s.m.* See eilitriom, *s.m.* A plank or board on which a dead body is placed. 2 Hearse.

eileanaidh, *s.m.* Diminutive of eilean, *s.m.* Little island. *Ross* and *Cromarty.*

eilidheadh, *s.m.* Fallow ground.

eilich, (MS), *v.a.* 2 Alienate.

eilidheachd, *s.f.* Information. 2 Plea. 3

See eileachd above.

eilthirich, (MS), *v.a.* Alienate.

eirblich, (MS), *v.a.* Maim.

eireannach, *a. Arran* for eidheannach, *a.* Of, or belonging to ivy.

eiribinn.? meaning = †airmid, an obsolete word for honour. *Celtic Review, v.* 123.

eiribleach, (MS), *s.m.* strain.

eiridneach, *a.* 2 Medicinal, having the power of healing. *Sàr-Obair.* 3 Restorative (MMcL).

èirigh, *s.f.* 4 (MS) Ledge.

eirionnach, (DMK), *s.m.* Churn. *West coast of Ross-shire.*

eis, *s.* Venison soup.

eisealachd, (MS), *s.f.* Requisiteness.

eiseanach, (DC), *s.m.* High wave. In a storm, now and then, a higher wave than others comes. *Mc. Mh.* A calls such a wave "cùlanach."

eisgeil, (MS), *a.* 3 Cynical.

eisimealach, *a.* 5 (MS) Mealy-mouthed.

eisp, *s.m.* See ìosp, *s.m.* Clasp for a padlock on a door.

eistreach, *s.m.* Rough stormy ebb, seabeach. *Sàr-Obair.*

eiteach, (DC), *s.m.* Stumps of burnt heather. Eiteanach, (DC), s.m. also.

eiteal, (DC), *s.m.* Gruel.

eòlanach, (MS), *s.m.* Adept.

eòlanachd, (MS), *s.f.* Habitude.

eòlan mòr, *s.m.* Cod-liver oil.

eòlas-beum-sùla, (DMK), *s.m.* The knowledge or faculty by which an occult practitioner can remove a mote from the eye of a patient, by chanting an incantation. It is not necessary that the practitioner should see the patient. The distance between the two is also immaterial.

eòlas-casg-fola, (DMK), *s.m.* The knowledge or faculty of stopping haemorrhage from any part of the body by the occult practitioner plucking the herb of Crowfoot (Ranunculus) in the name of the three persons of the Trinity, while his attention is concentrated on the affected part of the patient, and earnestly wishing it to be cured. It is not necessary that the former should see the latter.

eòlas-sguchaidh, (DMK), *s.m.* Knowledge or faculty of curing a sprain by tying on the affected part a woollen thread of a certain colour, over which the occult practitioner chanted an incantation. It is not necessary that the latter should see the patient. Indeed the greater the distance between them, the more easily is the cure effected.

eornach, (DC), *s.m.* Ruins, debris.

eubalta, (close *e*), (CR), *a.* Grand. *North end of Arran.* 2 Strong, capable. *Shiskine. Arran.*

eufacas, *s.f.* See èifeachd, *s.f.* Effect, consequence, efficacy.

eug-comhairleachas, *s.m.* Inflexibility.

eugnais, s. Want. *Arran.* As eugnais, for as eugmhais, without, deprived of.

eunach (spelling ?), *pr. pt.* Wearying. 'Chan 'eil thu ag eunach', *you are not wearying. Perthshire.*

eun-buidhe-'n-t-sneachda, (AH), *s.m.* Snow-bunting.

eun-chuing, (MS), *s.f.* Bird-cage.

eusbach, (CR), *s.m.* Regrettable pity. 'B'e eusbach gu'n', *it is a pity that*; b'eusbach sin, *that was unfortunate.*

F

fabharaich, (MS), *v.a.* Agrace.

fachach, *s.m.* 5 Little, insignificant man. *Sàr-Obair.*

fa chomhair, *adv.* 3 Level.

fàd, *s.m.* (*pl.* fòid) 4 Divot used in thatching.

fadhar, *s.m.* See faobhar, *s.m.* Edge.

fadhar, (MS), *s.m.* Collision.

fadhlainn, (DC), *s.f.* 2 Sandy point.

fàgail, *s.f. ind.* 5 Legacy. ''S gach buaidh a b' àillidh bh' air Diàna gu lèir mar fhàgail tha aig Mòir', *and all the most beautiful attributes which Diana had my Marion possesses completely as they are.* William Ross, 28.

fàgalas, (MS), -ais, *s.m.* After-wit.

faghaid, *s.f.* 7 (MS) Cry.

faghairt, *v. Perthshire* for farraid, *v.a.* Ask.

faghairtich, (MS), *v.n.* Anneal.

faiceannta, (MS), *a.* Showy.

faiceant, *a.* Gusty. Bu cholgail faiceant' an stoirm feachdaidh, *fierce and gusty was the hostile storm. West coast of Ross-shire.*

faichean, *s.m. Argyll* for foichlean, *s.m.* Sprout of corn above the ground.

faicidh, *s.* An interesting survival in the tale of "Gaisgeach na sgèithe deirge", of the old 3rd person singular present indicative active, which has become the future tense in modern Gaelic. *Celtic Review* xii, 357.

faicsinneach, (MS), *a.* 7 Aspectable.

faigseach, *a.* Approximate.

faigseannach, *a.* Approximate.

failbhe, No. 32 on D, p.76 should be failbheag, *s.f.* Ring-bolt.

failbheachan, (DU), *s.m.* The plural is failbheachanan. Ear-ring.

failcion, (CR), *s.m.* Pot-lid. 2 Kneecap. *Arran.* Sgullan no failcion a' ghlùin, *Knee-pan.* For failcean, *s.m.* See D, p.404.

fàileadair, (MS), *s.m.* Perfumer.

fàileanach, *a.* Fragrant.

faileas, (DMK), *s.m.* Lightening. 'Tha faileas ann', *it is lightening.*

failleanaich, (MS), *v.n.* Burgeon.

fainn-riochdach, (MS), *a.* Annulary.

faircil, (AC), *s.* Stoup-measure. Faircil agus breacag arain, *a stoup of water and a bannock of bread. Carm. Gadelica.* I.164.

faircioll, (DC), *s.m.* Vessel for drinking out of. *Lewis.*

faireachair, (CR), *s.m.* Mallet. *Arran.*

faireadair, (MS), *s.m.* Sentinel.

faireagan, *s.f.* Diminutive of faireag, *s.f.* Gland. JGC. W. 99.

faireamhanadh, (MS), *s.m.* Vision.

fairich, *v.a. & n.* 6 (DU) Get a bite when fishing. 'An d' fhairich thu?', *have you got a bite?*

fairil, (DC), *s.m.* Tongs for holding hair while it was being dressed, at the time when men used to wear a queue. Lùb fairil, *a temporary knot. Argyll.*

fairleachadh, (CR), In *Arran.* 'Ruith e mar a dh' fhairleachadh e', *he ran at his utmost speed*; ruith mar a dh' fhairleas thu, *run as hard as you can* (fairtlich.)

fàisnich, (MS), *v.a.* Betoken.

faist, *a.* At anchor, moored. *Rob Donn.*

faiteal, *s.* Hearty, cheerful salute. Friendly talk. *Sàr-Obair.*

faitheachd, *s.f.* Divination. Dèan faitheachd, *divine.*

fàitheam, *s.m.* See faitheam, *s.m.* Hem or border of a garment.

faitheamaich, (MS), *v.a.* Tack.

faithir, (MS), *v.a.* Advise.

faithreachadh, *s.m.* See faireachadh *s.m.* Watching, waking. 2 (MS) Affection.

faithrich, *v.a.* Prove.

fàl, (AH), *s.m.* Complexion. 'Tha fàl ruadh air', *he has a red complexion*; tha fàl a màthar oirre, *she has her mother's complexion.*

fàl, (CR), *s.m.* Halo round the sun or moon. *Arran.*

falach a' phaipeir, *s.m.* An indoor Uist game corresponding to "Hunt the thimble." All the players, with the exception of one, went out of the room, while the exception hid the paper. The rest then came in to search while the person who had hidden it called out teth! teth!, if anyone was near it, or fuar! fuar! to anyone far away from it. If anyone found the paper he sat down without saying anything and the game continued until all had silently taken seats or given up the hunt. Then the first to sit down stayed in the room for the next turn. *Uist Games* in *Celtic Review*, No. 16.

falach bheag, (DU), *s.* The game of "Hide and Seek." *Uist.*

falach-cuain, *s.* A seaside phrase for "Hide and Seek", the in-country equivalent being *car-mu-chnoc.* Thug e car-mu-chnoc asda, *and* rinn e car-mu-chnoc orra.

falach-fait, *s.m.* A Uist game much the same as falach-fead, "Hide and Seek." One player is chosen who covers his eyes while the rest go to hide. On a given signal, usually a whistle, he looks for them and when he finds one, that one is out of the game. The game continues until such time as they are all found, when the first one to be discovered takes his turn as searcher. *Uist Games* in *Celtic Review*, No. 16.

falachd, (MS), *s.f.* Animosity.

fàladair, *s.m.* 5 Turfer.

falanach, (AH), *a.* Red complexioned.

fallus-na-clòimhe, *s.* Natural oil of wool.

falmadair, *s.m.* 4 Whip-staff.

falruig, *s.f.* An fhalruig is the transverse beam or beams to which the double or single stakes are fixed, for tying cattle, in the older constructed byres. This term was obtained from an old and highly intelligent farmer who was a school-master in his younger days and whose native place was near the east end of *Loch Tay.* In the narrow thatched buildings, the space between the rafters or *cabair* and the top of the wall, was often made up with divots. So possibly the term arose from the beam extending from wall to wall, across the building.

faltraich, *v.a. Badenoch & Strathspey* for fairtlich, *v.a.* Overcome.

famh-mhugach, *s.* Mole.

famhsgul, *s.m.* Hurry, confusion. *Argyll.*

famh-shlighe, *s.* Mole-track.

famh-threabhadh, *s.m.* Mole-track.

fanarach, *a.* Desirous of. 'Bu dùthchas o do sheanair dhuit bhi fanarach air gruagaich', *you inherited from your grandfather to be desirous of a maiden.*

fancaich, (MS), *v.a.* Restrain.

fannachd, (MS), *s.f.* Deadness.

fann-choslaich, *v.a.* Adumbrate.

fann-choslas, *s.m.* Adumbration.

fannleir, *v.a.* Adumbrate.

fannsgal, see famhsgul above.

faoban, (WC), *s.m.* Cake suddenly and imperfectly toasted. 2 Last-baked cake. *Poolewe.*

faobhadach, (MMcL), *s.m.* Carcase.

faocnadh, *s.m.* Trying to skin an animal with a blunt knife. GSI, xiv. iii.

faodhailt, *s.f.* See faghaid, *s.f.* Hunting. D, p.402 and above.

faodhar, *s.m.* Knock.

faodharsach, (MS), *s.m.* Dabbler.

faodharsach, (MS), *a.* Frivolous, futile. 2 Shallow-brained.

faodharsachd, (MS), *s.f.* Futility. 2 Fantasy.

faog, (DC), *s.m.* A lump in cooked food, as in porridge. 2 A knot in thread.

faogach, *a.* Lumpy, pustular, applied to skin.

faogharsanachd, (MS), *s.f.* Nugacity.

faoid, (DC), *s.f.* Leader-drain. 2 Canal.

faoinear, (MS), *s.m.* Trifler, fribbler, dupe, object of scorn.

faoiteag, (DC), *s.f.* Cowrie shell.

faolainn, *s.f.* Stony beach. 'Thrus mi fiasgain air an fhaolainn', *I gathered mussels on the stony beach.*

faol-allaidh, *s.* Wolf, wild dog.

faomadh, *s.m.* *Lewis* for aomadh, *s.m.* Inclination, bending, drooping. Fainting from closeness or from excitement. Falling.

faoragach, (DC), *a.* Abounding in hard blades of grass.

faotharsach, (MS), *s.m.* Invalid.

farabhallag, (DMC), *s.f.* Covering of the eye. 'Air an fharabhallag àrd', *on the upper covering of the eye.*

farachan, (DC), *s.m.* 4 Mallet for beating the bark of oak-trees.

faradh, (DMK), *s.m.* Bier. *Caithness.*

fàradh, (DU), *s.m.* Horizon. Sky-line.

fàrag, (DMK), *s.f.* A worm that burrows in the hide of cattle when they are in low condition in the late spring and early summer. *Caithness.*

farbhasaich, (MS), *v.a.* Surprise. 2 Haze.

farclais, *s.f.* See far-chluais, *s.f.* Listening unperceived. Eavesdropping. Overhearing.

far-ghuilbneach, (DC), *s.m.* Whimbrel. Literally, *mock-curlew.*

fàrlaras, (MS), -ais, *s.m.* Abutment for supporting a wall of a house.

farmadaich, (MS), *v.a.* & *n.* Envy.

farragradh, *s.m.* Provacation, enmity. 2 Report, surprise. *Sàr-Obair.*

farraideach, *a.* (See fairdeadh, *s.*) Inquisitive, prying.

farsalman, (DMK), *s.m.* Snaod-casan of a hand-line. *Gairloch.*

farsan, (MS), *s.m.* Range.

farsanach, *a.* 2 (MS) Giddy-paced.

farsanaich, (MS), *v.n.* Hover.

farsannanachd, s.f. Ramble.

far-sgeul, (MS), *s.* Episode.

farspag, (DMK), *s.f.* Great black-backed gull in the first year of its age. *West coast of Ross-shire.*

farsuingich, *v.a.* 2 (MS) Raise.

fasgadair, *s.m.* 2 (MS) Blood-sucker.

faslachd, (MS), *s.f.* Porousness.

faslaichte, *a.* Porous.

fàsgain, (MS), *v.a.* Curry.

fasgathaich, (MS), *v.a.* Overshadow. 2 Hive.

fàth-chul, *adv.* Out of sight. 'Nach leig dh'a deòin air fàth-chul', who will not willingly let me out of sight. W. Matheson (editor) *The Songs of John MacCodrum*, Edinburgh, 1938, p.98, 1.1428.

fathadh, *s.f.* See fallaid, *s.f.* Light shake or dip of anything.

fàthaim, *s.m.* See faitheam, *s.m.* Hem or border of a garment.

fathrusg, (MS), *s.* Trash.

fathrusgach, *a.* 2 (MS) Scaly.

fè, (DJM), *s.f. ind.* Broken ground on a moor. 2 Hag. *Lewis.*

feachdadh, *s.m.* Beseiging, investing. *Rob Donn.*

feachdanta, (MS), *a.* Brave.

feadan na h-àth, (DMK), *s.m.* Narrow passage leading from the fire to the pit of a kiln. *Caithness.*

feadan-uisge, (DJM), *s.m.* A streamlet in a narrow channel.

feadaraich (or feadairich), (DU), *v.a.* Whistle. 'Feadaraich e', *whistle it* (that is to say, a tune that has been mentioned.)

fead-chluais, (DU), *pr. pt.* 'A' feadchluais', *eavesdropping.*

feairrdich, (MS), *v.a.* Reclaim, improve.

fealag, (DC), *s.f.* Smart dodge, trick.

feall-bhreitheach, (MS), *a.* Arbitrary.

feamainn, (DJM), Cut or gather seaweed. 'Tha iad anns an fheamainn', *they are cutting or gathering seaweed.*

feamanach, *s.f.* Kintyre for feamainn, *s.f.* Seaweed.

feanndagach, *s.* Great nettle. *Colonsay.*

feanndagach-leamhuinne, *s.* Small nettle. *Colonsay.*

feanndagach-nimhinneach, *s.* Hempnettle. *Colonsay.*

feanntag, s.f. Lorn for deannatag, s.f. nettle.

feanntagach, a. Lorn for deannatagach, a. Abounding in nettles, or like a nettle.

fear-àicheadh, (DU), s.m. Atheist, unbeliever, infidel.

fear-aideachaidh, (DU), s.m. Professor of religion, communicant. One who is a professing Christian.

fear-brèige, (DJM), s.m. Liar. Fir brèige is a name applied in Lewis to Druidical stone circles.

fear-cèile, s.m. Gossip.

fear-coimhead na h-ùirnigh, the rooster cock (literally, the watchman of prayer.)

fear dhùsgadh nan creideach, s.m. rooster cock (literally awakener of believers).

fear dhùsgadh nan naomh, the rooster cock (literally awakener of the devout).

fear-faire, s.m. Rooster cock (watchman).

fear faire na h-oidhche, s.m. The rooster cock (watchman of the night).

fear faire nan tràth, s.m. Rooster cock (watchman of the watches).

fear giùlan uisge, s.m. the sign Aquarius in the Zodiac.

fear ionadach, s.m. Lieutenant.

fear iùil, s.m. Grieve.

fear seannsaidh na maidne, rooster cock (the morning sainer).

fearail, a. 4 (MS) Athletic.

fearas-chuideachdail, (MS), a. Humorous.

fearas-mhòr, (DMC), s.m. Upstart pride, patronage (in its degraded sense), condescension of the same degraded type, pomp.

feargaich, v.a. 4 Affront.

fearnadh, (DC), s.f. Placenta mulieris, the female afterbirth.

fearsaid an t-seic, s.f. Spindle or axle of flyers in a spinning-wheel.

feartail, a. 5 (MS) Effectual.

feàthach, a. 2 Cloudless.

feicheantas, s.m. See fèicheannas, s.m. Friendly dispute.

fèilidh, (MS), a. Accessible. 2 see fialaidh, a. Bountiful, hospitable, liberal.

fèilidheachd, s.f. See fialaidheachd, s.f. Bounty, hospitality, liberality.

fèilleilealachd, s.f. Vendibleness.

fèiltealachd, (MS), s.f. Saleableness.

fèineach, a. See fèineil, a. Selfish.

fèin-ghluaisneach, (MS), a. Automatic.

fèiteach s. 'Bha fèiteach air an orghan'. Wm. Ross 86.

feith, s. Mizzy.

feith-dhìreach, (DMK), s.f. The oesophagus.

feitheamhach, (MS), a. Attendant.

fèith na fola, (DMK), s. The carotid artery, which butchers open when bleeding an animal.

fèith-na-h-iosguid, s. Hamstring of a horse.

feodhasaich, (MS), v.a. Reclaim.

feoirleagan, (WC), s.m. See feurlagan, (DMK), s.m. Field vole. West coast of Ross.

feòraich, v.a. 2 Seek. Duanaire, 3.

feòraiche, (MS), s.m. Asker.

feuchadair, s.m. 5 Index in writing.

feumalachd, s.f. 3 (MS) Availment.

feurachan, s.m. See feuran, s.m. Green grassy field. Chives.

feurlagan, (DMK), s.m. Field vole. West coast of Ross.

feur-sàile, s. Sea-plantation. Colonsay.

feusagaich, (MS), v.a. Beard.

fhacaig. Jura, North Argyll and part of Wester Ross for fhaca, the aspirated form of faca, the past interrogative of faic, v. See. 'Am faca tu e?, Cha'n fhacaig', did you see him?, I did not see him.

fiabhras-ruadh, (an fh-), (MS), s.m. Anthony's fire.

fiach, adv. Very. 'Tha mi fiach toilichte', I am very pleased; tha e fiach beag, it is very small. It does not aspirate the word following. Islay.

fiaclan, (DMK), s.m. Water in which the mouth of a dog suffering from rabies (hydrophobia) is washed after inflicting a bite on a human being. Lochbroom.

fiaclan an t-seic, s. See fiaclan na teic, s. The teeth of the flyer of a spinning-wheel. D, p.290, No. 25.

fiaclachas, (MS), s.m. Jaggedness.

fiadhaire, (MS), s.f. Fallow ground.

fiadhaireachd, (MS), a. Inarable.

fiadhantachd, s.f. 2 (MS) Extravagance.

fiadharaich, (MS), *v.a.* Afforest.

fiadh-chullach, *s.m.* [In the Appendix Dwelly suggests that this word, which MacLeod & Dewar give as a meaning *a wild boar* is not correct. He states that *cullach* means a castrated boar, and therefore the word fiadhaich – wild – cannot be applied to it. As, however, neither MacLeod & Dewar nor Dwelly state that *cullach* is a castrated boar, it may well be that MacLeod & Dewar's actual definition is correct.]

fiafrachadh, *s.m.* Question.

fiafrachd, (MS), *s.f.* Inquisitiveness.

fial, *s.f.* 6 Complacence.

fial, *a.* 5 (MS) Blythesome.

fialaidh, *a.* 2 (MS) Ample.

fialaidheachd, *s.f.* 3 (MS) Gallantry.

fiamhaich, (MS), *v.a.* Daunt. 2 Affray.

fianntachd, *s.f.* Story-telling, the recital of Fingalian stories.

fiaradair, (MS), *s.m.* Perverter.

fiarag, *s.f.* 6 Pastern of a horse.

fiathaich, *v.a.* 2 (MS) Becalm.

fid, -ean, *s.m.* Hole in a green plot of land filled with water, slime *et cetera.* 'Bhàthadh a' chaora 'san fhid', *the sheep was drowned in the hole.*

fideach, see fid above.

fideag, *s.f.* 8 Stack of corn. *Sàr-Obair.*

fidhleir, s.m. 2 (DU) Crane fly. "Daddy long legs."

fidrich, *v.a.* 2 (MS) Ask.

figheadair, *s.m.* Spider. *Islay* for figheadair-fodair, *s.m.* Spider.

figheadair-ròmach (ò as in brònach), *s.m. Balquhidder & Breadalbane* for figheadair-fodair, s.m. Spider.

fileadh, (DU), *s.m.* Act of looking hungrily for food, as an ill-bred dog does in a strange house. Dè am fileadh a th'ort?

filidh, (DU), *a.* Hungry applied to a dog, as above.

fine, *s.f.* 5 (MS) Virgin.

finilte, (DMK), s. Poultice. *Caithness.*

fioghaire, (MS), *s.m.* Comparison.

fioghaireach, *a.* Figurative.

fioltag, *s.m.* Fastener for sheep while they are being shorn.

fionag, *s.f.* For fineag, *s.f.* Cheese-mite. 2 Animalcule. 3 Miser. 'Na fhìonag

dhriopail gheur-chuisich', *a wretched subtle miser.* R. 24.

fionnadh, *s.m.* 'Fhad's a bhitheas falt no fionnadh 'fàs air Mac Gàidheil', *as long as Highlanders have hair or beard grow on them.*

fionnuaireachd, (MS), *s.f.* Cold. 2 Shade, shadiness.

fior, *a.* True. Gu fior, *adv.* Truly.

fior-cheàrnach, (MS), *s.m.* Rectangle.

fior-cheàrnach, *a.* Rectangular.

fior-iasg, (DMK), *s.m.* Fish of the salmon kind.

fiorlaid, (DMK), *s.f.* Firlot, measure containing 1.5 bushels 3 quarts. *Caithness.*

firigean, *a.* Gaelic spelling of *firkin.*

fiùchd, *s.f.* Coalition, conspiracy. *Rob Donn.*

fiùghanta, (MS), *a.* Remunerative.

fiùthantas, (MS), *s.m.* Bounty.

flasg, (DMK), *s.* Rushes dressed and prepared for making into ropes. *Caithness.*

flathail, (MS), *a.* 10 Blithesome.

fleadhaich, (MS), *v.a.* Convive.

fleasgachas, (MS), *s.m.* Bachelorship.

fleasg-ghrìogaig, (DMK), *s.f.* Necklace of beads.

fliopar, (AH), *s.m.* Slap in the face or side of the head.

fliùbh, *s.m. Gairloch* for liùbh, *s.m.* Lythe (fish).

fliughan, *s.m.* See fliodhan, *s.m.* Little wen or excrescence.

flùr-an-lochain, s. Water lobelia, *Lobelia dortmanna.*

flùr-na-cubhaig, *s.* Cuckoo flower. Ladies' smock. *Cardamine pratensis.* 2 Ragged Robin. See currachd na cubhaig.

flùr-na-gaoithe, *s.* Wind flower, Wood anemone. *Anemone nemorosa.*

flùr-na-grèine, *s.* Rock rose, see grian ròs. 2 Artichoke, see farrusgag.

flùran cluigeanach. Round-leaved bellflower. *Campanula rotundifolia.*

flùran-seangan, *s.* Sheep's sorrel. See ruanaidh.

fodar, *s.m.* See note under connlach above.

foghail, *s.f.* 4 (MS) Merriment.

fogharaiche, (MS), *s.m.* Harvest-man.

fòghlaichean, *pl.* of fòghlach, *s.m.* Rank grass growing on dunghills.

foghlainne, (MS), *s.m.* Novice. 2 Academician.

fòghlainne, (MS), *s.m.* Catechumen.

fòghlainneach, (MS), *a.* Academical.

fòghlainneachd, *s.f.* Apprenticeship.

fòghlainnich, (MS), *s.m.* Apprentice.

foghlan, (DMK), *s.m.* Whitlow. *West coast of Ross.*

foghluin, *s.m.* Apprentice, pupil. *Sàr-Obair.*

foghluinn, (MS), *s.m.* Beginner.

foghnachduinn, *s.f.* Competency.

fòid, *s.* 'Dà fhòid air aon', arrangement of peats when being dried See mòine.

fòid-buinn, *s.* Door-step.

foidean-rèisg, *s.pl.* Turfs from the heath. W & S, ii. 114.

fòidear, (MS), *s.m.* Plough-boy.

fòidearachd, (DU), *s.f.* The act of following a plough with a spade to turn over pieces of ground only partially cut.

fòidearaich, *v.a.* Turn over clods improperly turned by the plough.

fòidich, (MS), *v.a.* Plough.

foighideachas, (MS), s.f. Long-suffering.

foighidinn, (MS), *s.f.* Quietness.

foighidneach, (MS), a. Sedate. 2 Gentle. Gu foighidneach, *gently.*

foighinneach, *a.* Sufficient.

foighinneachd, *s.f.* Sufficiency.

foighinnteach, a. See foghainteach. 6 Forcible.

foileagan, *s.m.* Thick oat-cake prepared in the palm of the hand and baked in the embers.

foinneachan, *s.pl.* Warts. JGC. W. 94.

foinneamh, (MS), *a.* Athletic.

foinne-foladh, (MS), *s.m.* Ambry.

foireignear, (MS), *s.m.* Ravisher.

foireiteachadh, (MS), *s.m.* Confiscation.

foireitich, (MS), *v.a.* Confiscate.

foirlion, (MS), *v.a.* Cloy.

foirlionadh, (MS), *s.m.* cloyment, satiety.

fòirne, *s.pl.* Set of rowers, crew, brigade, troup. *Sàr-Obair.*

fòirneachd, (MS), *d.f.* Intrusion.

fòirnear, (MS), *s.m.* Intruder.

fòirneartair, (MS), *s.m.* Burdener.

fòirneartmhor, (MS), *a.* Burdensome.

foisdineach, *a.* Coy.

foisich, (MS), *v.a.* 2 Balm. 3 Becalm. 4 Allay.

foislichear, (MS), *s.m.* Analyser.

fois'nteachd, *s.f.* See foisneachd and foisdineach, *s.f.* Calmness, sedateness.

fòit, (DU), *int.* Exclamation uttered when a heated body is applied to the skin.

foith, gen. fothaigh, *s.f. Gairloch* for faiche, *s.f.* Field, green lawn. "Gabh an fhoith.", said when ordering somebody out of the house. Literally, *take the green.*

fosaich, (MS), *v.a.* Abide.

fosgailleachd, *s.f.* Looseness.

fosgalan, *s.m.* Porch, as in a crofter house.

fos n-ìosal, *adv.* See os ìosal, secretly.

fracan, (G), *s.m.* Fragment.

frafan, *s.m.* Jointed rush. *Colonsay.*

fraighe, *s.f.* Scabbard, sheath. 2 Protecting wall, shelter. *Sàr-Obair.*

frangaich, *v.a.* Frenchify.

fraoch-badanach, *s.m.* Common heather or ling. *Colonsay.*

fraoch-gucanach, *s.m.* Cross-leaved heath. *Colonsay.*

fraochran, (DU), *s.m.* Toe-cap of a boot or shoe.

fraoidhneasaich, (MS), *v.a.* Befringe.

fraoinidh, *s.m.* Place of shelter in the mountains. See fraon, *Beinn Dorain* line 70.

fraoth, (MS), *v.a.* Assuage.

freasdalach, (MS), *a.* Aidant.

fridh (for frith), *s.* Omen. JGC. S. 250.

frionasach, *a.* 5 (MS) Harsh.

frionasaich, (MS), *v.a.* Gall.

frith, *s.f.* Acuteness. 2 Gifts (supernatural) to find out hidden matter. e.g. the power to tell the exact situation and occupation of absent acquaintances.

fritheil, *v.n.* 3 (MS) Abide.

fritheireachd, *s.f.* Irritation.

frithillidh, (AH), *a.* Fitful, irritable, susceptible, fretful, fidgety, eccentric.

frithirich, (MS), *v.a.* Fret.

frithlisg, *s.f.* 2 (DMK). Earthworm. *West coast of Ross.*

frithmheachd, (MS), *s.f.* Barb.

frithneasach, *a.* See frionasach, *a.* Angry, vexed.

frith-sheirbhiseach, (MS), *s.m.* Factotum.

frodh, *s.* Method called proof of ascertaining the quantity of grain that a stock of corn will yield before it is threshed. 'Tha e a' frodh as a' chruaich', *he is proofing the stack. Caithness.*

frodhadair, *s.m.* Proof-man. See under frodh, above. *Caithness.*

froigeach, (MS), *a.* Solitary.

froisich, (MS), *v.a.* Bedabble.

fuabhaireach, (MS), *a.* Barbarous.

fuagarach, (MS), *s.m.* Flier, absconder.

fuagarradh, (MS), *s.m.* Alarm.

fuagradh, *s.m.* 3 (MS), Placard.

fuaidean, *s.pl.* Hands of a plough.

fuaidne, *s.f.* 4 Excrescence.

fuaimheireach, (MS), *a.* Truculent.

fuainne, *s.m.* See foinne, *s.m.* Wart.

fuaith-leus, *s.m.* Adumbration.

fualar, *a.* Urinary.

fuaradh, *s.m.* See D, p.460. May mean either starboard or port. 'Air fuaradh ort', *to windward of you*; an taobh leis ort, *to the leeward of you.*

fuarag, *s.f.* Cream whipped with the *loinid* or frothing-stick to which new oatmeal is added. *Caithness, Sutherland & Lewis.*

fuaraiche, (MS), *s.m.* Cooler.

fuaraidh, *a.* 4 Fusty.

fuarthaidheachd, (MS), *s.f.* 4 Coldness. See fuarachd, *s.f.* Coldness.

fuarthuidheachd, *s.f.* Coldness.

fuasgailte, (MS), *a.* 6 Absolute.

fuathalachd, (MS), *s.f.* Averseness.

fuathantachd, (MS), *s.f.* Abomination.

fuathasachd, (MS), *s.f.* Astonishingness.

fùcadair, *s.m.* 2 Napper of cloth.

fùchadaich, *s.f.* Rummaging, pushing heavily. *Arran. Celtic Review*, iv. 276.

fudaidh, *s.m.* Idiot.

fuileachas, *s.* See fuilteachas, *s.m.* Bloodshed, slaughter.

fuileachdach, (MS), *a.* 4 Bloodthirsty.

fuileadair, (MS), *s.m.* Blood-letter.

fuilteachas, (MS), *s.m.* Bloodiness.

fuinnsich, (MS), *v.a.* Potch.

fulasgach, *a.* Rocking, tossing. ''S na

cuileanan gu fulasgach', *and the whelps tossing to and fro.* (Angus MacLeod) *Beinn Dorain.*

furachas, (MS), *s.m.* 3 Advisement.

furaist, (DMK), *s.f.* Gun-wad. *Sutherland.*

furasdachd, *s.f.* 2 (MS) Pliancy.

furasdaich, (MS), *v.* Facilitate.

furabhailteach, (MS), *a.* Affable.

furbh-fhàiltich, (MS), *v.a.* Huzza.

furfhailteach, (MS), *a.* Blithe.

furman, (MS), *s.m.* Cricket.

G

gab èasguidh, *a.* Snapping. *Beinn Dorain.*

gabhag, (DMu), *s.f.* Lane, alley.

gabhaidh! *int.* Strange!

gabhaidheachd, *s.f.* 5 (MS) Marvellousness.

gabhaltachd, *s.f.* 7 (MS) Ableness.

gabhar-riabhach, (DC), *s.* Snipe.

gabhas, future subjunctive of gabh.

gabhdlais, (DMK), *s.f.* Silly talk. *West coast of Ross-shire.*

gàdag, (DC), *s.f.* A rope two fathoms and as much more in length as would suffice for a knot. The length suffices as a measure for the bulk of sheaves given by crofters in a township to the township bull, whose feeding is a matter for all the crofters in a township. See raoid, D, p.749. 2 Cleft-stick fork-shaped for tugging thistles and other weeds out of the ground.

gailleag, (DC), *s.f.* Filip.

gadlachan, (DMu), *s.m.* Withe for carrying fish in the hand. 2 The fish thus carried.

gadmunn, *s.m.* 3 (DC) Sundew, *drosera.*

gagail, (MS), *s.* Dysphony.

gàidh, (DMK), *a.* Surprising. 'Is gàidh sin', *how surprising that is! West coast of Ross-shire.*

Gàidhlig, A', *s.* A' Ghàidhlig Dhuitseach, *the unknown Gaelic tongue.*

gaidseag, (DU), -an, *s.f.* A long step, stride.

gailleabhach, *a.* Gusty.

gaille-bheinn, *s.f.* Huge billow. 2 Snow-storm. *Sàr-Obair.*

gaineachail, (MS), *a.* Sandy.

gaineamhach, *a.* 3 (MS) Gritty.

gaineamhachail, (MS), *a.* Sandy.

gaineamhachd, (MS), *s.f.* Grittiness.

gainmheil, (MS), Sandy, arenose.

gairbhionn, *s.m.* See gairbhean, *s.m.* Complaining. See D, p.471.

gàir-chliù, (MS), *s.m.* Acclaim.

gàirdean, *s.* Upright supports of flyers of a spinning-wheel.

gairisteanachd, (MS), *s.f.* Prodigiousness

gairistinnich, (MS), *v.a.* Convulse.

gairn, (DC), *s.m.* The otter. *Skye.*

gaisgeadh, *s.m.* See gaisgeachd, *s.f.* Heroism, bravery.

galathad, *s.f.* See galad, *s.f.* A familiar term of address to women and girls, used only in the vocative case, "a ghalathad!"

galeog, (MS), *s.f.* Drink.

gall, (G), *s.m.* Bough.

gallaglas, (MS), *s.m.* Gallowglasses.

gall-fheadan, *s.m.* 2 Clarionet. *Sàr-Obair*

gàmhlasach, *a.* 3 (MS) Ill-natured.

gamhntaich, *s.pl.* Stirk-shaped small island rocks. *Place Names of Argyll.*

gamuidh, *s.* Crest of a horse. See D, p.376.

ganntarach, *a.* 2 Indigent.

ganra-gort, *s.* Corn-craik.

gaoirean, *s.m.* Dry dung of animals. *Place Names of Argyll.*

gaoirid, *a.* See goirid, *a.* Short.

gaoitheanachas, (MS), *s.m.* Foppery.

gaolachadh, *s.m.* Embrace.

gaolanach, (MS), *a.* Amorous.

gaol-griasaiche, (DU), *s.m.* 'Cho teth ri gaol-griasaiche', *as hot as the small polishing iron*, which is used by a shoemaker to polish the welts of boots, and not to refer to the intensity of the sutor's love.

gaorrachadh, (MS), *s.m.* Putrefaction.

gaorraich, (MS), *v.a.* Bedraggle, be-dung, befoul, begrime.

gaoth, (DU), *s.f.* 6 Repugnance. 7 Smell. 'Tha gaoth agam roimhe', *I feel repugnance towards him.*

gaothaiche, *s.f.* 4 Mouthpiece of a bagpipe. (See D, p.722).

gaothaireachd, (MS), *s.f.* Flatulence.

gaotharlanach, (MS), *a.* Shallow-brained

gaotharlanachd, (MS), *s.f.* Fantasy.

gaotharlanaich, (MS), *s.m.* Whiffler.

garadh, (DC), *s.m.* Warming. This word is only applied to human beings. For other things blàthachadh, s.m. is used (blàiteachadh in Argyll).

garadh-cùil, (DU), *s.m. Gairloch & West of Ross* for garadh-cinn, *s.m.* The dyke separating the arable land from the moor or common pasture.

gar an, *conj.* Although not. The transla-tions of 'Thug siod togbhail air m'inn-tinn gar an d'fhaod mi chàch inn-seadh', is *That raised my spirits though I could not tell it to others. Gillies* 31.5. Gar an, conj. Although not. "S ioma marcaiche stàtail gar an àir mi ach cuid diubh.', is *and many stately knights although I name but some of them. Turner* 62. I. Lom.

garbh, *a.* 9 Huge. 10 Grained. 11 Turbid.

garbhbeirteach, (MS), *a.* Stern.

garbhuinn, (DC), *s.m.* Wooded dell through which a river flows.

garbh-ghucag, s.f. 2 The first distillation of the *sma' still* when distilling whisky. John Campbell, one of the last smug-glers and a native of the north side of Lochtay, used this word when speaking about the liquor that first came through the worm.

garrach, (DC), *s.m.* Young carrion-crow

garain, *gen. sing & n.pl.* of garran, *s.m.* Den. See D, p.479.

gas, *adv.* 'Cha bhi gas ort', *there will be nothing wrong with you*; a bheil gas air thoiseach orm?, *is there anything be-fore me.*

gasgan, *s.m.* 8 Green pasture. *Sàr-Obair.*

gasganach, *a.* 3 White-tailed like a deer or rabbit. *Donn. Bàn.* 4 Tailed. *Beinn Dorain.* L. 53, 77, 231.

gàth, (DC), *s.f.* Drip of rain from eaves.

gathan dealain, (DMK), *s.pl.* X-rays.

gatharainn, *s.m.* Otter. *Skye.*

gath-droma, *s.m.* Ridge-pole.

geal, (DC), *s.* The Moon. *Hebrides.*

geal, (DU), *v.a.* Whiten, bleach, suffer

blight. 'Gheal an t-arbhar', *the corn suffered blight.*

geal, *a.* Term of approbation. 'Mo ghille geal', *my good lad.*

gealltanach, *a.* 5 Promissory.

geambairn, *s.* Confinement, prison. *Sàr-Obair.*

geamh, (AC), *s.f.* Winter. "Se'n geamh so 'ghlas mo chiabhag', *this winter* bleached my locks. Jaine Carmichael (Sìn Iain Mhòir) *Barcaldine.*

geamhlaich, *v.a.* See geimhlich, *v.a.* Chain, bind with chains.

geamhta, (DC), *s.m.* Sturdy boy. *Argyll.*

geamhtag, (DC), *s.f.* Sturdy, bouncing girl.

geamhuil, *s.m.* See geimheal, *s.m.* Fetter, chain, custody.

geanag, (DC), *s.f.* Midwife. *Knoydart.*

geanail, *a.* 7 (MS) Placid.

geàrr, *v.a.* Geàrr fead. Whistle.

gearradan, *s.m.* Connecting pipe of a still. See D, p.730.

geàrr-chomach, (MS), *a.* Short-waisted.

gearsom, *s.m.* See geàrr-suim, *s.f.*

geaslag, (DC), *s.f.* Fairy spell.

geaslanachd, (DC), *s.f.* Divination, foretelling. 'Geaslanachd na Callainne', the divination of Hogmanay. The direction of the wind at that time afforded scope for predicting the weather of the coming year. The Argyll version is as follows:
Gaoth an ear sneachd is gaillionn.
Gaoth a deas teas is toradh,
Gaoth an iar, iasg is bainne,
Gaoth a tuath fuachd is crannadh.
The east wind, snow and storm,
The south wind, warmth and fruit,
The west wind, fish and milk,
The north wind, cold and decay.

gèilleadh, (DU), *s.m.* A foolish superstitious belief.

geiltich, (DU), *v.n.* Feel happy, rejoice. 'Gheiltich mo chridhe ris', *my heart rejoiced at it.* [leg. eiltich].

geimheal, (MS), *s.m.* Prison.

geir, (DMK), *s.f.* Pain experienced in the wrist of persons manipulating the pruning hook. Used with the article, a' gheir. *Caithness.*

gèis, (DC), *s.f.* Wisdom.

geiteanach, *a.* Orderly, frugal.

geobhastan, *s.m.* Wild Angelica. *Colonsay.*

geodail, (DC), *s.m.* Dialect, provincial pronunciation.

geug, *s.f.* 6 (DC) Family. *Argyll.*

gèug, (DMK), *s.* Good humour, cheerfulness. 'Tha gèug air', *he is in good form. Sutherland.*

geurachd, *s.f.* Observing, looking at. *Islay.*

ghon, *adv.* To, toward. *West of Ross* for *chun.* 'Tha e 'dol ghon a' bhaile', *he is going to the town.*

giamhag, *s.f.* Fear, panic, sudden alarm. *Sàr-Obair.*

giarag, *s.f.* 6 (MS) Skittishness 'Tha giarag air', he is slightly under the influence of drink. "Balmy."

gibeach, *s.m.* Long wool.

gibeag, *s.f.* 10 Tuft. JGC. S. 166. Gibeag mhurain, a brush made of sea-bent.

gibeag-fhlaisg, (DMK), *s.f.* Handful of rushes, seasoned and prepared for making into ropes. *Caithness.*

gibean, *s.m.* 8 (DC) St. Kilda pudding made of the crop of a solan goose filled with a mixture of fulmar fat, oatmeal *et cetera.* Said to be most sustaining and efficacious against coughs and kindred lung troubles.

gille-flipidh, (AH), *s.m.* See gille-flidir, *s.m.* Message-boy, courier.

ginteach, *a.* Genitive in grammar.

giobagach, *a.* Like lint. *Oran an t-Samhraidh.*

giobain, *s.m.* See gibean, *s.m.* A hump on the back.

giocaireachd, (MS), *s.f.* Riot, extravagance.

gioganachd, *s.m.* Flattery, prickliness. *Celtic Review* v. 346.

giollachd, (G), *v.* Prepare.

giollan, (DMK), *pl.* of gille, boy. *Caithness.*

giomaileid, (MS), *s.f.* Screwer, possibly a gimlet.

gioragach, *a.* 4 (MS) Skittish.

gioraig, *gen* of giorag, *s.f.* Dread, fear. 'Dol 'san iomairt gun bhonn gioraig', *entering the fray without any sign of fear.* William Ross, p.29.

giorasach, (DMK), *s.m.* Hare. *Caithness.*

gis, *s.* Doctair bi gis, a quack doctor, (*A doctor by guess*, a comical mixture of Gaelic and English. Not uncommon) Bi gis, *at a venture.*

giug, (DMK), *s.* Offal of a fish. Giug sgadan, offal of herring. *Caithness.*

giuigire, (G), *s.m.* Invalid.

giùirne-mu-ghiùirn, *s.* Augur-dust. Out of alphabetical order on D, p.496, being placed after *giùrnan*, but it ought to follow *giuirne* on the left-hand side of page 496.

giullan, *s.m.* 11 (CR) A bachelor of any age in *Kintyre*, though he be 90.

giuran, *s.m.* 4 Cow parsnip. *Colonsay.*

giùrnaich, *s.f.* Constant minute work. 2 Constant motion and stir. *Rob Donn.*

glac, *v.a.* Take. Ghlac e an cuan, *he took to the sea.*

glacadan, *s.m.* 3 Spirit receiver of a still.

glagan, s.m. 4 Chattering. *Smeòrach Chlainn Raonuill.*

glaislig, *s.f.* See glaistig, *s.f.* Supposed she-devil or hag in the shape of a goat.

glaisnig, *s.f.* See glaistig also.

glàm, *v.a.* Drink greedily. *Mac Mhaigh. Alasdair.*

glamhadh, (DU), *s.m.* See glàmadh, *s.m.* Metaphorically a sharp rebuke. The first *a* is very short. *Gairloch.* 2 Voracious bite or snap.

glamras, *s.m.* 3 (MS) Tweezers.

glan, *a.* Good-looking, handsome, as in *Duine glan, nighean ghlan.* It has been noticed that Wester Ross people living at Middle River, Cape Breton Island, Nova Scotia, pronounce the *l* and *n* of this word as in English.

glaodhachd, (MS), *s.f.* Stickiness.

glaodhan, *s.m.* 6 (MS) Pulp.

glaoim, *s.f.* See D, p.500. The *tingling sensation* in the ears was always supposed to be a forerunner of the death of a relation or acquaintance.

glas, (DC), *a.* 4 Blue colour of woad.

glasrach, *s.m.* Woad. *Isatis tinctoria* CGI. 216.

gleacanach, *s.m.* 3 Rival.

gleadhrachan, *s.m.* See gleadhran, *s.m.* Rattle, noise.

gleò, *s.m.* 7 (AH) State of being half asleep and half awake, dullness, stupor, lethargy.

gleogaid, *s.f.* 3 (AH) Woman who is habitually inclined to talk with an air of superior wisdom.

gleòghar, *s.m.* See gleadhar, *s.m.* Noise. See D, p.501.

glidheach, (DC), *a.* Astray, wrong.

gliogoisgeag, *s.m.* See MacCruslaig 's na mucan, MacCruslaig and the pigs. Once a favourite game in Uist. See *Celtic Review* No. 16.

gliom, *s.m.* 2 Leap, kick, any sudden motion or spring. *Rob Donn.*

glogruinn, *s.f.* See glogluinn, *s.f.* The rolling of the sea in a calm.

glòmadh, (AH), *s.m.* 2 Morning twilight. Glòmadh an là, Dawn.

gluasad-sgrìobhaiche, *s.m.* Cinematograph.

glularan, *s.* The packing between the outer and inner walls of a house.

glum, *s.m.* Gloomy forbidding look.

glumachd, (G), *s.f.* Puddle.

glutaranadh, *s.* Packing between the outer and inner walls of a house.

gnàth-obair, (AH), *s.f.* Pastime, hobby.

gnàthalachd, *s.f.* Grace. R. page 11.

gnobag, *s.f.* 4 (AH). Prim and tartish woman.

gnogach, *a.* 6 Dumpy, stumpy. 'Cho gnogach ri stòb siolla', *as stumpy as a gill-stoup.*

gnoiseanach, *a.* Mouthed. 2 Snouty. 3 Garrulous.

gnudh, *s.m.* See gnudhadh, *s.m.* below.

gnudhadh, (DMK), *s.m.* The slush from drifting snow in the winter. Pronounced *grudhadh. Caithness.*

gnùg, -ùig, *s.f.* Morose, cast down, sullen countenance. 2 Sullen look or expression. 3 Wrinkle. 4 Lie. 5 Straitness.

gnùg, -ùige, *a.* Morose. 2 Weak. 3 Wrinkled.

gnùgach, -aiche, *a.* 3 Wrinkled, furrowed. 4 Inhospitable. 5 Weak, feeble.

gob, (DU), *s.m.* Toe of a stocking.

gobha-dubh-nan-allt, *s.m.* See gobha-dubh-an-uisge, *s.m.* Water-ouzel.

gobhachan, *s.m.* Skip-jack insect JGC.

S. 228.

gobhalagan, (DMK), *s.pl.* Row of wooden posts, having their upper ends forked, set in the ground at intervals, with the cross-pieces resting on the forks, on which fishermen hung their nets to dry. *West coast of Ross-shire.*

gobhar, s. Goat. 7 Obsolete for horse.

gobhar-beag, (A' gh.) *s.* A very fine single star, the principal one in the constellation of Auriga, the Charioteer, and one of the finest stars in the whole northern sky.

gòbhlaid, *s.f.* Goblet. *Perthshire.*

gocairneach, *s.m.* Short, stout, straight, bold, determined-looking man. G.S.I., xiv, iii.

gocan, *s.m.* Young of the *glaistig*, the supposed she-devil or hag in the shape of a goat. JGC. S. 161.

gocan, *s.m.* 5 Perky little fellow. JGC. S. 176.

gogadaich, (DU), *s.f.* Cackling of hens, crowing of a cock, cry of grouse and other birds. Gogadaich a' choilich-fhraoich, *the cackling of the moorcock. Gairloch.*

goic-mhoit, s. Tossing of the head in pride. *Allt an t-siùcair.*

goiceag, s.f. A stout paunchy woman. *Uist.*

goid a' chrùin, *s.* A game once played in Uist, like *cluich an taighe.* See p.52. Rounders.

goillse, (DC), *s.f.* Alternate sunshine or shower. April-like weather.

goillseach, (DU), *a.* Showery. Latha goillseach, *a showery day.*

gòraileas, *s.f.* See gòraiche, *s.f.* Folly, silliness.

gorrlann, i.e. gobhar-lann, *s.*, stable. See gobhar 7 above.

gothar, *a.* See gaothar, *a.* and gaoth-mhor, *a.*, pronounced *gaothar.* Windy.

gràdh-saothraiche, *s.m.* Amateur.

grainnseag, *s.f.* 6 Cowberry. *Colonsay.*

gramaisean, *s.pl.* Spatter-dashes. *Rob Donn.*

graodhaich, (DC), *s.m.* Cream with oatmeal. See *fuarag. Kintail.*

greannanach, *s.m.* Unkempt cow-herd 'Cha b'e 'n greannanach bà coltas faicinn mo ghràidh', *It were no unkempt cow-herd the seen appearance of my love. Duanaire.*

greim-fuaigheil, *s.m.* Stitch.

greim-snàthaid, *s.m.* Stitch.

greoig, (DU), *s.f.* Mess, any hand-work botched or badly performed. See gròig, s.f. 4 Mess.

greòlagan, (DMC), *s.m.* Gathering together of birds or beasts, as when they are terrified.

greosach, (WC), *a.* Not tight or compact, as a creel, not well made or spun, as thread. 'Nach i a rinn an obair ghreosach', *What a slovenly job she made of it.*

greòsgach, (DNC), *a.* Open, as badly baked bread or badly woven cloth. Aran greòsgach; clò greòsgach.

griadach, (DC), *s.m.* A female child before baptism.

grianan, *s.m.* 14 (AH) Felicity, delight. 'Tha e ann an grianan a shaoghail', *he is in the seventh heaven of delight.*

grìlean, *s.f.* See grìleag, *s.f.* A grain of salt. Any small matter.

grìneachan, *s.m. pl.* of grìn, the Gaelic spelling of English green. Plot of ground, lawn. 'Gach sràid a's àillidh grìneachan', *every avenue with its own lovely lawns.* (Angus MacLeod) *Donn. Bàn,* p.96.

grinne, (AH), *s.m.* Bundle of hazel or other wands or withes, scraped free of bark and ready to be made into a basket or creel.

grinne-caoil, *s.m.* Bundle of scraped wands or withes.

grinn-ghruagach, *a.* Fine-haired.

grinn-obair, *s.f.* Dexterous use of the hands, as though by machinery.

griobag, (AH), *s.f.* A prim, tartish and ungracious woman.

griobhadh, *s.f.* See grìobhag, *s.f.* Hurry, confusion. 2 Timidity. MacAlpine gives *genteel hurry.* See D, p.527.

grìoch, (DMC), *s.* Hind.

griogal, (DMC), *s.m.* A clumsy, useless fellow.

gròbte, *a.* Grooved in joinery.

griogaran, (DMK), *s.pl.* Pleiades *Caithness.*

grìosag, (DMC), *s.f.* Anything roasted on embers. Grìosag bhàirneach, *limpets roasted on embers.*

grìs, *s.* Gaelic spelling of *grease.*

groigeanachd, *s.* Botched work.

groigeasach, *a.* Surly, peevish, grim. Another form of gnoigeasach, *a.* See D, p.310. 'Tha mhaoileach bheag bhranngach 's i noigeanach groigeasach', *the little snarling bald one ugly and surly.*

gròmag, *s.f.* See ròmag, *s.f.* Athole brose.

gropach, (DMC), *a.* Mean, scrimpy.

gropan, (DMC), *s.m.* Small round knoll.

grualan, *s.m.* See cluaran, *s.m.* Thistle. *Lochalsh.*

grùd, (DC), *s.m.* Sediment. 2 Contemptible man.

grùig, *s.f.* 5 (DMC), lowering of the eyebrows.

grunndail, *a.* 6 (DMC) Intelligent.

guairn, (DC), *s.m.* Wood refuse from an auger, gimlet or saw-drift.

gucag, (DMC), *s.f.* Egg-shell placed incorrectly under 9 Guc (D, p.532). 2 (DU) Bead on whisky, also placed incorrectly under 11 Guc. (D, p.532).

gudaboc, (DC), *s.m.* Snipe.

guireatair, *s.m.* Incubator.

gulb, (DC), *s.m.* Nose. 2 "cork".

gulm, (DMC), *s.m.* Black ashes of paper or of any other substance. 'Chaidh e 'na ghulm', *it was burnt to ashes.*

gunna-cnagain, (DMC), *s.m.* Pop-gun.

gùn-goirid, (DMK), *s.m.* Bed-gown. Worn by women by day and night. *Caithness.*

gunn'-uisge, (DC), *s.m. & f.* Squirt, syringe.

gus, *adv.* Untl. 'Gus an do chaill sinn cliù na rìoghachd', until we lost the kingdom's honour. McI. 19. 32.

I

iadhadh, *s.m.* 12 (DMC), Desisting, ceasing. Gun iadhadh, *incessantly.*

iar-bhuille, *s.* 3 (DMC) Death stroke.

Uist.

iarnaigeadh, *s.m.* (DMC) What has been ironed.

iarradach, *a.* 3 (DMC) Of a begging disposition.

iarrtanach, (DMC), *a.* 2 Desiring.

iarunn-loisgte, (DMK), *s.m.* Branding-iron. 'Tha 'n t-iarunn-loisgte agam air', *my brand is on it. West coast of Ross-shire.*

iarunn-siubhail, *s.m.* Axle of the driving-wheel of a spinning-wheel.

iasg-geal, *s.m.* All over the Northern counties this term is restricted to salmon or fish of the salmon kind. It is not applied there to any other kind of fish whatever.

iathlaideach, (DMC), *s.m.* Slow-going person. It is erroneously spelt *ialaideach* on D, p.539, the word it refers to being *èalaidheach*, not *èalaideach*, as there given.

i'car, *s.m. Arran* for ìochdar, *s.m.* The bottom, lowest part.

ilimeag, *s.f. Badenoch, Strathspey, North Argyll, Wester Ross, North Sutherland* and *Lewis* for imleag, *s.f.* The navel.

ilimich, *v.a. Badenoch, Strathspey, North Argyll, Wester Ross, North Sutherland* and *Lewis* for imlich, *v.a.* Lick with the tongue.

ìm, *s.m.* Butter. 'ìm buaile gun bhi air a thruailleadh', *fresh butter taken from the newly-made churnings with the butter-milk adhering to it*, and placed on the table for use, especially for invalids.

imeach, *a.* See iomach, *a.* and iomadh, *a.* Much, many, divers.

imeachd, *s.f.* 13 (AH) Act of operating, as a purgative medicine. 'Tha 'chungaidh ag imeachd', *the medicine is operating, working.*

imich, *v.n.* 6 (AH). Operate, as a purgative medicine.

imleagach, *a.* 3 Having a large navel.

impire, *s.m.* Emperor.

impireachd, *s.f.* Empire.

impireil, *a.* Imperial.

inbhir, *s.m.* is the correct spelling not *ionbhar, s.m.*, as given in D, p.353. Confluence of rivers.

ineach, *s.m.* Great wood-rush. *Colonsay.*

inneadh, (DMC), *s.m.* Scarcity in woof of cloth. 'Tha 'n t-inneadh air a' chlò', *the woof is not sufficient for the warp of the tweed.*

innibh, (DMC), *s.f.* See inbhe, *s.f.* Quality, dignity, rank.

innspead, (DC), *s.m.* A knife used by tinkers when making horn spoons for cutting and paring the horns.

iob, (DC), *s.f.* Snipe. *Perthshire.* 2 Now applied in derision to a woman who is quiet and restrained – one whom "no one knows how to get at".

iodhalach, *a.* 3 (DMC) Made much of.

iolamaid, *s.f. Wester Ross* and *North Sutherland* for iomlaid, *s.f.* Exchange.

iolaman, *s.m.* 2 Covering of skin for a vessel in which milk or other fluid is carried. *Rob Donn.*

iolach, *s.f.* 4 (DMC) Long ragged garment.

iolagach, (DMC), *a.* Light-headed, merry, happy-go-lucky.

iolraig, (DC), *s.f.* Doubt, quandary.

ioma-bhaidh, *s.* Excessive love.

iomarachd, (DC), *s.m.* Superfluity.

ioma-bhuail, *v.a.* Strike frequently.

ioma-bhualadh, *s.m.* Striking frequently, thumping.

iomach, *a.* 3 Speckled or spotted, as the face of a sheep. Mult iomach, *a wedder with a black and white face.*

ioma-ghnèitheachd, *s.f.* Manifoldness.

ioma-ghointe, *past. pt.* of ioma-ghon, *v.a.* Wound severely, below. Pierced with many wounds. Severely wounded.

ioma-ghon, *v.a.* Wound severely.

ioma-ghonadh, -aidh, *s.m.* Act of inflicting many wounds or of wounding severely.

ioma-ghuin, *s.f.* Severe wound. 2 Agony. 3 Battle.

iomain, *s.f.* 8 Shinty, see camanachd.

iomarachd, (AH), *s.f.* Direction, bearing, course, drift. 'Gabh a suas air iomarachd a' chnoic ud, agus tachraidh nead smeòraiche ort', *go up in the direction of that knoll and you will find a thrush's nest.*

iomas, *s.m.* Tribulation, trouble, confusion. *Rob Donn.*

ionachaill, *s.f.* See eanchainn, *s.f.* Brains.

ionbhar, *s.m.* A bad form of inbhir, *s.m.* Confluence of rivers.

ionchaill, *s.f.* See eanchainn, *s.f.* Brains.

ioraim, *v.a. Wester Ross* for iomair, *v.a.* Employ, row a boat.

ioramadh, *s.m. North Sutherland* for iomradh, *s.m.* Fame, report.

ioramall, *s.m. Wester Ross & Lewis* for iomrall, *s.m.* Error, wandering.

iorcachd, (DC), *s.m.* (?*f*) Surliness.

isean, *s.m.* Young of the glaistig. See above. JGC. S. 161.

iucadan, (DMK), *s.* Upper shell of the clam-shell or scallop-shell (Used with the article, *an t-iucadan.*)

iunndachas, *s.m.* Gleaning.

iunntachd, *s.f.* Gleaning.

iunntas, -ais, *s.m.* Gleaning.

L

Là, *s.m.* Day. In some grammars, day is said to be used in the singular, with numerals generally requiring the plural, except trì, naoi and deich, but it is really governed by these three numerals in the nominative plural and by others in the genitive plural.

laban an Ultaich, *s.m.* The Ulsterman's bed. Not uncommon in the 17th century. See *Archaeological Review*, vol. 4, page 429. It was a bed of straw in a small room, covering the whole floor, in which the husband and wife and sometimes a guest or two slept.

lachasach, *a.* Accommodating, liberal, indulgent. *Rob Donn.*

làd, *v.a.* Pommel. JGC. S. 173.

lag-an-òtraich, *s.f.* The site of the midden, usually a hollow situated opposite the door. *Wester Ross.*

lagh, *s.* Law. Generally masculine but feminine in *Sutherland* and *Badenoch.* (DMu).

lalus, s.m. Self heal. CG. II 330. 2 Ribwort plantain.

lamrach, (DC), *s.m.* Parboiled mess.

lamrachadh, *v.n.* Parboiling.

làn, *a.* Perfect in Grammar.

langadan, (DMK), *s.m.* Rope placed on one of the forelegs and one of the hind legs of an animal to impede its locomotion and thus prevent it straying. *Caithness.*

langasaid, *s.* Chain tether of a horse. JGC. W. 118.

laodaich, *v.a. & n.* See lùghdaich, *v.a. & n.* Lessen, diminish.

laoghadair, (DC), *s.m.* A mould used by tinkers for shaping horn spoons. The word is laighilt in *Argyll.*

laoigh, Na, *s.m. pl.* The calves. Two stars in the Constellation of the Little Bear.

laomaidh, (DU), *a.* Fat, applied to soil.

lapan, (DU), *s.m.* Avoidable misfortune, accident. 2 Defect. 'Thàinig lapan air', *he has sustained an accident (misfortune)*, in person or property; bha lapan air, *he was crippled* (in body).

lapanach, (DU), *a.* Unfortunate, accidental. Gnothach lapanach, *an unfortunate event.* The idea is that the worst feature about it, is that it might have been prevented.

lasaran, (DU), *s.m.* Match.

lathadh, (AH), *s.m.* State of being benumbed with cold. 'Tha mi air mo lathadh', *I am benumbed or helpless with cold.*

lathaich-mhòine, (DMK), *s.* Peat-moss, place where peats are cut. *Caithness.*

lathaist, (MMcD), *s.m.* Lathing.

lathaistear, *s.m.* A person who fixes up lath wood.

lathus, (WC), *s.m.* 2 Sticks placed longitudinally on a thatched roof, to keep the thatch on. 3 Lath.

le, *adv.* 7 (WC) Since. 'A bheil fada le rinn thu e?', *is it long since you did it?* *West coast of Ross-shire.*

lèabag-atha, (WC), *s.f.* Little insect found in sheep's livers.

lèabag-leathann, *s.f.* 2 (WC) Turbot.

lèabag-rapach, (WC), *s.f.* Lemon-sole. *Gairloch.*

lèabag-thuathal, (WC), *s.f.* Sole. This fish is so-called because of its wry-mouth.

leabaidh, *s.f.* 3 (AH) Space or opening left in a boat's cargo to admit of baling.

leabaidh-bhreac, (WC), *s.f.* Bed where men and women slept in a circle, feet to feet, which was common at one time in the Highlands.

leabaidheag, (WC), *s.f.* Little bed.

leabaidh-thaoim, (WC), Space left in cargo, as of seaweed, for baling.

leabhar, *s.m.* Book. It is feminine in the North Highlands generally (DMW) with *gen-sing.* leabhrach. Àm na leabhrach, *the hour of family worship.* (Lit; of the Book).

leac-an-dorais, *s.f.* Flagstone laid just outside the doorstep.

leac-an-teintein, *s.f.* The hearth-stone, a large flag set upright in the centre of the floor, against which the fire is placed. *West coast of Ross-shire.*

leac-bhannach, (DMC), *s.f.* A flat stone for supporting bread while it is being baked.

leac-bhuinn, (DMC), *s.f.* Flat stone in or under the out-door of the house.

leaganach, (DU), *s.f.* Shifting while fishing from one place to another. When fishing haddock and whiting with the anchor down, the fisherman occasionally shifts to new ground. 'Thug e leaganach', *he has shifted* (to new fishing grounds).

leannan-falaich, (WC), *s.m.* Fairy sweetheart – said of anyone whose sweetheart is not publicly known.

leann-tàth, (WC), *s.m.* Twist of a rope, string *et cetera.* 'Thàinig e às an leann-tàth', *it came untwisted.*

leasgadan, (DC), *s.m.* The flat shell of a clam. (Diucal & diucadan in *Uist.*)

leid, (DC), *s.m.* 3 Temporary fireplace, a few stones placed for resting a pot above a fire, as for washing clothes outside within convenient reach of water. 4 Fire-place of a still (D, p.730).

leig, *v.a. & n.* 'Leigidh sinn sin seachad', *we will let that pass.*

leigis, (DC), *s.m.* 2 Knife of adapted shape for paring and shaping the inside of a horn spoon – used by tinkers.

lèine-bheag, (WC), *s.f.* 2 "Dicky", the Irishman's shirt.

lèine-shona, (DC), *s.f.* Caul. An infant who is born with this membrane covering its head, was looked upon as being lucky and happy.

leipeid, (DMK), *s.f.* Delay, not turning up at the proper time. This is applied particularly to a funeral when those attending it do not arrive punctually. 'Tha leipeid an car leithid seo', *delay is incident to occasions of this kind. West coast of Ross-shire.*

leis, *prep. pron.* On account of. 'Cha b'urrainn e faotainn troimh 'n choille leis cho tiugh 's a bha i', *he could not get through the wood on account of its thickness.*

leòmhann-chraobh, *s.m.* Griffin. *West H. Tales,* ii 434.

leothras, ⅟₁₆ of a davoch, an old measure of land. D, p.719.

letheachas, *s.m.* See leathachas, *s.m.* Partiality, unfairness.

leth-aodach, *s.m.* 2 (WC) Half-waulked cloth.

leth-chù, *s.m.* 2 (WC) Mongrel or cross-bred dog.

leud-deiridh, *s.* After-leech of a sail.

leus-gealaich, (WC), *s.* Crescent.

liabag-bhrathann, *s.f.* See lèabag-bhrathainne, *s.f.* Turbot.

liabag-leathann, *s.f.* See leabag-leathann, (DC), *s.f.* Halibut.

liaghra, *s.f.* See D, p.588.
parts of a liaghra.
1 Stob na liaghra, *s.m.* Pin on which the reel revolves.
2 Am bonn, *s.* The stock.
3 Na trì casan, *s.f. pl.* The three feet.
4 Ceirsle, *s.f.* The clew.
5 An iarna, *s.* The hank.
6 Liadhan na crois, *s.f. pl.* The blades or ladles of the cross.
7 Biorain, *s.m. pl.* Pins to stretch the hank.
8 Na tuill, *s.m. pl.* Holes for pins.

liath, *a.* 6 (AH) In dyeing this word describes a very light blue colour. Liath is dubh, *light blue and black.*

liathadh ort! (WC), *int.* A bad wish.

May ill luck befall you!

liath-shad, *a.* compound of *liath,* grey and *sad,* throw. 'Gaorr a 's eanchainn 'nan spadal, 's nan liath-shad feadh mòintich', *filth and brains being struck about, thrown all grey throughout the moor.* ('Brosnachadh nam Fineachan').

leac, *s.f.* Flag, slab. The genitive is *lice* and the dative is *lic.*

linninn, *s.m.* Arran for *linig, s.m.* Lining.

linntean, (AH), *s.m.* Shoemaker's waxed thread.

linntein, *s.m.* See linntean above.

liobaid, (WC), *s.f.* Delay.

liobaideach, (WC), *a.* Dilatory, lazy. Nach e tha liobaideach!, *how lazy he is!*

lìon-cladaich, (DU), *s.m.* Cod nets. Used originally in all the Western Highlands and later adopted by East coast fishermen.

lìon-liùthaichean, *s.m.* See lìon-cladaich, *s.m.* above.

lionn-tàth, (DC), *s.m.* Lime made from sea-shells. *Uist.*

liucadan, (DC), *s.m.* Concave washer on a nail, as used in boat-building.

liùgach, *a.* 8 Lame, JGC. S. 85. 9 (DU) Slow in motion.

lodag, *s.* Scoundrel.

lògais, (DC), *s.m.* Water-lily. Hoof of a foal. 3 Gutsy boy. 4 Short squat woman. 5 Junk, anything shapeless.

loirig, (DU), *v.a.* Souse in water.

loit, (AH), *s.f.* Questionable company, "a bad crew". 'Thuit thu anns an droch loit', *you have fallen into shabby company.*

loith, (DMC), *a.* See loibheach, *a.* Foetid, somewhat rotten.

lom, *a.* Calm. Muir lom, *a calm sea.*

lomach-air-èigin, (DMC), *adv.* By the skin of the teeth.

lomadh, *s.m.* 7 (DMC) Process of separating the chaff from the grain to be sown by beating it with a *buailtean* or wooden flail.

lomarra, (DM), *a.* Bare, shorn, stripped, naked. 2 Unclad, unadorned, plain. 3 Unembellished. 'Crunnluath lomarra 'ga phronnadh', *a quick measure unembellished* (bagpipe) *tune, being pounded (or pulverized). Filidh,* p.67.

loma-làn, (DU), *a.* Completely full.

lom-sguabadh, *s.m.* A ˋclean sweep, devastation.

lom sguabta, *a.* and *past pt.* Perfectly bare, utterly deprived of one's possessions.

lon, *s.* Kind of hair rope. See ribeag *s.f.* Hair, little hair. D, p.758.

lon, (TS), *s.m.* Horse-play.

lonadair, *s.m.* Voracious creature.

lonadal, *s.* See lonach, *a.* Greedy.

long, *s.f.* 3 Toy boat.

longag, (MMcD), *s.f.* Sling for throwing stones.

loramadh, *s.m. Sutherland* for lomradh, *s.m.* Fleecing, shearing.

loron, (DC), *s.m.* Bird when in the shell. *Uist.*

los, *s.m.* Power of destruction. *W. Highland Tales,* iv. 423.

lot, *s.m.* 6 (DMC) Fool. 7 (DMC) Quantity of any liquid on the ground. 8 Stinging.

lotach, *a.* 4 Stinging.

lotadh, *s.m.* 4 Stinging.

lòth, (DMC), *a.* See lobhach, *a.* Rotten.

lòthar, *a.* Bright.

luadhadh, *s.m.* In most places, the waulking-board is now placed two-and-a-half feet from the ground and the operators sit, instead of kneeling to the work. Waulking with the feet has also been practically discontinued now. (1911).

luaidhrean, *s.m.* Slow motion, loitering.

luaineach, *a.* 8 (DMC) Careless, unconcerned.

luaisgeach, (DMC), *a.* Restless.

luaithrean, *s.m.* Haste, hurry. 'Dèan luaithrean leis', *hurry up with it.*

luath-aireach, *a.* Meddling, interfering.

luathragan, *s.m.* Haste, quickness.

lùbach, *s.f.* 5 (DU) Door-chain (the small chain fixed into the outside of the door and secured over a staple in the wooden upright. The door was locked by putting a padlock through the staple. It is common in barns).

lub-muran, *s.* A rope of bent. See lùb-

mhurain, *s.f.* Rope of grass plaited or woven in a horse collar.

luchag, (DMK), *s.f.* A pinch of anything, such as snuff. *West coast of Ross.*

luid, *s.* (DNC) Clown.

luideach, *a.* 6 (DMC) Stupid, clownish.

luideagan, *s.m.* 2 (DMC) Stupid fellow.

luidean, *s.m.* 2 (DMC) Term applied to a person or creature in a drenched condition.

luidhean, *s. pl.* Hinges of a door. *Beauly* and elsewhere.

luidhearachd, *s.f.* 4 (DU) Act of stirring up mud and water, messing.

luighean-toisich, *s.m.* Coronet of a horse.

luim, *s.m.* 3 (DMC) Opportunity, chance.

lùireach, *s.m.* 8 (DMC) Weakling. Note that *lùireach,* 1 to 7 are given as *s.f.* See D, p.609.

luis, *s. coll.* 2 Swarm of bees. *Rob Donn.*

lunnsaid, (DMK), *s.f.* Tub. *Lochalsh.*

luran, (DC), *s.f.* Young female seal.

luran, *s.m.* 3 (DC) Young male seal.

lus-analach (DU), *s.* Panting after exertion.

lus-Bàchair, *s.m.* Golden samphire. Livingston, 124.

lus-a'-chrodain, *s.m.* Bog asphodel.

lus-an-talaidh, *s.m.* Early purple orchis. JGC. W. 106.

lus-an-toraidh, *s.m.* ? Foxglove.

lus nam meall, *s.m.* Common mallow.

lus nan sibhreach, *s.m.* Great yellow loosestrife.

M

mac-meanmhuinn, *s.f.* Imagination, R. 64.

mada-galla, *s.m.* See madadh-allaidh *s.m.* Wolf. T. 46.

madra-croinn, (DC), *s.m.* Marten cat.

magadan, *s.m.* Snipe (bird).

maide-aide, *s.* A cross-piece joining the two door posts at the top. Literally 'hat-stick', so-called from its coming into contact with hats of people who were not accustomed to bow down on entering a house. See D, p.923.

maide-ceangail, *s.m.* The part of the couple that was fitted in the wall of an old Highland house. It was a most important item in the house. It contained pegs on which to hang odds and ends, notably the *binid* (rennet) was almost invariably suspended from it. (DMK).

maide-gobhlach, (DMK), *s.m.* Beam of wood balanced across a low wall with a boy perched on each end of it weighing each end down alternately with a see-saw motion. *Lochbroom.*

maide-milis, (DU), *s.m.* Roots of bird's-foot trefoil. The fibrous root is sappy and was often chewed.

maide-pronnaidh, (DMK), *s.m.* Potato-masher. *Strathglass.*

maide-slabhruidh, *s.* Cross-stick laid on two upper rafters (*taobhain*) from which to hang the hook and chain over the fire. See D. p.923.

màirnealachd, *s.f.* Weather wisdom.

maisean, (DMK), *s.m.* An amiable and virtuous man. *Caithness.*

maisil, (DC), *v.* Die. *Knoydart.*

malard, (AF), *s.m.* Drake, mallard.

maogh, (DC), *s.m.* Watershed. *Skye.*

maoilean, *s.m.* 8 (DU) Polled cow.

maois, *s.f.* 8 (DC) Rope for placing round a mass of seaweed in a bay to keep it from being carried away by the tide.

maoiseach, *s.m.* 5 (DC) A goat in milk.

maoislinn, (DC), *s.m.* Unripe corn pulped for food.

maoil, *v.a.* & *n.* 3 (DU) Cut one's hair. 'Cò a mhaol thu nach d'thug na cluasan diot? Am madadh ruadh nach d'thug na casan dhiom'. A common greeting to a person who has had his hair cut recently and also his appropriate response.

maol-dòmhnaich, (DC), *s.m.* Generally a male child before baptism. In Skye the name is given to a foundling who had to be kept by the poor-box of the church. In English the name is rendered as Ludovick.

maor-chladaich, *s.m.* 3 Receiver of wrecks.

maor-gruinnd, *s.m.* Ground officer on an estate.

maorach-iasgaich, *s.m.* Shell-fish for fishing bait.

maothan, *s.m.* 'Cha ghearain i maothan', *she will not make her breast moan. Beinn Dorain,* 1.58.

mar. *conj.* 'Mar gu'n rachadh cù ri caoraich', *as a dog would go after sheep.* McI. 141.

marachd, (G), *s.f.* Luck.

marag-geòidh, (DMK), *s.f.* Pudding made in the stomach of a goose, consisting of the blood and fat of the goose with seasoning. *Caithness.*

marag-truisg, (DMK), *s.f.* Pudding made in the stomach of a cod consisting of the liver of the cod, oatmeal and seasoning. *Gairloch.*

Mart-gearr-adharcach, *s.m.* Shorthorn cow.

mart-laoigh, *s.m.* Cow with calf at foot.

mart-maol, *s.m.* Polled cow.

ma's ta e, (G) *Before he's able.*

màs an taighe, *s.m.* Lower end of the house.

masanaich, *s.f.* Mockery, derision, turning another into ridicule. *Rob Donn.*

masg, (DMK), *s.* Mesh of a net. *Sutherland.*

math, *a.* In *Arran:* 'Is math an sàs so am buntàta a lobhadh, is math an sàs so an gort a fhroiseadh', *this* (*weather*) *is enough to rot the potatoes, to shake the standing corn*; is math an sàs sibh mo chuir a mach air an doras = *you are enough to drive me out of the house* (*with noise*) or to make me homeless (*with your extravagance*); nach math an sàs sin a thoirt breitheanais air an talamh; *is not that enough to bring judgment on the earth*; cha mhath gun = *it is to be hoped*; *negatively*; cha mhath gu'n do thachair a bheag dha = *it is to be hoped that nothing has happened to him*; glè mhath = *good enough*; math math = *very good.*

math-shluagh, *s.m.* 3 Congregation. 'Nam faicte mo leannan 'sa mhath-shluagh Di-dòmhnaich', *if my sweetheart* *was seen in the congregation on Sunday.* Moladh Mòraig, 217.

màthair-shìomain, *s.* Heather rope laid about three feet above the eaves (outside) and round which the loops are bound before weights are put on. 2 Stretch of heather rope extended horizontally below the row of weights. (AH) See D. p.923.

meagadaich, *s.f.* Call of a goat.

meall-eochd, *s.* Serpent's spittle becoming solid. JGC. W. 86.

meallach, *s.m.* Colloquial for mùrach *s.m.* Sand-hill on the sea-shore.

meanan-adhair, (DC), *s.m.* Snipe (bird).

meanan-sàibh, *s.m.* Saw-dust.

meang, *s.f.* Gun mheang gleus, *without fault of tune.* R. 7 and 13.

meanmuin, (DU), *s.m.* In *Gairloch* this word equates with meanma, *s.m.* 12 Titillation of the nostril, which when felt, is supposed to portend the arrival or sight of a relative or acquaintance. This is the only use of this word there.

mearrachasach, *a.* Joyous. *Beinn Dorain.*

meath-chridheach, *a.* 2 Readily moved to pity.

meath-dhuine, (AH), *s.m.* Coward, weakling. 2 Unprincipled person. 'B'e sin comaine 'chur air meath-dhuine', *that would be conferring a favour on an ungrateful and contemptible person (who would never require it.)*

meilcheart, (DC), *s.f.* "Grease" in horses, inflamed and painful skin of the feet after long standing or walking.

mèilleachan, *s.m.* Young of the *glaistig.* JGC. S. 161.

meinealas, (DC), *s.m.* Disposition, nature.

meud-mhòir, (AH), *s.f.* (Accent on the second syllable) Haughtiness, loftiness, high notions, vainglory.

meur-nan-con, (DMK), *s.* Brow-antler of a stag.

meuran-nan-cailleachan-sìth. Foxglove. See lus-nam-bàn-sìth. JGC. S. 26.

mial. McBain prefers this spelling to miol, *s.f.* Louse.

mial, (DMK), *s.* Disease in the form of a growth in the lower gum of horses.

mialachd, see mìothlachd, *s.f. ind.* Offence, displeasure, resentment.

miamh, (AC). 2 Smut. *Carmina Gad.* 2.162.

miapadh, *s.m.* Disgracefulness. D. p.651. 'Chaidh e air mhiapadh', *he lost his head through fear* (DMy).

mì-fhallan, (HSD), *s.m.* Unwholesome, unsound, unhealthy. HSD also gives *'mis fallain'.*

milereach, *s.m.* Sea marram. Sheep's fescue grass.

mileur, *s.m.* Sea marram. Sheep's fescue grass.

mileurach, *s.m.* Sea marram. Sheep's fescue grass.

mineag, (DC), *s.f.* Sheep on its first lamb.

minidh-teine, (DMK), *s.* Primitive awl, consisting of an iron cylinder of the requisite thickness used in an incandescent state for boring holes in wood *et cetera.*

miodhag, (DMK), *s.f.* Thug e miodhag asam', *he nipped me.* Caithness.

miorar, (DMK), *s.f.* Vessel made of wood, used for setting milk. Also miorar-bhainne. (Scots, *lifter.*)

miorcan, *s.m.* Lewis for mircean, *s.m.* Badderlocks, hen-ware (seaweed.)

miosad, *s.f.* Degree of badness. 'Am miosad 's an donad mar a bha cuilean a' mhadaidh-ruaidh', *the bigger the worse as the fox's whelp.*

miosguinneach, *a.* Malicious.

mìr, (DMK), *s.* Pile of corn or hay stowed in a barn. *Lochalsh.*

miragaidh-fad, (DMK), *s.f.* The middle finger. *Lochbroom.*

mireag ort (oirre). A pet expression used to, or of, a cow.

misde, *comparative* of olc, worse, worst. 'Bu mhisd 'e thusa d'a dhìth', *he was the worse of not having you. Duanaire* 6.6.

miseag, (DC), *s.f.* A goat on her first kid.

mìsleanach, *s.m.* See mìslean, *s.m.* Sweet meadow grass. *Anthroxanthum odoratum.*

mobach, *a.* Tumultuous.

modh, *s.m.* Mood of a verb.

mogan, *s.m.* Old stockings with feet and soles or some other material, as tweed or felt cut to the size and sewn on. They were usually worn at haymaking as they were a protection against thistles, stubble and so on. *Perthshire.*

moineag, (DC), *s.f.* Young female seal.

moinean, (DC), *s.m.* Young male seal.

moin-iobach, (DC), *s.f.* Shaped peat, *Lismore.* As this island contains no real moss-land from which peats can be cut, the natives used to gather mud from any bog and shape the mass into peats with their hands.

molltair, *s.m.* Mould. Coinnlean-molltair, *s.f. Moulded candles* in distinction to "dips".

monabhur, (DC), *s.m.* See monmhar, *s.m.* Murmur, uproar.

mòrach, *a.* Capable of, able to. 'Bidh thu mòrach air an tuirs (= turuis) am màireach', *you will be capable of the journey tomorrow. Glendochart.*

morgha, *s.m.* See morghath, *s.m.* Fishing-spear, trident.

mòrlanachd, *s.f. ind.* This should read *Free* labour performed by tenants for their landlord. See D. p.672.

mo ruar! *int.* Term of commiseration, Mo ruar mise leat! *pity me with you!*

mosag, (DC), *s.f.* Snipe (bird).

mosan, *s.m.* Pith of wood. 2 Porous part of a bone.

mosganach, *a.* Pithy (of wood). 2 porous, as the inner part of a bone.

muc-àil, *s.f.* Sow with young. *Perthshire.*

muidhe, *s.f.* Churning.

muileann, *s.m.*, also used as *s.f.* with *genitives* muilne and muillne. A mill. *The parts of the mill mentioned below:*
1. Crann-sheall, a small piece of wood tied to the string connecting with the sluice which, when released, let water into the mill.
2. Garbhile, or garbhile mhòr, the water wheel outside the mill.
3. Ma seach car, a turn in the opposite direction to that made by the bigger wheel.
4. Maide-sgailcinn etc., sticks set in a certain position and worked by the motion of the mill, striking the bin

containing the parched corn and thus feeding the mill stones at proper intervals.
5. Min bhàn, white meal.
6. Cho garbh ri earball a' chapuill bhàin, *as thick as the white mare's tail*; meaning, the meal coming down to the receiver in a spout that resembled his grey mare's tail in appearance.

'Thug e tarruing air a chrann-sheall is chuir a' gharbhile mhòr a muigh car dhi, is chuir a' gharbhile bheag ma seach car dhi. Thòisich an sin ghrimeil a' ghramail, bhuile am maide sgailcinn air a' mhaide sgilcinn is sputa a' mhin mhìn gheal bhàn cho garbh ri earball a' chapuill bhàin againn fhèin', he gave a pull on the toggle and the large water wheel outside gave a turn and the small wheel gave a turn in the opposite direction. Then it began to grunt and groan, the cross-sticks struck the corn bin and produced a spout of white meal as thick as our own white mare's tail.

mullach an athair, *s.m.* The Zenith.

mùr, (G), *s.* Leprosy. JGC. W. 100.

murtaig, (CR), *Blair Athole* for biurtaig *v.n.* Gaelic version of *burst.*

muthail, (DC), *v.* Die. *Skye.*

N

namhag, (DC), *s.f.* Home-made boat, canoe, coracle.

naosgan, (DC), *s.m.* Snipe.

nausg, *s.m.* See gobhar-athair, *s.m.* Snipe.

neartail, *a.* Emphatic in *Grammar.*

neo-chinnteach, *a.* Indefinite.

neòineag, *s.f.* Daisy.

neo-shannsar, (WC), *a.* Unbecoming.

neo-shaothrachail, (WC), *a.* Worthless.

nighe, *s.f.* (DU) Washing.

nighe, *a.* Pertaining to washing. Beannighe, *s.f.* A washerwoman. Taighnighe, *s.m.* A wash-house.

nodag, (DC), *s.* Snipe.

nuadhag, *s.f.* Bride. *Old Highlands*, 226.

nuallan, *s.m.* 2 Cry of the roebuck.

nuasg, *s.m.* See gobhar-adhair, *s.m.* Snipe.

O

obair, *s.f.* Work. The genitive singular in *Poolewe* is na h-obrach. (WC).

ofrail, *s.f.* 2 (WC) Money for the church collection.

ogluidh, *a.* 7 (DC) Passionate.

oidhche, *s.f.* Oidhche mhath *leibh,* is also for good night to you, and the more common form. *Oidhche mhonaidh,* (WC), is the annual night when all the crofters meet to settle and adjust the souming, hill-pasture, or common grazing.

oidhche-nan-càlaigean, (DC), *s.f.* The night of presents, Christmas eve. *Uist.*

oidheam, *s.m.* 6 (DC) Rumour. 'Chuala mi oidheam', *I heard a rumour.*

oidheirpeach, (AH), *s.m.* Industrious fellow (said of a man who struggles bravely against overwhelming difficulties).

oid-oilean, (AH), *s.m.* A professor (in a university).

oirbhideach, (DC), *s.m.* A township-constable or ground-bailiff. *Uist.*

oitir, *s.f.* (DC) Bank or ridge in the sea. Oitir-èiteag, *pebble-ebb*; oitir-mhùrsgain, *razor-fish ebb*; oitir shrùban, *cockle-ebb.*

òl, *s.m.* Drinking. In D. 708 *dunaidh* should be corrected to *dunach.*

ola, *s.f.* Oil. Ol' armaidh, oil for mixing with wool before it is carded; ola smeuraidh, oil and tar mixed together for smearing sheep.

òlach, (DC), *s.m.* One of noble birth. *Perthshire.*

òlach, (DU), *s.m.* 'Is aighearach an t-òlach thu!', *you are a jolly liberal fellow!*

ollamhnachadh, *s.m.* 4 (DMC) Whipping, mauling.

ollanachadh, *s.m.* 4 (AH) Severe thrashing.

ollanaich, *v.a.* 5 Thrash, belabour with a rod or stick.

onfhadh, (AH), *s.m.* 8 Breath, lung, energy. 'B'e ministear cho math onfhadh 's a chuala mi; bha onfhadh math aige; cha robh onfhadh circ' aige; bha e mach d' onfhadh mu'n d'ràinig e 'm mullach'. *He was a minister with as good breath (pair of lungs) as ever I heard; he had good breath (a good pair of lungs); he didn't have the breath of a hen; he was out of breath before he reached the top.*

onoid, *s.f.* 2 (DMC) Sluggish female.

òrd-chlach, (DMK), *s.m.* Mason's hammer.

òrd-gobhlach, (DMK), *s.m.* Claw hammer.

òrd-mòr, (DMK), s.m. Blacksmith's hammer.

òrdan, *s.m.* 4 (DMC) Order, condition. An deagh òrdan, in good condition.

òrensin. *Moladh Mòraig,* 100 for 'orange-an', oranges, in 'Phoebus dath nan tonn air fiamh òrensin', *and Phoebus (the sun) colouring the waves with the hue of oranges.* (Completes the note in D, p.711).

oscar, *s.m.* 6 (DMC). A lean or diseased creature.

oscarra, *a.* See oscarra and oscarach *a.* 8 Diseased-looking.

P

pailliunaich, *v.* Live in a tent, dwell. 'Phailliunaich e 'nar measg'. *He (Christ) dwelt among us.*

paindeal, *s.m.* 2 (AH) Strait waistcoat.

paipeir taighe, *s.m.* Wallpaper.

paul-truisg, (DMK), *s.m.* A greatly emaciated cod-fish. It generally hugs the shore and in some places it is called a "harbour master." *West coast of Ross.*

pealaidh, (DC), *s.f.* Water sprite, kelpie.

peinnichean, (WC), *s.pl.* of peinneag, *s.f.* Chips of stone for filling crevices in a wall. D, p.720.

pic, *s.m.* Gaff of a sail.

pill, *v.a.* Relapse.

pilleadh, *s.m.* and *pr.pt.* Relapsing.

pìob-na-coimh-sheirm, *s.f.* Generally called the *union pipes.* This name has no connection with the union between Great Britain and Ireland, as some suppose, but the name is a corruption of *uileann,* elbow, because they are blown by bellows pressed by the elbow.

pìob-staile, (MS), *s.f.* Rostrum.

piollaidh, (MMcD), *s.m.* The Devil.

piosagraich, *s.f.* Hissing. 'Biodh gannra gorm na piosagraich/A nis agad mar chlàrsair', *The blue gander on hissing bent/May thou have now as harper.* Calder, *Gaelic Songs by W. Ross,* 136.

pisearachd, *s.f.* Curative measures against spells. *Arran. Maclagan's Evil Eye,* 6.

pisreag, s.f. Power of taking away produce. *Kintyre. Maclagan's Evil Eye.*

plath, (DC), *s.f.* Stench, smell as of rotting seaweed.

pleat, (WC), *s.* Cheek, impudence. 'Nach ann air 'tha 'm pleat!', *what impudence he has!*

pliut, *s.m.* 3 (DU) Cat's paw.

ploc, *s.m.* 18 (DMK). Shinty-club. *Caithness.*

ploic, (WC), *s.f.* The mumps. also masculine. With the article, a' phloic or am ploic.

poc-buidhe, (DMK), *s.m.* The stomach of a deer, which is a tit-bit and the perquisite of the stalker.

potag, (DC), *s.f.* Oatmeal and whisky mixed – a handful of oatmeal made into dough with water and eaten. The people of Trotternish, Skye, are called "potagan", because they eat *potag* in the morning before going out into the open air.

prac, (DC), *s.m.* Kain rent. The part of the rent paid in kind as hens, sheep and so on. 2 Tax on guests at a wedding to pay for a fiddler or piper. 3 A priest's tax – *prac na h-eaglais.*

praiseach, *s.m.* 5 (DC) Corn-bin made of straw.

preasan, (DMK), *s.pl.* Articles of dress to the value of £5 which the bride-groom presents to the bride in anticipation of their forthcoming marriage. Used with the article. Scots 'braws'. *West coast of Ross.*

prillè, prillè, *int.* Accented on the last syllable. A call to calves. *Islay.*

primeir, *s.m.* Gun, *ludicrously* so called. *Rob Donn.*

pruiseo, pruiseo, *int.* Pronounced prooshaw, with the last syllable accented. Call to horses. *Islay.*

pullaid, (CD), *s.f.* The lifting-stone found in many old parishes, near the parish church. Raising it off the ground was a sign that one was fit to take his place as a man. (*Perthshire.*) Usually called *clach togail.*

purrag, (DC), *s.f.* Soil in crevices of rocks, such as limestone, which soil is very weak until it is exposed to the air. (*Talamh gnothaidh – Lismore*).

puthail, (DC), *s.m.* Wall-recess. Press.

R

ràbhadh, (DMK), *s.m.* Vital spark. It is said of an animal that is dying, 'Tha 'n ràbhadh ann fhathast', *he still has a vital spark. West Coast of Ross.*

rabhadh, (MS), s.m. 7 Proclamation.

rabhas, -ais, -an, *s.m.* Notification, message. 2 Intelligence. Information about anything lost.

radh, (DC), *s.m.* Times, season, e.g. Samhradh, geamhradh.

ràing, (DMK), *s.* Ring of meal that forms around the edge of the upper mill-stone when the mill is grinding. *Caithness.*

raith, (DC), *s.m.* Tether-pin.

raoith, (DC), *s.m.* Tether-pin.

ràth, (DC), *s.f.* Burying place. *Lewis.*

reachd, *s.* Movements of clouds, used by weather prophets when speaking of the direction or speed with which winds are moving. *Glenlyon.*

ream, *s.* Convenience, facilities. *Rob Donn.*

reige, *s.m.* Dimmont tup with only one

testicle (MMcL). See D, 165, under *caora*.

riachlaid, *s.f.* Old tattered garment. *Rob Donn*.

rialtach, *a.* See riaghailteach, *a.* Regular, according to rule.

ribeide, (WC), *s.f.* Going wild or clean to the dogs. 'Chaidh e gu ribeide riasg', *he went to the dogs.*

ribheid, *s.f.* 10 Reed of a bagpipe, See D, p.722.

riof, (MMcD), *s.m.* Riof an duirn, wrist.

riofan, (WC), *s.m.* Roll of carded wool as it leaves the cards.

rionn, (AH), *s.m.* Film of fat on the surface of hot broth or another liquid.

roimhean, *s.m.* Relative *in grammar*.

roinn, *s.f.* Point when threading a needle, when they say about the thread, 'thoir roinn air', *put a point on it.*

roinn-oisne, *s.* Part of the roof of a house. See D, p.922.

roinneach, *a.* Distributive.

roiseanach, (DU), *a.* Muddy. 'S math mur òl thu 'phaidhir bhròg athair do spògan roiseanach, *it will be well if you do not drink the pair of shoes belonging to your father with the flailing legs.*

roith, (DC), *s.m.* Tether-pin.

rolag, *s.f.* 6 Ball of hair. JGC. W. 278.

romhanaich, (DC), *s.f.* Muggy weather, still and damp. Romhanaich na Samhna, *the muggy weather of Hallowmas.*

rònag, *s.f.* Ball of hair put in the milkpail on Lùnasdal or the Thursday after. JGC. W. 11.

ronn, *s.m.* Slaver, spittle. Pìobair nan ronn or pìobair ronnach, *a slovenly piper.*

ruaim, (DC), *a.* Muddy, dark. Uisge ruaim, *muddy water.*

ruaim, *s.m.* 3 (DC) Impatient boy. 4 (DC) Unrespectful man.

ruais, *s.m.* (DC), Impatient boy. 4 (DC) Unreposeful man.

rudaidh, *s.f.* (dim. of rud) Little thing.

rugha, *s.m.* Smith. 2 Reciter. *West Highland Tales.* iii, 409.

rùghan, (DC), *s.m.* Wind-row; rickle peats are set up on end and mutually supporting one another with peats

across the top so as to dry.

ruid, (DC), *s.m.* Swell of the ocean.

ruidhne, *s.f.* Yeld cow.

rùig, *s.m.* Ridgling.

rùilich, *v.* Search. Uist for rùraich, see rùdhraich, *v.a.* Search, grope.

rùis, (DC), *s.f.* Rye-meal and oatmeal mixed together.

ruite, (DMK), *s.m.* High wave.

rungadh, (DMK), *s.m.* Rumbling noise caused by the movements of gas in the intestines. *West coast of Ross.*

rustal, (DC), *s.m.* Single-stilt plough.

S

saidheachan, *s.p.* Couples of a house. See D, p.922.

sàileach, *a.* High-heeled, of shoes.

salachar-ronnaig, (DU), *s.f.* Falling star, meteorite.

samhanach, *s.m.* Savage, giant, monster. 'Chuireadh tu eagal air na samhanaich', *you would frighten the very savages. Islay* and *Argyll.*

samhladh, *s.m.* Simile *in grammar*.

samhrachadh, *s.m.*, and *pr. pt.* of samhraich. Summering.

samhraich, *v.a.* To summer.

saobhadh, *s.m.* 11 (AH) Omen, portent, augury, sign, precursor.

saodh, *a.* Premonitory. 'Tha e saodh', *he is "fey".*

saoidhean, *s.m.* Coal fish in its second year. See ceiteanach and smalag, *ss.m.*

saor-geal, (DU), *s.f.* Joiner. Saor-cathraichean, carpenter, boat-builder.

saosadh, *v.* Outlining a lazy-bed by a spade-cut. *Uist.*

sapag-upag, *s.f.* Trifling superstition. JGC. W. 56.

saplas, *s.m.* Soap-suds.

sasmaid, (DC), *s.m.* See sosmaid, (DC), *s.m.* Hash of meat? Mixture of fragments of food. *Argyll.*

seamlag-dhearg, *s.f.* Red clover. Not seamrag. *Trifolium pratense.*

sèanas, *s.m.* See sianas, *s.m.* Hate.

seang-na-coise, (AH), *s.* Instep.

seiceag-bheag, (DMy), *s.f.* Woman's stays.

seid, (G), *s.* King frog or toad.

seisdear, (DU), *s.m.* Condition, form. 'Dè'n 'seisdear 'sam bheil thu?', *What trim are you in?*

sepachan, (WC), *s.m.* A feather mop.

seunas, *s.m.* See sèanas, *s.m.* above.

sgàilean-grèine, *s.m.* Sunshade, parasol.

sgàireach, (AH), *a.* Descriptive of a mouth in which the upper teeth and gums are unduly visible when it is open. Usually applied to a woman.

sgait, (DMK), *s.f.*, pl. -ean. Tail of the old long *casag.* Now applied to the tails of a dress- or frock-coat.

sgaitch, (DMK), *s.* Saw-pit. *Wester Ross.*

sgaitcheadh, *s.m.* Hoeing and weeding potatoes before earthing. 'A' sgaitch-eadh a' bhuntàta', *hoeing the potatoes.*

sgarta, *a.* Abstract *in grammar.*

sgartach, *a.* Abstract *in grammar.*

sgàthach, (DC), *s.m.* for sgathach, *s.m.* fence made of loppings.

sgailgeag, *s.f.* Charlock, wild mustard. *Sinapis arvensis.*

sgeirean, *s.m.* Sea sandwort, *Honckenya peploides.*

sgialt, *s.f.* For ciall, *s.f.* Sense.

sgiath-ime, *s.f.* Slice of butter.

sgiathan-maghain, (DC), *s.m.* Bat.

sgionn, (DC), *s.m.* Marten cat. *Skye.*

sglaib, (DMK), *s.* Garrulity, especially of a female.

sgleogan, (DU), *s.m.* Any object de-fatted.

sgòd-dheiridh, *s.f.* Clew-piece of a sail.

sgòd-thoisich, *s.* Clew.

sgoich, (DC), *s.f.* The heart, kidneys and liver of a sheep left in the carcase when it is hung up to harden. An old superstition in Argyll and also in Ireland, was that no part of these should be given to a boy, until he had developed so far as to be able to pronounce the word "sgoich". If a boy did partake before that, it was sup-posed that he would never beget children.

sgoid, *s.m.* Driftwood. *Lewis.* Sgoid-cladaich, *shore driftwood.*

sgolbag, *s.f.* The first finger.

sgonnag, (DC), *s.f.* The chief rafter in a gable-less house. It was placed at the end where strength was most needed.

sgòth, *s.f.* Is given in the Dictionary, p.830, as meaning a boat with stem and stern vertical in Gairloch. In the Appendix, however, it is stated that 'sgòth never means a boat, but a cloud, *gen. sing.* sgòthan, *n.pl.* sgòthan. † [The word for boat has a short *o*].

sgrios, *s.m.* 4 (DU) Crowd of small objects.

sgroigean, (DC), *s.m.* Knob or catch on iron, wood *et cetera. Uist.*

sguile, sguilean, s.m. Wicker fishing-lines basket. *Lewis* usage. See D, *sgùlan.* (MS 14958).

sguill, *s.m.* Clown.

sianas, *s.m.* The space between the two front teeth when it is wide. The person so affected is considered to be lucky. *Fionn.*

siantachan-a'-chlòir, *s.* is another name for *bonnach fallaid, s.m.* Fallaid, *s.f.* is the refuse of meal left on the baking board after a batch of bread has been baked. An interesting custom used to prevail in the Outer Hebrides, any remains of meal on the board being made into a cake in the palm of the hand, and set to fire among the other and larger cakes. This custom had its origin in the superstitious belief that doing thus with the remains, kept the store of meal from wasting. No thrifty wife would think of dusting the baking-board into the meal girnel. JGC. S. 232.

siantaidh, *s.m.* Stands for *fiantaidh* i.e. fiannaidh, s.m. Fingalian, giant, hero.

siath, *s.* Sprain. Màiri Siath, Mary of sprains. *Maclagan's Evil Eye,* p.99.

similear crochaidh, An, *s.* This was made of thin wood or canvas to confine the smoke. Generally, but not always, exists when the fire is at the end of the house.

sin, *a.*, *adv. Harris* people and others pronounce this word *sean* both as an *a.* and an *adv. Uist* people pronounce the *a. sean,* but the *adv. seanach,* e.g. *an seanach.*

sìne. Used incorrectly for sìthne, *gen. sing.* or sithionn. Venison.

sineadh, *s.m.* Bar of metal. *West Highland Tales* iii 40.

siochaire-baic, (AH), *s.m.* Should be siochair-baic. See D, p.841.

siod, *Uist* people say *siodach.*

siodach, see *siod.*

siolpan, (DU), -ain, *s.m.* Stick for threshing corn, the beating part of a flail.

siom, *s.m.* Image reflected by a blade with a high polish. *West Highland Tales* iii 385.

siomain-fraoich, *s. pl.* Heather ropes used to keep the thatch on the house. (WC).

sionnach, *s.m.* 6 Valve in a bellows.

siostacota, *s.m.* See siosacot, *s.m.* 2 Waistcoat. Some parts of *Skye.*

siota, *s.* 5 Shelf. 6 Sail after-part.

slabhcan, *s.m.* See slabhagan, *s.m.* A kind of seaweed.

slacardaich, *s.f.* See slacarsaich, *s.f.* Thrashing, beating, battery. D, p.849.

slachdrach, *s.f.* See slacaireachd, *s.f.* Thrashing, beating.

slàlus, *s.m.* Self-heal. CG II 330. 2 Ribwort plantain. CG II 330.

slat-bhuinn, *s.f.* Boom of a sail.

slige-coilleag, *s.* Cockle shell. JGC. W. 22.

slim, (AC), *s.*Bog violet. CG. 1 206.

slinneanan, *s. pl.* Withers of a horse. See D, p.376.

slisneach, *s.m.* Self-heal. CG II 330. 2 Ribwort plantain. CG II 330.

smàlta, (G), *v.* Put out.

smògran, *s. Air a smògran* is used by *Wester Ross* people as the equivalent of *air a mhàgan,* on all fours.

snag, *s.f.* 2 clink. JGC. S. 183.

snàthadag, (DU), *s.f.* Sting of a bee, wasp *et cetera.*

snàthgail, (DU), *v.a.* This is the better form of snàgail, *s.f.* Creeping, slow motion.

snàthgaladh, (Du), *s.m.* This is the better form of snàgaladh, *s.m.* Thread wound round a fishing-hook to attach it to the hair-line.

so-atharradh, *a.* See so-atharrach, *a.* Alterable, easily moved.

sochairidh, (WC), *s.f.* Bashfulness. A bheil an t-sochairidh a' cur ort?, *are you bashful or timid?*

sochairidh, *a.* Bashful.

sodail, *v.* Should be siodail. *Fionn.*

soilleir, *a.* 11 (AH) Fair. Falt soilleir, *fair hair.* cruth soilleir, *fair complexioned.*

soirbheas, *s.m.* 'Cha'n 'eil mòran soirbheis ann', *there is not much wind;* dè'n rathad tha'n soirbheis?', *what direction is the wind?* See D, p.871.

soitheach, *s.m.* Used in *Poolewe* for a ship but not for any other vessel.

soitheach-tomhais, *s.m.* Measuring vessel generally containing a bushel. Soitheach sìl, *a bushel of corn.*

solusach, *a.* Duine solusach, *an enlightened, well-informed man.*

sonn, *a.* Hidden, mysterious. Saighead sonn, *an elf bolt, a bolt from the blue;* bogha sonn, *a reef in the sea* (known only by waves breaking over it).

sòthan, (AH), *s.m.* Dried stool of bent grass used for scrubbing purposes as a substitute for a scrubbing-brush.

spag ri tòn, (DC), *s.f.* Snipe.

spaitch, *s.* (? sgaith) Saw-pit. *West coast of Ross.*

spaitcheadh, *s.m.* Process of hoeing and weeding potatoes prior to earthing up. 'A' spaitcheadh a' bhuntàta', *hoeing the potatoes.*

spannachadh, (AH), *s.m.* Tight-lacing. 'Tha i 'ga spannachadh fèin tuillidh 's a' chòir', *she practises tight-lacing to an undue extent.*

speiceain, *s. pl.* Pieces of wood on which coffins are borne to the grave. GS, I. xiv.

speilidh, *s.m.* For spaoilidh, gen. sg. of spaoileadh, *s.m.* Wrapping. Brat speilidh, *a rug used for keeping horses warm.* (WC).

spiod, (DU), *v.a.* 2 Pluck at a person's hair or clothes surreptitiously.

spiolg, (WC), *s.f.* Any shred of flesh. Said of a very thin piece. 'Cha'n 'eil spiolg air', *there is not a shred of flesh on it.*

spiontag, *s.f.* 4 (WC), A kind of maggot in beef or cheese. Addition to spiontag. See D, p.884.

spleadradh, *s.m.* Smash. JGC. S. 224.

spor, *s.m.* Gunna spuir, *a flint-lock gun.*

spreachail, *a.* See spraiceil, *a.* Reprimanding severely or harshly. D, p.887.

spreadhan, (WC), *s.m.* 4 Broken pot used instead of the crùisgean, an oil lamp or cruise.

spreadhanan, (WC), *s. pl.* Broken pieces of anything. 'Chaidh e 'na spreadhanan', *it was broken in pieces.*

sràibh-dhriùchdain *s. pl.* See drùchdan, drop, D. 363. *"Sràibh-dhriùchdain dhonna thiachduidh, Fo shinean cìochan d'fheòir." Allt an t-siùcair.*

sreath, *s.f.* Bitch. 'Sreath chuileanach', *a bitch with a large litter.*

sriutan, (AH), *s. pl.* The "kinks" of whooping cough. [Scots *kink-hoast*, whooping cough].

srùlach, *a.* See sruthlach, *a.* Washing, rinsing, scouring.

stail, s.f. A still. See also A' phoitdhubh, *the 'sma' still*, D, p.730.
The parts of a still:

1. *Anger an uisge-bheatha*; the spirit receiver.

2. *Bord guaile, Am*; the lid of the still with a hole in the centre into which the *clogaid* was inserted.

3. *Bucaid an leanna* or *an spuidsear*; the bucket for baling or emptying the beer out of the *dabhach* (Vat) into the *stail* or still.

4. *Bucaid a' bhùirn* or *spuidsear a' bhùirn*; the bucket for supplying the worm-cask with cold water out of the cold water tub. The *bucaid* or *spuidsear* was used in Lewis instead of the discharge cock (charger or filler) and the chute for supplying cold water distilling was retained in canes and in accessible jars where water had to be carried.

5. *A' chliath*; the worm. This was a copper pipe in four coils and was placed inside the worm cask or tub. One end connected with the *feadan* on top of the cask and the other end comes out two inches above the bottom.

6. *An clogaid*; the still head in the

shape of a lum hat, was inserted into the hole in the lid and was full of steam.

7. *Am feadan*; the connecting piece between the still head and the worm.

8. *Measair a' bhùirn*; the cold water tub, which was always kept full to supply the worm cask with cold water to condense the steam into spirit that was in the worm.

9. *Smuggan*. The spout into which a large needle was inserted with a woollen thread attached on which the spirit was dripping into the spirit receiver. The U of smuggan is pronounced short.

10. *Stannda-na-clèithe*; the worm stand or worm tub. The above names were given to Dwelly by Mr Donald Murray of Aberdeen who hailed from Lewis. He, in turn, obtained them from his uncle Mr Roderick Murray who used to distil whisky himself and was the last, as far as is known, to have distilled whisky in Ness. Mr D. Murray added that although *bucaid* or *spuidsear* was the term most commonly used, the correct Gaelic name for *bucaid* was *taoman*. Thus *taoman leanna* and *taoman a' bhùirn* were the old Gaelic names.

stall, *s.m.* Space between the door and fire in "black houses".

starradh, (AH), -aidh, *s.m.* A fresh topic abruptly introduced into a conversation.

steilleag, (DU), *s.f.* Tongue of a boot or shoe.

sticeadh, (DU), *s.m.* Scalloping or notching paper.

stiùireamaiche, *s.m.* A steersman.

stiùramaich, *s.m.* A steersman.

struacan, *s.m.* Snoring. 'Tha struacan aige', *he is snoring. N. Uist.*

stubach, *a.* Short-tailed.

stùbhach, *a.* Short-tailed.

snigh, *v.a.* Drop, let fall in drops, ooze through in drops.

suircean, (MMcD), *s.m.* See surcain, *s.m.* A piece of skin or wood with a sharp peg placed in it point upwards for attaching to a calf's snout to prevent it sucking its mother.

T

tabhaich, *s.m.* See tathaich, *s.m.* Supernatural, knowledge of the absent.

tabhaill, *s.f.* Sense. Gun tabhaill, *without sense*; air mo thabhaill, *highly pleased.*

tabharadh, *s.m.* See tabharnadh, *s.m.* State of being haunted. 2 Apparition.

tabhasg, *s.f.* See tathasg, *s.f.* Shade, spirit.

tadadh, A', *pr. pt.* of tataidh, *v.a.* Attract, attach to one's self.

tadhal, *s.m.* 6 Football. Cuir tadhal (taoghall), *play at football*; cuir 'thadhail ('thaoghaill), *drive home, as a football.*

tairbhean, (DMK), *s.* A disease to which calves are subject. *West coast of Ross.*

tairbheartachd, *s.f.* Plenty, abundance.

taobhan ullaich, *s.m.* Roof-tree of a house. See D, p.922.

tarbh-oighre, *s.m.* Bull supposed to serve cows grazing near to lochs in which they are supposed to live.

teamhradh, *s.m.* Royal residence. *West Highland Tales* iii, 344.

thiibh [dat. pl. of *ti*, point, square on board]. 'Ruaig air dìsnean, foirm air thiibh'. *Iain Lom* R. McD, p.172.

thireil, A! Interjection of surprise (AH). 'A thireil, cha'n fhaca mi each riamh cho luath ris an fhear seo!' *Goodness, this is the fastest horse I ever saw!* A thireil perhaps means a Thì rathail, Providence.

tiaraineach, *s.* An eighteen-month old *othaisg.* See D, 165, under *caora.* MMcL suggests it derives from *an t-sia-raidheach*, the six-quarter old one. (MS 14958).

tiorman, (AH), *s.m.* 5 A person who talks in a "dry, wordy, verbose fashion".

tiormanachd, (AH), *s.f.* "Dry", wordy talk.

toirsgian, *s.f.* Peat-spade, peat-cutter or peat-knife.

Parts of a peat spade, (DMy):
2. Ceum, step for the foot (AH), *North Argyll.* Elsewhere this is *smeachan.*
4. Lùdag, point of the blade (AH) *North Argyll.* Elsewhere this is *bàrr na sgèine.*
6. Osan, socket in blade-iron, in which the handle and step are inserted. (AH). *North Argyll.* Elsewhere this is *na h-ailean.*

topag, (DMK), *s.f.* The nest of a wild bird, scraped out of the ground before the eggs are deposited in it. *Lochbroom.*

trom-duirghe, *s.* Used for clach-luaidhe (a cod-line sinker) by some people in *Barra.*

tuaireapadh, (MMcL), *s.m.* Mishap.

tuathanachas, (WC), *s.f.* Farming, agriculture, husbandry. Given as *s.m.* in the Dictionary, p. 978.

tuireadan, (AH), *s.m.* See turraban, *s.m.* Rocking motion of the body when sitting. See D, p.984.

tuirnealaich, (MMcL), *s.f.* Dizziness.

tùislein, (AH), *s.m.* Case of accouchment. 'Bha tùislein aca 'san taigh ud shuas an raoir', *they had a case of accouchement in yonder house last night.*

tulach, (WC), *s.f.* Hillock, knoll. Given as *s.m.* in the Dictionary, p. 982.

tulachainn, (TS), *s.* Back wall of a house. (WC) Gable of a house.

tumadh-chaorach, (WC), *s.m.* Sheep-dip.

turach, (MMcL), *s.m.* Anger on being without tobacco. 'Tha'n turach air', *he is angry at being without tobacco.*

U

Uachdar, *s.m.* Top, surface, summit. Plural may be uachdair (WC) as well as uachdaran. See D, p.985.

uaghaidh, *s.f.* Cave, cavern, den. The genitive is *na h-uaghach* (WC).

uamhag, *s.f.* Hollow. Occurs in its
Anglicized form in names of places
such as *uags* and *wags*.

ubhal, *s.f.* Apple. *Lochalsh.*

ùig, (AH), *s.f.* 3 Recluse.

uil'-ìoc. Mistletoe, *Viscum album.* Its
gender is feminine, according to William Cameron of *Poolewe.* In the
Dictionary, p.993, it is simply *s.*

urchair, *s.f.* Shot, cast, throw, push. Its
plural is *urchairichean* in *Poolewe* instead of *urchraichean*, given in the
Dictionary on page 998.

ùrlar, *s.m.* 11 Floor of a boat (WC). 12
Cross-sticks of a wooden bed (WC).

urras-beatha, *s.m.* Life insurance policy.

ùr-sneachd, *s.m.* Fresh snow, new-laid
snow is ùr-shneachd in *Poolewe.*
(WC).

INDEX (Chiefly of English words)

holder 59
Fury 6, 7
Furze 8
Fusty 73, 82
Futility 77

Gabbling 22
Gable 101
Gad-fly 24, 51
Gaelic, Unknown 82
Gaff 61
Gaff of a sail 55, 95
Gainsay 4
Gall 53, 71, 72
Gall (verb) 81
Gallantry 34, 80
Gallow-glass 83
Gammon 52
Gannet 11
Garb 23
Garment, Long ragged 88
Garment, Old tattered 97
Garrulity 98
Garrulous 85
Garter 59, 60
Gasconade 9
Gathering together, of
  birds & beasts as when
  terrified 86
Gazeful 66
Gazer 66
Gemination 44
General 10
Generative 9, 50
Generosity 26
Genitive (grammar) 84
Genius 74
Gentle 81
Gentleman 15
Gesticulation 44
Get a bite (fishing) 76
Get out! 72
Get the better of 58
Ghost 11
Giant 97, 98
Giantess 20
Gibbous 62
Gibbousness 62
Gibe 26
Giddiness 43
Giddy 34
Giddy-paced 22, 78

Gifts 81
Gig 62
Gimlet 84
Girdle cake 30
Girdler 60
Girl, Headstrong 37
Girl, Poor little 73
Girl, Sturdy bounding 84
Girth 2
Girth belly-band 34
Girth-saddle 15
Girth-saddle, Bent ridge of
  a 1
Girth saddle timbers 2
Glaciation 67, 75
Glacier 75
Gladness 5, 9
Gladsome 4
Gland 76
Gleaning 69, 88
Glee, Great 65
Gleeful 13
Gloominess 14, 72
Gloomy 14
Glove, Fisher's 61
Glutton 18
Go back 8
Go to the dogs 97
Goal 19, 54
Goat 38, 86
Goat call 93
Goat-hag 85
Goat in first kid 93
Goat leader 38, 47
Goat, Three-year-old
  castrated 1
Goatfell pebbles 50
Goats 48
Goats rutting 29
Goblet 86
Golden samphire 91
Good 56
Good, Devilish 69
Good-for-nothing 17
Good-looking 85
Good-night 95
Goodness gracious! 6
Goose, Laying 31
Gooseberry 60
Gorse 8
Gossamer 61
Gossip 79

Governable 70
Governing 46
Gowned 74
Grace 9, 85
Grain, Inferior 67
Grain, Peeled 28
Grain, Undressed 25
Grained 83
Grampus 41
Grand 76
Grange 18
Grant 1
Grass, Abounding in hard
  78
Grass, Decayed 26
Grass in pools 21
Grass, Sweet meadow 93
Grateful 62
Gratification 55, 72
Gratify 55, 72
Grave-plot 44
Grease 60
Grease, Gaelic spelling of
  87
"Grease" in inflamed and
  painful skin of horses feet
  93
Greasy 15
Great 9, 12
Great mace weed 63
Greed 13
Greedy 27, 91
Green 5
Green dye 6
Green patches 7, 86
Greenish 31
Grey 33
Grieve 47
Grieve (noun) 79
Griffin 90
Grim 87
Grimace 45
Grin 31, 59
Grinning 71, 72
Gripe 7
Griper 7
Grittiness 83
Gritty 83
Groaning 4
Groat or 4d piece 54
Groat land 58
Grooved (joinery) 86

Keeping 57
Kelpie 95
Key for flyer 59
Kick 85
Kick, Little 32
Kicker 32
Kicking 32
Kiln, Parts of a 16
Kiln passage 78
Kind 13
Kindly 14
Kindness 45, 50
Kindred 14, 36
"King's Game" 66
"Kinks" of whooping
  cough 100
Kitten 43, 45
Knack 53
Knavery 52
Kneading trough 11
Knee-cap 76
Kneed 53
Knife, Peat 101
Knife, Sharp 5
Knife, Tinker's 88, 89
Knob or catch 74, 98
Knock 77
Knoll 45, 87, 101
Knot 18
Knot, Temporary 76
Knotted 9
Knowledge 8

Labour, Free 94
Labour, Statute 44
Labra 16
Lad 29
Lad, Mischievous 11
Lady 19
Lamb enclosure 58
Lamb, Fat 49
Lamb, Pet 31
Lame 60, 90
Lament 53
Laminania digitata 73
Lamprey 25, 67
Land, River 21
Land roller 62
Land, Sloping 52
Land, Unploughed 20
Land yielding two crops 17
Landrail 31

Landslip 31
Lane 82
Lapful 34
Lapis Lazuli 50
Lapwing 64
Large litter 63
Lascivious 5
Lassie, Smart 62
Lasting, Not 69
Late 6, 13
Lath 89
Lathing 89
Laughable 72
Laughter, Idiotic 31
Law 88
Lawn, Green 86
Lawyer 00
Lazy 5
Leader 38, 49
Leader of birds 47
Leader of cattle 29, 46
Leader of horses 47
Leader of men 46
Leading 4
Leaky 65
Leanness 11
Leap 85
Leaping 29
Leavings 17
Ledge 75
Ledge-path 17
Lee side 23
Leech 67
Left earth-board 59
Leg, Wooden 45
Legacy 76
Legerdemain 51
Lemon sole 89
Lend 8
Leo constellation 58
Leprosy 94
Lessen 89
Let that pass 89
Lethargic 33
Lethargy 33, 85
Letter X 10
Letter ending 25
Level 56, 76
Level plain 64
Levelness 56
Liar 79
Liberal 79, 88

Liberality 79
Libidinous 12
Lick up 67
Lick with tongue 87
Lie in wait 7
Lieutenant 79
Life 7, 25
Life insurance policy 102
Life-rent 26
Light 22
Light, Faint 50
Light-headed 88
Light, Spot of 39
Lightening 76
"Lights" 71
Like that 65
Likeable. Not 72
Likely 65
Likely, More/most 70
Lime 90
Limpet 19, 32, 36
Linen band for an infant's
  head 61
Linen, Rough 44
Ling 81
Lining 90
Lint-like 84
Lintel 14
Lip, Blubber 25
Lip, Smacking noisily 28
Liquid, Quantity of 91
Liquorice, Wild 44
Litigant 3
Litter/brushwood in boat's
  bottom 23
Little or much 7
Little, Very 14
Livelihood 26
Lively 19, 27
Liver 3
Livestock 26
Lizard 4, 15
Loach 32
Load of hay/straw 44
Loaf-bread 15
Lob-worm 27
Lock 18
Loftiness 93
Log 27
Loitering 91
Long-suffering 81
Longing 5

St. John's wort 9, 43, 74
Stab with horns 34
Stack, Oblong 65
Stack of hay, Conical 73
Stack, Proving 82
Stag 3, 4, 29, 31, 37, 44, 49
Stag's brow-antler 93
Stag 5 years old 65
Stag-hound 15
Stag's switch horns 37
Stag's head with switch
  horns 37
Staggering 32, 71
Stake 17, 24, 49
Stall of a byre 17, 19, 33,
  34, 35, 36
Stall-tie 24, 46
Stall-tree 17, 24
Stallion 4
Stamping 32, 45, 50
Standing 44
Staple 73
Star, Falling 97
Star, Small 29
Starboard/port 82
Stargazer 19
Start 17
Stay 12, 13, 59
Stays of a female 98
Steamboat funnel 59
Steep 8
Steep place 68
Steersman 23, 100
Stem 23
Stem, Soft vegetable 36
Stench 96
Step 101
Step, Long 82
Step, Narrow 9
Stern 23, 83
Stick, Threshing 99
Sticks striking bin to feed
  mill 94
Stiff 7, 40
Still discharge cock 29
Still head 100
Still lid 100
Still, Parts of 100
Still pipe 84
Still, Shoulder of 100
Still, Spirit receiver 85, 100
Stinging 91

Stirk-shaped 83
Stirring mud & water 91
Stirrup 2, 49
Stitch 86
Stoat 44
Stock 63
Stock, Live 26
Stock of *liaghra* 90
Stocking toe 85
Stockings, Old footed 94
Stone 9, 16, 30, 35, 52
Stone, Black 38
Stone, Boundary 5
Stone, Cabalistic 73
Stone circles 79
Stone circles, Place of 44
Stone, Dressed or
  sculptured 51
Stone outside house, Flat
  89
Stone, Flint 5
Stone fort 75
Stone, Grinding 51
Stone, Healing 50
Stone hollowed for barley
  54
Stone, Lifting 96
Stone supporting bread 89
Stone, White 34
Stonecrop 26
Stones, Witches 50
Stook-hoods 2
Stork 58
Storm 75
Storm finch 8
Storm-petrel 5, 8, 11
Stormy petrel 5, 8
Story-telling 80
Stot 5
Stout 40, 61
Stoup measure 76
Straight as a stick 66
Straightness 69, 85
Strain 75
Strait 64
Strange 8, 82
Strangeness 54, 73
Stranger 17, 65
Stratagem 11
Straw 16, 23
Straw/fodder 57
Straw for thatch, Long 37

Straw rope circle 38
Stream, Shallow 51
Stream under heather 43
Streamlet 78
Strength 38
Strength, Trial of 50
Strenuous 43
Stretch 64
Stretches 2
Strictness 70
Stride 82
Strife 13
Strike frequently 88
String of fish 17
String of herrings 17
Stripped 90
Strong 24, 64, 65, 70, 76
Stronghold 64
Strum 68
Stubble 5, 57
Stubborn 69
Stubbornness 4
Stump 49
Stumpy 85
Stupid 91
Stupid fellow 71, 91
Stupor 85
Sturdiness 38
Sturdy boy 84
Sturgeon 31
Subject to 54
Subsiding 69
Substantive "*achd*" 2
Successless 74
Suck 53, 67
Sudden 7, 12
Sudden alarm 82
Suet, Full of 28
Sufficiency 81
Sufficient 81
Sulky 5, 30, 74
Sullen 5, 74
Sullen look 85
Sullenness 12
Summer 97
Summer, Beginning of 48
Summer town 1
Summering 97
Summit 25, 101
Summon 19, 21
Summoning 22
Sun & shower, Alternate

INDEX TO MANUSCRIPT 14958